The
FALSE
PROMISE

of

GREEN
ENERGY

The
FALSE
PROMISE
of
GREEN
ENERGY

**ANDREW P. MORRISS, WILLIAM T. BOGART,
ROGER E. MEINERS, AND ANDREW DORCHAK**

CATO INSTITUTE

WASHINGTON, D.C.

Library of Congress Cataloging-in-Publication Data

The false promise of green energy / Andrew P. Morriss ... [et al.].
 p. cm.
 ISBN 978-1-935308-41-6 (hardback : alk. paper) 1. Clean energy industries. 2.
Renewable energy sources. 3. Environmental sciences--Vocational guidance.
4. Green movement. I. Morriss, Andrew P., 1960-

 HD9502.5.C542F35 2011
 333.79′4—dc22

                                                                    2010047745

Printed in the United States of America.

                              CATO INSTITUTE
                     1000 Massachusetts Ave., N.W.
                         Washington, D.C. 20001
                              www.cato.org

Contents

1. How We Live: Reality and Utopia

The promise of building a new economy based on green energy is enticing—enough well-paid, mentally satisfying jobs that help, not hurt, the environment. A switch to green energy will produce many "green jobs," an alluring prospect in a lack-lustre economy. Double-digit unemployment rates of recent years will be vanquished; clean electricity will come from wind turbines and solar panels; homes, offices, and public buildings will be cool in the summer and warm in the winter without the annoyance of high utility bills; and neighbors will grow our healthy, delicious food, free from potential toxins. And these benefits are within easy reach—we can have them if we just borrow a few hundred billion dollars from the great-grandchildren, invest them wisely in the right technologies, and then enjoy the rewards of our efforts for generations to come.

There's an old joke about two economists walking along a city street. One spots a $20 bill on the pavement and points it out to his friend. The other walks right by the money without picking it up, saying to his friend, "If it were there, someone would have already picked it up." The joke pokes fun at economists' belief in "efficient markets," the idea that if there is an opportunity to make money, market pressures will push someone to do it. As a result—and contrary to the signs stuck to utility poles around the country—there are few opportunities for easy money with little effort. The idea of efficient markets captures an important insight from economics. In sum, there aren't many $20 bills on the sidewalk, and someone would certainly pick one up quickly if there were. Proponents of green energy programs would have us believe that there are many $20, $50, and even $100 bills lying about in America. If only we would build windmills, add solar panels to deserts, stuff insulation into buildings, switch our cars to run on biofuels, build more light rail, ride the train more, eat more locally grown produce, and buy more goods produced in America instead of overseas, we'd discover that the money we spent on those things would be quickly recouped by energy savings, greater wealth, reduced environmental damage, and better health. Green energy proponents don't quite promise an "ecotopia," but, as we describe in Chapter 2, they promise something almost as good.

In effect, what green jobs proponents argue is that there are many benefits to be had at little risk if only we will invest a few hundred billion dollars in capturing it. Because they are positive the investments are a sure thing, proponents urge us to borrow money from future generations, confident that not only can we pay them back with the savings in energy, environmental, and health costs but that we will also leave future generations better off if we invest their money in green programs today.

Such bets on the future payoff from investments today might be a good idea, or they might be the equivalent of investing in a fancy subprime mortgage derivative sold by one of the banks that required federal life support. If people or corporations want to invest their own money in producing alternative fuels or insulating their homes, we should wish them well and be eager to learn if their investments pay off. But green jobs proponents want to force people and businesses to take certain actions by regulatory edict and to invest other people's money, either raised through taxes today or, more commonly, from government bonds that have to be paid for in the future. Since we can't easily ask the people who will be paying for these investments, we have to decide today whether spending public dollars on programs is worthwhile. The three of us with children took a poll of our offspring. Unsurprisingly—these are *our* kids—they voted against borrowing against their earnings.

This book is an effort to help you decide whether green energy proposals are worthwhile. Three of us are either lawyers or economists or both, and all of us work at universities, making us professional skeptics. Our skepticism has led us to ask some questions about green energy proposals that we think their supporters haven't answered. These are questions you need to ask candidates for federal and state offices. Ask them to explain how rhetoric about a "green economy" will be translated into concrete actions. Ask what those actions will cost and how they will be paid for; what the benefits of those actions are supposed to be and how those benefits were calculated; and why the officials believe they have gotten their choices right.

This book draws upon, updates, and expands upon our previous research.[1] In Chapter 2, we discuss where green energy proponents want us to go and suggest an alternative based on markets. In the remainder of the chapter, we look at where we are, asking how green our economy is, and taking a look at why some of those $20 bills aren't actually lying on the sidewalk. Chapter 3 examines the claims for green energy, as a critical part of the green program focuses on transforming energy use and sources. Chapter 4 attempts to unpack what proponents mean when they call something "green," finding many contradictions and inconsistencies in the proponents' definitions. Chapter 5 discusses the use of economic models and the mistakes in green jobs proposals that result from improper use of models, making such predictions an unreliable basis for public policy. Chapter 6 focuses on green economy advocates' anti-trade agenda, a potentially costly problem if the proposals are implemented.[2] Chapter 7 continues the discussion of the peculiar assumptions about economics that are imbedded in much of the discussion, assumptions that display a profound rejection of elementary economic logic in favor of assertions about economic and environmental gains that are supposed to happen because the supporters want them to happen. Chapter 8 debunks some of the claims about the economic stimulus effect of green spending. Chapters 9 and 10 look at transportation issues, including the role cars and trucks play in our economy and the dismal economic record of mass transit systems. Chapter 11 takes a look at the politics of green energy proposals, explaining some of their problems as the result of efforts to build a political coalition that can muster the votes in Congress and state legislatures to unlock the public treasury. Chapter 12 concludes with thoughts about the economy and the environment and a checklist of questions readers can use to do due diligence on future green jobs proposals.

There are real environmental problems that deserve study and solution. That will happen by economic and technical progress, not mandates from politicians driven by special interests. We begin with a look at where we are today. If we are going to assess green energy proposals, we need to know how green our economy is already.

Energy Use

Energy affects everything we do. Economist Robert L. Bradley Jr. coined the term "the master resource" to describe energy's role in our economy, and the phrase captures the critical function of energy.[3] When we go to the store to buy something (or click on "buy it now" online), we use energy to make the purchase and bring it to our homes. Energy also goes into all the goods we consume. Using Department of Commerce data, American Enterprise Institute researchers Kenneth Green and Aparna Mathur calculated the indirect energy content of a variety of consumer goods in 2006.[4] As an example, they describe the energy embodied in a cotton T-shirt:

> Energy is required to grow and harvest the cotton; transport it to a factory; make, package, and transport the chemicals used to bleach, dye, or condition the cotton; run the machines on which the t-shirt is processed; create packaging materials; ship the t-shirt to the store; and keep the heat and lights on in the store.[5]

Green and Mathur calculated that nearly half (46 percent) of the energy we use is used indirectly in the production of food, medicines, and consumer goods. This is important because anything that increases the price of energy will also increase the price of goods that use energy indirectly. Thus, if energy costs were to increase because of forced use of more expensive renewable energy, not only would the price of electricity rise, but so would the price of food, medicines, and consumer goods, such as cotton T-shirts. Those price increases would disproportionately affect the poor. Green and Mathur found the ratio of indirect energy expenditures to income to be four to five times as great for the poorest 10 percent compared to the richest 10 percent of our population. Other analyses reach similar conclusions about the widespread nature of indirect energy use.[6]

Beginning with energy is appropriate because energy is at the heart of efforts to "green" the economy. Advocates tout sources of green employment in building, operating, and maintaining approved energy facilities, such as wind turbines and solar photovoltaic (PV) panels, as both sources of employment themselves and as a means of greening energy-using industries.

Four important things are missing from any discussion of green energy, however. First, Americans currently get just 0.6 percent of total energy from wind and solar power.[7] Add in hydroelectric power, even though many environmentalists oppose many conventional hydroelectric projects, and the percentage rises to 3 percent, still a tiny fraction of U.S. energy demand.[8] Moreover, energy produced by wind and solar is still considerably more expensive than coal, natural gas, or nuclear-generated power. Conventional coal-generated electricity typically costs 25 percent of solar PV and 66 percent of on-shore wind. (See Table 1.3.) An energy strategy that relies on rapidly scaling up such small sources is unrealistic in the short to medium term, a problem that green energy proponents gloss over with assumptions about rapid deployment of new technologies.

Second, wind and solar electricity production differs significantly from energy production using coal, natural gas, hydro, or nuclear power. Coal, natural gas, large hydro, and nuclear power plants can work almost continuously, providing power day or night, on windy days and still days, whether it is sunny or raining. Neither wind nor solar is produced continuously or at the flick of a switch—the wind must blow or the sun must shine. As a result, they add new complexity to managing the power supply. Wind- and solar-produced electricity is likely to be generated far away from the existing grid of wires that distributes electric power throughout the United States, requiring expensive investments in new lines. Any strategy that relies on dramatic increases in wind or solar production of electricity must take these problems into account—and green jobs advocates largely do not take this complex (i.e., costly) issue seriously.

Third, even those energy facilities that green proponents are most fond of—wind farms and solar PV fields—are not uncontroversial once someone plans to build one in someone else's backyard. Windmills can cause "shadow flicker," kill birds, and create visual and noise pollution that annoys neighbors.[9] Solar PV fields can interfere with endangered species' habitats. Both require lots of new transmission lines that will have to cross people's properties. As a result, expanding such facilities is much harder than green energy advocates suggest.

Fourth, defining what energy counts as "green" is difficult and symbolizes the problems in reconciling the interest groups within the green jobs coalition. Is nuclear power "green?" *Green Jobs in U.S. Metro Areas*, a report prepared for the U.S. Council of Mayors that studies the impact of green jobs on U.S. cities, suggests that existing nuclear plants are, but new ones would not be, so no more should be built. Many green groups oppose all nuclear energy. In general, nuclear power confronts green energy advocates with a difficult question about trade-offs—more nuclear power plants would undoubtedly reduce carbon dioxide emissions, a key goal for most green interests. But nuclear power has environmental downsides, such as the disposal of long-lived radioactive waste products. Nuclear power is not the only form of energy that poses trade-offs, however. Producing solar PV panels can involve considerable hazardous waste that requires disposal; the larger land footprint of solar panel farms increases their environmental impact; and the sunny regions best suited for solar power are often environmentally sensitive deserts. There are similarly complex trade-offs about the use of biofuels and hydro power.

Here we look at the realities of energy production and use in the United States and the rest of the world and compare that to green energy advocates' proposals. We think that the data suggest that green energy proponents have been peddling an unrealistic vision of energy production and use and are suggesting measures that will require either dramatically increasing the cost of energy or significantly cutting its use. Both would mean a reduction in the standard of living. The impacts globally would be even worse, as increasing energy use generally—and increasing use of electricity in particular—is an important way to improve the quality of life for people in developing economies.

The Big Picture on Energy

Before we can evaluate the claims about energy made in support of green programs, we need a clear picture of where we are today. We begin with where the federal Department of Energy experts say we are and where we are going in terms of energy production. From Figure 1.1, we can see how important conventional energy sources are, with coal, natural gas, liquids (petroleum based), and nuclear providing over 94 quadrillion BTU while biofuels (such as ethanol) and renewable energy sources provide just under 7 quadrillion BTU.

Figure 1.1
Primary Energy Use by Fuel (quadrillion BTU), 2008

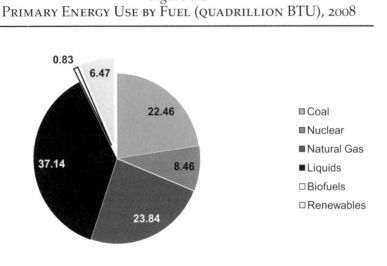

- ▨ Coal
- ▪ Nuclear
- ▪ Natural Gas
- ▪ Liquids
- ▫ Biofuels
- ▫ Renewables

Source: Energy Information Administration, *Annual Energy Outlook 2010*, Fig. 1, http://www.eia.doe.gov/oiaf/aeo/execsummary.html.

Figure 1.2 shows that this proportion of traditional sources to "green" sources is not likely to change dramatically between now and 2030. Indeed, the increase in energy from renewables and bio-fuels over that time is about the same size as the increase the U.S. Energy Information Administration predicts for nuclear and coal. The EIA does not have a crystal ball for making such forecasts, but its predictions are based on energy expertise, data, and careful statistical analysis, rather than on hope and an optimistic attitude, as are many of the predictions in the green energy literature. Importantly, unlike the interest groups touting green energy spending plans that will funnel public money to their own pockets, such as the American Solar Energy Society, the EIA has no horse in this race. Regardless of what our energy future looks like, there will likely be an EIA gathering data. Its predictions are thus a valuable benchmark against which to compare predictions of special interest groups.

If we look at electricity, the picture is even clearer. As Figure 1.3 shows, for electricity generation, the overwhelming majority comes

7

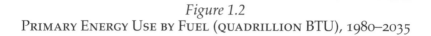

Figure 1.2
PRIMARY ENERGY USE BY FUEL (QUADRILLION BTU), 1980–2035

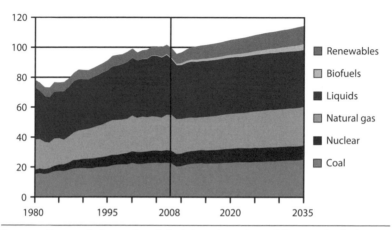

SOURCE: Energy Information Administration, *Annual Energy Outlook 2010*, Fig. 1, http://www.eia.doe.gov/oiaf/aeo/execsummary.html.

Figure 1.3
ELECTRICITY GENERATING CAPACITY (GIGAWATTS), 2008

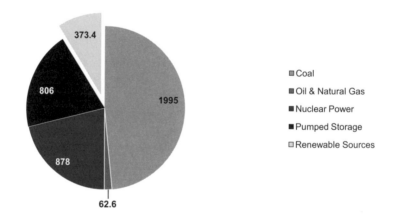

SOURCE: Energy Information Administration, *Annual Energy Outlook 2010*, http://www.eia.doe.gov/oiaf/aeo/electricity.html.

Figure 1.4
RENEWABLE ELECTRICITY SECTOR, NET SUMMER CAPACITY,
ALL SECTORS (GIGAWATTS)

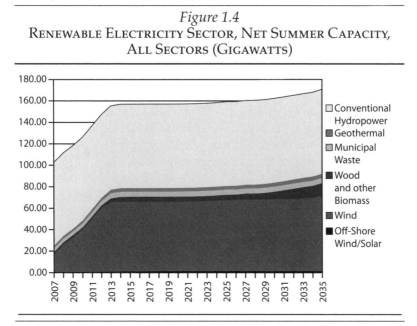

SOURCE: http://www.eia.doe.gov/oiaf/aeo/aeoref_tab.html. See Table 16.

from coal, nuclear power, and oil and natural gas.[10] Just over 10 percent comes from any form of renewable energy. When we look at the types of renewable energy used to generate electricity (see Figure 1.4), we can see that over 70 percent comes from "conventional hydro"— precisely the type of renewable energy that environmental groups are opposed to expanding and some are working to eliminate. Solar's contribution is tiny. And even by 2030, a very long time in the forecasting business, only wind shows a sharp increase in power generated, nearly all of which comes about within the next decade in EIA's predictions. The EIA forecasts that the share of energy generated by wind rises only from 0.8 percent of total generation in 2007 to 2.5 percent in 2030.[11]

Why is wind forecast to increase its capacity so sharply in the next few years? The major reason is government mandates and subsidies. Table 5.1 at page 101 lists the subsidies for various fuels in dollars per kilowatt-hour (kWh) of energy produced and shows that wind receives subsidies courtesy of taxpayers more than 10 times greater than nonrenewable fuels when adjusted for the total amount of energy production. This adjustment is crucial to comparing subsidies, since the amount of energy produced by different sources is so dramatically different. Refined coal and wind receive similarly high levels of subsidies per kilowatt-hour.

We will review issues related to subsidies in more detail later, but for now note that it pays to be suspicious of programs that are driven by subsidies rather than by market demand for three reasons. First, if an energy source is being subsidized, the price does not reflect the cost, so people use more of it than they would if they paid the real price. Since green energy advocates are generally fans of increasing conservation, subsidizing any form of energy is inconsistent with the market signals necessary for reducing consumption (e.g., direct higher prices for users, not subsidies from taxpayers). Second, once a subsidy is available, an interest group quickly organizes to protect its members' continued receipt of the subsidy, and it becomes difficult to wean the subsidized from the flow of public dollars. Finally, if the subsidies do disappear, or a better subsidy is offered elsewhere, firms chasing subsidies are quick to decamp. For example, BP shifted its wind power spending from Britain to the United States because American subsidies were more generous than British ones.[12]

Finally, Figure 1.5 shows the dependence of the U.S. transportation sector on gasoline and diesel. Ethanol and biodiesel, both inferior fuels in many respects (as we will describe later), have only a tiny fraction of the transportation fuel market, despite being heavily subsidized. In part, this reflects two important facts about the transportation sector. First, the United States has a massive investment in the use of gasoline and diesel fuel that cannot be readily transformed to shift consumption to ethanol, biodiesel, or other fuels. There are 160,000 miles of gasoline pipelines, 380,000 gasoline storage tanks, and 120,000 service stations in the United States. This infrastructure ensures there is fuel ready when motorists and truckers pull their vehicles into a service station. Almost none of it can be readily used for ethanol or biodiesel; costly conversion is required.

Everything from pipelines to engines must be redesigned if more than 10–15 percent ethanol is used in the fuel mix, because existing valves and other parts risk corrosion. Nevertheless, EPA has again announced plans to increase the ethanol content of gasoline. In *The Great Ethanol Scam*, columnist Ed Wallace of *Business Week* catalogued accounts of ruined fuel pumps and expensive repairs caused by in-

Figure 1.5
TRANSPORTATION FUEL USE (MILLION GALLONS/YEAR), 2005

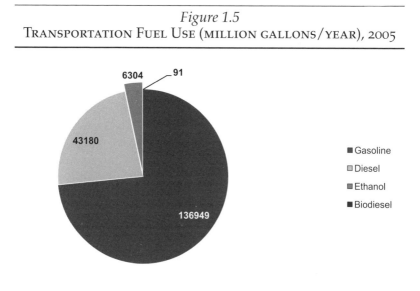

SOURCE: Energy Information Administration, *Biofuels in the US Transportation Sector (2007)*, http://www.eia.doe.gov/oiaf/analysispaper/biomass.html.

advertent use of higher proportions of ethanol in cars, boats, and small engines.[13] Wallace concluded, "Not one mechanic I've spoken with said they would be comfortable with a 15% blend of ethanol in their personal car. However, most suggest that if the government moves the ethanol mandate to 15%, it will be the dawn of a new golden age for auto mechanics' income."[14] In addition, ethanol's affinity for water makes it impossible to ship in existing pipelines or store with gasoline. Separate tanks and pipes must be built, raising costly, complex problems.

Biodiesel has fewer problems than ethanol, but it still has some serious drawbacks.[15] Like ethanol, biodiesel generally has a lower energy content per gallon (about 8–9 percent less), reducing the mileage for vehicles used it and can absorb water from the atmosphere, reducing the efficiency of the fuel, producing more smoke in exhaust, freezing fuel lines in the winter, and damaging engines. Most notably, biodiesel "gels" at higher temperatures than conventional diesel. Vegetable oil-based biodiesels, for example, generally start to gel at 32–40 degrees Fahrenheit; animal fat biodiesels gel at even higher temperatures. Some biodiesel advocates even suggest that users should install separate fuel tanks or fuel tank heaters to deal with this problem when using pure biodiesel.[16]

Shifting to mass use in vehicles that have the corrosion-resistant parts necessary for high percentages of ethanol, or the heated fuel tanks necessary for high percentages of biodiesel, seems unlikely because of the expense of duplicating the infrastructure necessary to fuel such vehicles across the country. More likely, alternative fuels will attract fleet operators (bus systems, trucking firms, delivery companies) that can spread the cost of building and maintaining a central fueling station over a large fleet. Biofuels are thus likely to remain only a small part of the transportation fuel market. We will discuss the prospects for changes in car and truck use in more detail in Chapter 9.

Energy in Our Lives

The typical American household consumes between 72 and 122 billion BTU of energy per year to heat and cool a home, power appliances, travel, cook, surf the web, and all the other activities of our daily lives.[17] On an individual basis, that works out to between approximately 26 and 53 billion BTU. Americans in the West and South use less; those in the Midwest and Northeast use more, largely reflecting the difference in heating needs. Table 1.1 compares energy use in 1980 and 2005 across the country and shows that energy, both as measured per person and per household, declined.

Those averages mask considerable differences. As the Tennessee Center for Policy Research discovered in a review of Al Gore's home utility bills for 2006, Gore's home used 221,000 kWh of electricity compared to the Department of Energy's calculation of 10,656 kWh for the average home.[18] (Surprisingly, after the report sparked charges of hypocrisy, Gore's energy use *increased* the following year by 10 percent[19].) To be fair, one key reason for Gore's outsized energy use was that the home is about four times larger than the average American's home and also served as an office for both Al and Tipper. Gore obtains carbon offsets and pays premium prices for energy generated from renewable sources, practices some have likened to the medieval church's sale of indulgences to wealthy sinners and which raise important equity issues.

Table 1.1
HOUSEHOLD ENERGY USE

Region	1980		2005		Per Household Change	Per Household Member Change
	Per Household (million BTU)	Per Household Member (million BTU)	Per Household (million BTU)	Per Household Member (million BTU)		
Northeast	138.3	49	122.2	47.7	−11.6%	−2.7%
Midwest	140.5	49	113.5	46	−19.2%	−6.1%
South	95.4	34	79.8	31.6	−16.4%	−7.1%
West	84.1	31	77.4	28.1	−8.0%	−9.4%

SOURCE: Energy Information Administration, *Residential Consumption Survey, Historical Data (1980)*, http://www.eia.doe.gov/emeu/recs/historicaldata/ historical_data80_02.html and http://www.eia.doe.gov/ emeu/recs/recs2005/ c&e/detailed_tables2005c&e.html (2005 Survey).

We use energy for many different purposes in our lives. People react to changes in energy prices in several ways. Some energy uses can be changed quickly—turning a thermostat down in the winter or up in the summer. Many uses of power are conveniences that can be readily dispensed with, such as leaving televisions or stereos in "standby" mode when not in use (when they typically consume about the same energy level as a 75- to 100-watt light bulb). The Natural Resources Defense Council, for example, recommends using power strips to completely shut off such equipment when not in use, and other such measures to reduce energy consumption.[20] Other uses are harder to change in the short term but can be changed over time—replacing a furnace or air conditioner with a more energy-efficient model or a car with a higher mileage one. For example, a new central air conditioner is 30 to 50 percent more efficient than a 15-year-old one. As a result, higher energy prices can bring conservation by sending individuals a price signal that conservation is more cost-effective.

Many environmental pressure groups don't want to leave conservation to individuals, preferring government mandates to change energy use. At the individual level, these include the federal government's energy-efficiency rules for washing machines, which have led to a shift toward requiring more energy-efficient (but more expensive) front-loading washers, and the phaseout of the sale of incandescent light bulbs after 2012, requiring more costly compact fluorescent bulbs (which present a hazard if a bulb breaks and releases the mercury each bulb contains). To a large extent, the choice we face on greening the economy is whether we will continue to rely on people and firms responding to price signals received in the market, or whether we will supplant those signals with decisions made by politicians and bureaucrats in Washington, D.C. In short, do we want government picking our light bulbs and washing machines or do we want to leave that to personal choice among alternatives provided by competitive sellers? Of course, individuals and groups of citizens may react to certain programs or government incentives. FirstEnergy had to cancel a planned distribution of 3.75 million compact fluorescent light bulbs (at a proposed cost of $21.60 per customer) after public outcry against the program.[21] Ohio residents, however, eagerly participated in the Ohio Energy Efficient Appliance Rebate Program, especially for the purchase of qualifying refrigerators, clothes washers, and dishwashers (and, to a lesser extent, water heaters).[22]

The Cost of Energy

Calculating the cost of energy requires considering construction, operating and maintenance (O&M), transmission investment, fuel costs, the cost of building transmission capacity to link plants into the national electric grid, and the amount of time the plant will be operating. Using EIA data, the Institute for Energy Research compiled the information in Table 1.2, which allows an apples-to-apples comparison of different means of electricity generation. The table shows the "levelized" cost per kilowatt-hour; "levelized" is economists' jargon for "comparable." Those costs represent the present value of the total cost of building and operating a generating plant over its financial life, converted to equal annual payments and spread over expected annual generation. Coal and natural gas plants, even when incorporating advanced technology to reduce greenhouse gas emissions, are cheaper than wind and solar. In short, coal, natural gas, and nuclear are all much cheaper, generating power at a quarter to a third of the cost of solar PV, less than half to half the cost of offshore wind farms, and 30–40 percent less than onshore wind farms. Some alternative energy sources (hydro, geothermal, and biomass) are cheap enough to compete with conventional energy sources, although the volume of energy produced by such plants remains tiny.

The higher cost of wind and solar is due to three things. First, their capacity utilizations are dramatically lower than for conventional energy sources (20–35 percent compared to 85–90 percent). Every dollar invested in a wind farm or solar PV facility thus produces less energy than one invested in a nuclear or coal plant simply because the renewable plants operate much less of the time. Solar plants don't work at night and wind farms don't produce energy when the wind isn't blowing. Moreover, because they operate less predictably (as they are dependent on weather conditions), wind and solar plants must be backed up by conventional plants if electricity is to be available when people want it. Second, both wind and solar require higher levels of maintenance spending than many other sources of energy, although solar has an advantage over wind here since it involves fewer moving parts. Third, some of the best locations for wind and solar energy facilities are located far from the existing transmission grid and so require considerable investment in additional transmission facilities, which often irks those whose land the power lines will run across.

If it is desirable for people to use wind and solar energy for electricity generation and they cost more to operate, taxpayers will have to subsidize them or few people will choose to buy them. Governments in many countries heavily subsidize wind and solar energy.[23] Table 1.3 lists the U.S. subsidies for all forms of energy for 2007, as calculated by the EIA. Wind, solar, and refined coal receive 20 to over 100 times the subsidies when compared to nuclear, conventional coal, hydro, or natural gas plants. Obviously, the value of those subsidies to wind and solar producers is considerable. Some wind producers, for example, are willing to sell their power at a *negative price*—to pay people to use it. Why? Because putting power into the grid is the only way they can receive the subsidy; it is profitable for some alternative energy producers to pay customers to use their energy at times so that they qualify for the subsidy. Moreover, subsidy-dependent producers are not viable once the subsidies disappear. We discuss wind and solar energy in detail in Chapter 3. The important point is that they are not cost-competitive with other forms of energy production using current technologies and at current resource prices.

Table 1.2
LEVELIZED COST OF NEW GENERATING TECHNOLOGIES, 2016 REVISED AEO 2009 REFERENCE CASE

U.S. Average Levelized Costs (2007 $/mWh) for Plants Entering Service in 2016

Plant Type	Capacity Factor (%)	Levelized Capital Cost	Fixed O & M	Variable O&M (including Fuel)	Transmission Investment	Total System Levelized Cost
Conventional Coal	85	64.5	3.7	23.0	3.5	94.6
Advanced Coal	85	75.6	5.2	19.3	3.5	103.5
Advanced Coal with CCS	85	87.4	6.2	25.2	3.8	122.6
Natural Gas-Fired						
Conventional Combined Cycle	87	23.0	1.6	55.7	3.7	83.9
Advanced Combined Cycle	87	22.4	1.5	52.3	3.7	79.9
Advanced CC with CCS	87	43.6	2.6	65.8	3.7	115.7
Conventional Combustion Turbine	30	41.3	4.6	83.6	10.7	140.2
Advanced Combustion Turbine	30	38.5	4.0	71.2	10.7	124.3

Advanced Nuclear	90	84.2	11.4	8.7	3.0	107.3
Wind	35.1	122.7	10.3	0.0	8.5	141.5
Wind—Offshore	33.4	193.6	27.5	0.0	8.6	229.6
Solar PV	21.7	376.6	6.2	0.0	12.9	395.7
Solar Thermal	31.2	232.1	21.3	0.0	10.3	263.7
Geothermal	90	86.0	20.7	0.0	4.8	111.5
Biomass	83	71.7	8.9	23.0	3.9	107.4
Hydro	52	97.2	3.3	6.1	5.6	114.1

SOURCES: Energy Information Administration, *Annual Energy Outlook 2009 (revised)*, April 2009, SR-OIAF/2009-03, http://:www.eia.doe.gov/oiaf/servicerpt/stimulus/index.html; http://www.instituteforenergyresearch.org/wp-content/uploads/2009/05/levelized-cost-of-new-generating-technologies.pdf.

Table 1.3
SUBSIDIES TO ELECTRIC PRODUCTION BY SELECTED
PRIMARY ENERGY SOURCES

Primary Energy Source	FY 2007 Net Generation (billion kWh)	Subsidies and Support Allocated to Electric Generation (millions FY 2007 dollars)	Subsidies and Support per Unit of Production (dollars/mWh)
Natural Gas and Petroleum Liquids	919	227	0.25
Coal	1,946	854	0.44
Hydroelectric	258	174	0.67
Biomass	40	36	0.89
Geothermal	15	14	0.92
Nuclear	794	1,267	1.59
Wind	31	724	23.37
Solar	1	174	24.34
Refined Coal	72	2,156	29.81

SOURCE: Energy Information Administration, *Federal Financial Interventions and Subsidies in Energy Markets 2007*, SR/CNEAF/2008-1 (2008).

How Green Can We Be?

The picture of energy use this data provides has three key features that are obstacles to the massive transformations in production and consumption that green energy advocates propose.

- *Changes in the mix of energy sources will come gradually.* Green energy proposals are full of exciting plans for massive shifts in the way we produce energy. Even if we throw the enormous sums of money green energy proponents suggest at changing how we produce energy, such shifts won't happen for decades. Our current mix of energy technologies is deeply embedded within our society and our economy. We need to focus on how to improve the reliability and environmental impact of our energy system, not propose massive change.

- *Electricity will largely be generated by a mix of coal, natural gas, and nuclear power plants for decades.* These technologies are well-tested, cheap to operate compared to the alternatives, and, for some, easy to expand. The alternatives are more expensive, harder to match to demand for power, and located far from the existing transmission infrastructure. Adding new sources to the generation mix is a good idea, as technology improves to make these technologies cost-competitive. Until they are, however, they cannot compete.

- *Most of the energy for transportation will continue to come from petroleum for decades.* Gasoline and diesel are excellent fuels—they contain considerable energy per unit volume, are easy to transport and store, and work in a wide range of vehicles. In addition, we have billions of dollars of infrastructure created to service, fuel, and use vehicles powered by these fuels. Thus far, the renewable alternatives are less convenient, more expensive, and inferior in a number of important quality dimensions.

What Then Should We Do?

Diversifying our sources of energy to include wind, solar, geothermal, biofuels, and whatever else scientists and engineers can invent is a good idea. Using energy from multiple sources would make us less vulnerable to price shocks like those we experienced in 2008 as the price of oil soared. But diversification makes sense only if the new sources of energy are cost-effective and reliable. Adding more expensive forms of energy into the mix is not a good idea.

The best way to encourage development of new technologies is not for the government to select some favored ones and subsidize them. Governments love to do this, because it allows politicians to hand out money to special interests. Remember the Synfuels Corporation? Congress and President Jimmy Carter wanted to spend $100 billion, back when that was a lot of money, on the creation of synthetic fuels from coal to replace oil. The project was unsuccessful, and President Ronald Reagan pulled the plug shortly after taking office.[24] Instead of letting Congress choose the next technology, we should leave that to market competition. Instead of wind energy producers such as GE spending money lobbying for tax credits, those companies should invest those resources in improving wind technology to make it more reliable and cheaper.[25] If we need to spur improvements faster, offering prizes for new technologies that meet specified criteria, such as the new X Prize for "clean, production-capable vehicles that exceed 100 MPG energy equivalent," can encourage technological development without committing the government to a particular technology.[26]

When governments choose technologies, they often fail for three reasons. First, government decisionmakers are insulated from market signals. Without having to respond to price changes, decisionmakers can't learn the important lessons about how they work. Second, the public resources governments make available are so addictive that firms reorient themselves away from producing to meet market demand toward pleasing the government decisionmakers who allocate funds. Every dollar spent on campaign contributions is unproductive of energy. But because those dollars yield reliable results of more subsidies and special treatment, while money invested in technology is risky, firms rationally invest in lobbying instead of R&D. Third, government decisionmakers own only those successes (and failures) that happen between now and the next election. Worrying about the economics of solar power in 2030 is well past the time horizon of anyone in government today. No one currently in office is likely to be held responsible for their decisions today when the results are in and the bill comes due 15 years from now. Markets, on the other hand, price in the future. If a company is making a big bet on solar technology, its stock price will reflect that. If solar seems like a good bet, the stock price will rise. If not, it will fall. Today's executives can be held accountable for that decision.

Here are three important steps governments can take to promote a more secure energy future:

End Subsidies. We need economically sustainable energy sources, not producers hooked on infusions of public money. Environmentalists are right to criticize existing subsidies for forms of energy they do not like (such as government caps on liability for nuclear plant operators). They're wrong to think that the answer to subsidies they dislike is getting their own. Instead, we need to get the government out of the energy subsidy business and allow all forms of energy to develop and compete. The heads of the Sierra Club and the Cato Institute jointly endorsed just such a strategy in a 2002 *Washington Post* op-ed.[27]

Distribute Information. Help consumers make intelligent choices by providing transparent information about the energy demand of appliances and other goods. The labels on appliances showing the annual cost of operation are a simple way to help consumers make informed choices when buying. Governments can take many steps to help make prices more transparent without mandating the technologies in use.[28] In particular, governments can encourage competition in energy markets, giving competitors the opportunity to explain to consumers the virtues of their energy-efficient products.

Set Standards. Governments are big consumers, buying goods and energy. In their roles as consumers, state and federal governments can spur private actors to innovate by buying better buildings, new energy systems for their facilities, and so on.[29] Of course, we need to be certain that governments aren't hoodwinked into buying poor quality merchandise masquerading as green goods. By offering to purchase goods that meet rigorous performance standards for energy efficiency and the like, governments can play a constructive role in the marketplace.

Green Living

Our straightforward overview of energy usage today, and of some of the major policy issues that have an impact on that sector of the economy, contrasts starkly with the green utopia envisioned by those advocating a radical transformation in how we work, live, and generate energy.[30] This book will delve into the world of "green energy" and the many policies—and the implications of those policies—that are commonly advocated. Before getting into those details, it is worth considering a bit of recent history about the green energy movement and its claims about employment.

In 2009, the *Merriam-Webster Dictionary* officially added "green-collar" to the common parlance, as an adjective meaning "of, relating to, or involving actions for protecting the natural environment."[31] The date of origin is 1990, perhaps part of the voluminous literature associated with that year's 20th anniversary celebration of Earth Day.[32] Nicholas Basta claims he coined the term "green-collar work force" to describe the field of employment associated with "environmental preservation and protection."[33] Basta noted a key distinction that resonates today: millions of "businesspeople, lawyers, government officials, researchers, and teachers" were green-collar workers, regardless of how they felt about the environment.[34] Basta found it difficult to assess the job market for green-collar scientists because "there is no definite count," forcing him to use the count of "pollution abatement and control" jobs as a proxy.[35] He noted that federal employment of green-collar workers was unpredictable and paid less than the private sector.[36]

As an environmentalist and sustainability expert, Alan Thein Durning probably was aware of green-collar jobs sooner than most people. In 1995, Durning heralded his seven sustainable wonders of the world in the *USA Today Magazine:* bicycles, ceiling fans, clotheslines, telephones, public libraries, campus interdepartmental envelopes, and condoms.[37] In 1999, he wrote a book touting "green-collar" jobs after examining five "down-on-their-luck" Northwestern locales (Ketchikan, Haida Gwaii, Hayfork, Boonville, and Bend) in an attempt to determine the interplay of employment prospects, environmental policy, and social justice. He described a shift from "old" extractive industries (such as timber) to a new economy (information technology, environmental conservation, tourism, and retirement communities). While viewing the traditional timber industry as nonsustainable, Durning admitted that it had provided a pathway to good-paying jobs that did not require a college education. For Durning, even the "new-economy" jobs, though they have less of a direct impact on the environment than the extractive industries, still have negative consequences: workers with resource-intensive hobbies; increased mobile source (car, boat) pollution from tourism and retirees; and disparities in wealth and access to new-economy jobs.[38] Durning thought that public will (political action) was necessary for the Northwest to successfully transition to an equitable, sustainable economy:

> In the end, fostering a green-collar economy boils down to a few personal questions. Will we choose to harmonize work and nature? Will we choose sufficiency or excess? Will we choose one Northwest or two?[39]

Durning published a report in 2005 that emphasized clean energy as the best path to prosperity and security for the Northwest region (Cascadia).[40] The report provided case studies that invoke empathy but did not provide a systematic approach to introducing green-collar jobs outside Cascadia. The extent to which Durning's call for green-collar jobs was heard outside the Pacific Northwest forest and the environmental movement (with the notable exception of a 1999 *Economist* article) is unclear.[41]

Perhaps the green-collar jobs migrated south to California. In 2004, Raquel Pinderhughes, professor of urban studies and planning at San Francisco State University, wrote a study on green-collar jobs in 22 economic sectors (from bicycle repair to whole home performance).[42] In 2009, Governor Arnold Schwarzenegger and the State of California created the California Green Corps, leveraging $10 million of federal stimulus money with an additional $10 million of private and public money to create at least 1,000 green jobs.[43] California's commitment to "wise" energy policy is not new. The state started regulating the energy efficiency of appliances, such as refrigerators, in the 1970s.[44]

In addition to state efforts, municipalities and city cooperatives have been pursuing a green economy for several years.[45] Chicago Mayor Richard M. Daley has worked on several green projects in his city.[46] Individual citizens have undertaken green projects as well. Omar Freilla applied the green jobs concept in the Bronx by creating a cooperative that recycled used building materials.[47] Taja Sevelle founded an international nonprofit organization called Urban Farming, which oversees community gardens in 14 cities in five countries.[48]

We have to go back to Oakland, California, to find one of the most formidable proponents of green-collar jobs. Van Jones, the man who literally wrote the book on green jobs,[49] got his start at Oakland's Ella Baker Center for Human Rights, teaching green jobs skills as a way to mitigate economic inequality.[50] He defined a green-collar job as "blue-collar employment that has been upgraded to better respect the environment, family-supporting, career track, vocational, or trade-level employment in environmentally-friendly fields."[51] (Jones served briefly in the Obama administration before a controversy over remarks about 9/11 that he made prior to joining the administration led to his resignation.)[52]

While the sentiment is in line with that of Alan Durning, the methodology of attaining a green economy is more detailed. Jones advocates building a coalition of labor, social justice advocates, environmentalists, and faith organizations working with the green business community to create a Green New Deal.[53] Government policy must help create the green economy by "setting standards, spurring innovation, realigning existing investments, and making new investments."[54] Jones looks to the Civilian Conservation Corps during the Great Depression, America's efforts in World War II, and the Apollo Project (the moon landing) as examples of how the government can influence positive change.[55] He even offered an idea that was the precursor to the "Cash for Clunkers" program.[56]

The Green Jobs Act of 2007 was passed as part of the Energy Independence and Security Act (Public Law 110-140). Then-Rep. Hilda Solis (now secretary of labor in the Obama administration) said that this federal legislation would advance national energy security and families' economic security: "Through targeted job training efforts, we can support both our nation's innovation and technological leadership and lift people out of poverty."[57] Then-Sen. Hillary Clinton of New York and Independent Sen. Bernie Sanders of Vermont included green jobs language in the Senate version of the energy bill.[58] President George W. Bush was pleased to sign "the first major energy security legislation in a decade" into law.[59] The law allocated up to $125 million per year for worker training and research in energy efficiency and renewable energy.[60]

Green initiatives grew hotter during the 2008 presidential campaign. Both candidates embraced a future green economy, with Sen. John McCain favoring market-based approaches and candidate Obama emphasizing governmental initiatives.[61] McCain's staccato listing of various types of alternative energy (wind, solar, tidal . . .) made each alternative energy source seem viable, scalable, and sure to be ready to go soon after Inauguration Day. Future president Obama promised a secure, clean energy economy and 5 million new green jobs.[62] The positive aspects of green policies appeal to many Americans on a visceral level: energy independence; pro-environment; and good-paying jobs that cannot be outsourced and don't require an Ivy League education.

In 2010, as the unemployment rate hovers around 10 percent, green jobs have added appeal. But there are major issues to cause concern. Highly credible sources, such as the Bureau of Labor Statistics[63] and the Specialist in Labor Economics at the Congressional Research Service, confirm that there has been no coherent definition of a green job.[64] While we will examine at length the problems of using an input-output model for forecasting green jobs, the CRS

report succinctly states that the North American Industry Classification System, which most agencies use for compiling statistics,
"does not identify separately so-called green industries," nor does
it have a "retrofitting" category.[65] While green jobs proponents like
the "progressive" think tank Center for American Progress[66] may explain their use of the input-output model as the best of not-so-great
options, one still must measure the total *net* jobs created (green jobs
added minus nongreen jobs lost) as a result of governmental policy.
While we will discuss at length the difficulties of scaling solar and
wind (much less cellulosic ethanol) to federal- or state-mandated
levels, the CRS report also notes that the major green jobs reports
predated the current recession as multiyear proposals, not quick
fixes for high levels of unemployment during a recession.[67]

The green energy mantra should be appealing. Many proponents
offer something desirable at no cost: high paying, environmentally
friendly jobs, power generated by the (free) wind and sun, and
pollution-free biofuels powering modern, high-speed trains carry-
ing commuters between well-insulated homes and energy-efficient
workplaces. Unfortunately this promised future is built on sand. The
analytical foundations upon which green economy advocates base
their predictions are deeply flawed. The concrete results of following
these policies will be a decline in living standards around the globe,
including for the world's poorest; changes in lifestyle that Americans do not want; and a weakening of the technological progress that
market forces have delivered, preventing us from finding real solutions to the real problems we face. The next 10 chapters discuss why
we think green programs have been oversold, showing the mistakes
that make the analyses upon which they are based unreliable. The
final chapter gives you a checklist of questions to ask about green
energy proposals to help make informed judgments about whether
these massive gambles with our future are appropriate.

2. Fables: Alternative Futures for Society

Before delving into details of the green energy and green jobs literature, it would be useful to summarize the most comprehensive piece in that area, the United Nations Environment Programme report.[1] It provides a sense of the scope of the transformation that would be required of the United States and world economies, as well as to the structure of society, to implement green energy and jobs proposals. These suggestions by the UNEP report are not the simple sort we hear most about, such as hiring the unemployed to weatherize schools. To reduce greenhouse gas (GHG) emissions on a large scale, such as 50 percent by 2050[2] or, even better, by 80 percent by 2050 as Al Gore and other politicians advocate,[3] the UNEP report explains that we must restructure almost everything about how we live.

The UNEP report stresses that new, green jobs will be created to achieve program goals. Some workers will switch from traditional production to greener production. The report notes, unlike most green jobs reports, that existing jobs will be destroyed as disfavored methods of production are forced to cease, replaced by new, preferred methods of production. It also explains that while some existing jobs will, after retooling, continue to exist, these are usually lumped into the category of green jobs since the change is forced by environmental objectives. The UNEP states: "it would appear that many existing jobs (such as plumbers, electricians, metal workers, and construction workers) will simply be transformed and redefined as day-to-day skill sets, work methods, and profiles are greened."[4]

How will all this happen? "Forward-thinking government policies" are "indispensable."[5] That is, strong government action is required. The policy changes called for by the report fall into nine categories:

- **Subsidies.** Subsidies for "environmentally harmful industries" will be terminated; the funds will be shifted to renewable energy, efficiency technologies, clean production methods, and public transit.

- **Carbon markets.** Carbon markets, such as carbon trading under the Kyoto Protocol, are not doing as much as needed, so they must be strengthened. In addition to carbon credits being traded, carbon must be taxed so revenues can be used as "adequate funding sources for green projects and employment."
- **Eco-taxes.** Eco-taxes must be initiated and used to discourage polluting and carbon-producing activities.
- **Government regulations.** "Regulatory tools" must be used "to the fullest extent" to force greener technologies. This includes expanded government land-use controls, revised building codes, more stringent energy-efficiency standards, and increased renewable energy production.
- **Electrical grid access.** Alternative energy production will be encouraged by guaranteeing access to electric grids at favorable prices for such suppliers.
- **Expanding recycling requirements.** Manufacturers will be required to take back their products after use, so producers will ensure that products will be recycled properly at the end of their useful life.
- **Mandatory eco-labeling.** Eco-labeling of products will be required, so consumers can make informed choices among alternatives given the environmental costs.
- **Shifting energy research funding.** Cut support for nuclear power and fossil fuel research in favor of greater funding for renewable energy and technical efficiency.
- **Changes in foreign aid.** Reorient foreign aid away from fossil fuel and hydro-electric power projects in favor of renewable energy sources.[6]

Note that the action items are all government mandates. This is because the report claims that environmental improvements that occur naturally "are insufficient and may simply be overwhelmed by continued economic growth." Not only will new kinds of jobs be created in place of old jobs, but for environmental (and human) sustainability, lower standards of living are an unfortunate fact. As such, the UNEP report calls for "retool[ing] not only the economy, but also economic thought" so that people will use "a different way of measuring human activity" and a "different theory," no longer focused on "quantitative growth" but instead on "a shift from the acquisition of goods" to "the continuous receipt of quality, utility, and performance."[7]

Mass production will generally end, as will the jobs that comprise the modern economy, according to UNEP. After all, we are no longer going to focus on "large scale purchases of 'stuff,'" but instead on "quality retail, in which the salesperson knows how to sell intelligent use rather than simple ownership."[8] Accompanying this major move away from impersonal big-box retailing, consumers will "obtain desired services by leasing or renting goods rather than buying them outright."[9] Such changes will mean many displaced workers, so we need to think of how to "share available work better among all those who desire work."[10]

Another major green jobs area is building. New buildings should have high green standards, but existing buildings can be retrofitted to be more efficient.[11] Emission savings can be significant, and the technology exists now to incur such savings, according to these reports. For example, retrofitting buildings to be energy saving will reduce GHG emissions by 29 percent.[12] The UNEP report estimates that this could create 2 million jobs in the European Union and the United States and, obviously, millions more around the world.[13]

Energy conservation is another major area of concern in the green jobs reports. Although private incentives to save resources are strong, the report asserts that they are insufficient to resolve the GHG problem. Transportation contributes about 23 percent of such emissions.[14] While aircraft today are 70 percent more fuel-efficient than those built 40 years ago, and continued improvements are projected, those are insufficient and will not halt emissions, the reports claim.[15] Car and truck traffic is also a major contributor. While engines are more efficient now than in the past and new engine technology is coming into play, given the rapid increase in demand for vehicles in China, India, and other parts of the world, the emission problem will not be "solved," if you believe the green jobs reports.[16]

Besides continued improvement in car and truck engines, there must be a push to public transit systems, UNEP reports.[17] For this to succeed, cities throughout the nation must have greater density, implying massive population shifts from the suburbs to central cities. Subways are not realistic in sprawling cities, so we must rebuild cities. Think of Manhattan, not Denver. "Denser cities and shorter distances reduce the overall need for motorized transportation."[18]

29

High-density living also means that walking and bicycling will become more realistic alternatives and will replace cars for many, according to the reports.[19]

All such changes should be done in a labor-intensive way. For example, the report decries the falling employment in the production of locomotives and rolling stock in China. Despite the growth of the rail network by 24 percent from 1992 to 2002, employment fell from 3.4 million to 1.8 million. "A sustainable transport policy needs to reverse this trend."[20] A senior manager at a Chinese rolling stock company, a state-owned enterprise, told one of the authors that the single biggest challenge for his company is to keep employment up (which the government prefers) as it continues to modernize and expand production. Most such state-dominated organizations have surplus inefficient labor despite the cuts already made. With modern production methods, it is dubious that more workers will be needed as the UNEP report hopes.

The UNEP also puts great stock on increased recycling of steel and aluminum to reduce energy usage as opposed to production of virgin metals.[21] In addition, it assumes new technology will allow for less pollution than traditional production. The same is true in other areas where recycling is technologically feasible. As we show below in more detail, there is a trend toward more energy efficiency in steel and aluminum production, but it is the result of market forces, not mandates. Millions of people are already doing recycling for a living[22]—but this includes people who scour garbage dumps around the world.[23] The employment problem is that, the UNEP explains, much existing recycling is small scale and not environmentally friendly.[24]

The UNEP report also takes aim at the world's agricultural system. A little over a third of the world's workforce is in agriculture.[25] Much of the work is on small plots of land, not the large industrial-scale farming in the United States that requires few workers. The continuous decline of the share of the workforce in agriculture poses a conundrum for the authors as they recognize the trade-off between large-scale, efficient modern agriculture and traditional small plots that still dominate in poor countries.[26]

Modern agriculture relies on inputs such as chemical fertilizers. Those are not green.[27] Further, existing global integration of agriculture means large companies "dictate 'take it or leave it' terms on those who actually grow the food."[28] That is, farmers who have found it to their advantage to contract with large companies must cease such activities so food is not carried off to Carrefour and other big-box retailers.[29] Farmers should focus on local production and consumption.[30] Small-plot agriculture is to be encouraged.[31] Large-scale meat production "is neither green nor decent"[32] and must come to an end in favor of a few animals on small plots of land that keep hundreds of millions employed.[33] Of course, with many people living in high-density cities, if agricultural production as we know it is undesirable because shipments across long distances is carbon-intensive, then we must have "sustainable urban agriculture" that will employ hundreds of millions, according to the report.[34] Unfortunately, the net effect of this proposal is to increase food prices, thereby injuring the poor most of all, and to reduce choices as people will be required to eat domestic products and not enjoy diverse foods from around the country, let alone around the world.

The last major sector considered in the UNEP report is forestry. Forests must be expanded and deforestation reversed in many countries.[35] Since this occurs primarily in very-low-income areas, the cost of moving from deforestation to forestation is estimated to be relatively small at $5–10 billion per year.[36] Keeping millions busy requires investment in agroforestry, such as expansion of fruit trees, but the report's authors admit that the fragmented nature of the industry makes solid projections difficult.[37]

The change to green jobs will not be easy, cheap, or voluntary. "Governments at the global, national, and local levels must establish an ambitious and clear policy framework to support and reward sustainable economic activity and be prepared to confront those whose business practices continue to pose a serious threat to a sustainable future."[38] What this means is that massive public spending is needed and many existing methods of production must be terminated by regulatory controls if we are to achieve the technological and economic transformations on the scale needed to achieve significant reductions in energy production and use, and to have the changes in methods of the energy that is produced.

The UNEP report explains the scope of what is at stake in the green jobs policy discussion; it does not pretend that this is a simple matter. In contrast to domestic reports we review here, which assert that green jobs programs are all win-win and claim to know exactly how many green jobs will be created decades from now, the UNEP report,

31

while comprehensive, does not pretend that the costs can be known exactly, nor does it sugarcoat some parts of the structural changes that would be needed to force massive change.

What the UNEP report makes clear is the broad scope of the change it proposes. Virtually every aspect of daily life—from where we live, where our food comes from, how we commute to work, to what we do at work—will be dramatically altered. Such massive social change is costly in both monetary terms and in the disruption of lives. Before launching a program to transform the lives of billions of people at a cost of trillions of dollars, we should be sure that not only is this the future we want but that the theory on which the vision is built is correct. The history of the 20th century is, in part, the history of failed efforts to remake societies according to visions that proved unsustainable. Before launching yet another effort, on an even grander scale, we need to thoroughly critique the vision. We turn to doing so now.

Ignoring Incentive Effects

The green jobs literature focuses heavily on public policies intended to induce greater energy efficiency, both to reduce GHG emissions from power generation and because it generally seeks to shift expenditures away from fossil fuels. However, energy efficiency occurs naturally as a result of market processes even without expensive government programs. Because the literature ignores this trend, which has occurred in multiple industries over many decades, the green jobs literature overstates the benefits of its conservation measures by claiming credit for conservation that would occur even without proactive public policy prescriptions.[39]

Because energy is costly, market forces provide incentives to produce and consume using less energy. These forces produce real change: from the late 1970s to 2000, energy utilization per dollar of real GDP produced in the United States fell by 36 percent.[40] Total energy usage increased because of economic growth over that time, but efficiency increased more than growth in all major energy-using sectors.[41] That is, as energy efficiency in production increases, the marginal cost of consuming energy per unit of output declines, thereby stimulating demand for energy as the cost of output falls (for many goods) and consumer incomes rise as the economy grows.[42] This trend has meant that past efforts to forecast future energy use have consistently overestimated future energy demands. During the 1970s, the United States had grave concerns about the sufficiency of energy sources. Oil prices hit an all-time high. OPEC reduced production. The domestic problem was exacerbated by price controls imposed by the Nixon administration, causing concern that the energy crunch could inflict major economic harm as far into the future as could be seen. Would there be sufficient energy to drive the economic engine? Some were convinced that could not be possible, so doom was on the horizon.[43]

Knowledgeable researchers in the late 1970s looked ahead to estimate energy use by 2000. Their conclusion was disturbing. It showed significant increases in energy would be needed. Looking back, we know that the estimates of that time proved to be 60 to 80 percent too high compared to actual use by 2000.[44] In other words, the experts, who knew efficiency in energy production and use would increase, still greatly underestimated technical progress in efficiency. Further, the apparent incentive to conserve energy should have been lessened because oil prices turned out to be much lower by the mid-1980s than were anticipated by scholars in the late 1970s based on that decade's oil shock. The situation is no different today. We find no good reasons to be concerned about energy security in the future, as supplies are abundant.[45] However, the future will not look like today because of innovations that emerge and that cannot now be known.

Given the bias against many technologies in the green jobs literature, as we noted earlier, we would expect the predictions made in it to be even more likely to discount incorrectly the chances of improvements in energy efficiency caused by market forces. Predictions of future energy efficiency depend on forecasts of technological change. But technical progress is a perpetual process, difficult to measure and difficult to force.

The green jobs literature is not the first time that government mandates have been proposed to reduce energy consumption. Mandatory energy savings have been popular since the oil shocks of the 1970s. Utilities were required at that time to engage in assorted "negawatt" programs that would result in less electricity being required over time.[46] Either due to political pressure to show good results, or simply poor ability to comprehend costs, the savings from the programs that emerged after the 1970s energy crisis shock were vastly overstated or, conversely, the costs were underestimated "by a factor of two or more on average."[47] The claims in the green jobs literature should be evaluated keeping in mind this record of failure by political planners of energy policy. Proponents of new policies bear the burden to explain how their proposals will succeed where past efforts did not.

Market competition creates incentives for firms to find more efficient ways to achieve results. Waste reductions in the private sector (improvements in efficiency) are pervasive. As the CEO of Boeing notes, the fuel efficiency of commercial aircraft over several decades has increased 70 percent. That is, "carbon emissions per mile flown have dropped 70 percent—all without a regulatory requirement for greenhouse gas emissions."[48] A decade ago, the Federal Reserve Bank of Dallas estimated that a bank transaction in person cost a bank $1.14 (ignoring the bank customer's time and cost of traveling to the bank in an emission-spewing vehicle) while an online transaction cost one cent.[49] A result of the electronic transactions was that many bank teller jobs were eliminated. Thinking of those as "jobs lost" is incorrect. Productive resources—humans—were released to other activities. Wealth increased. The same report noted that Wal-Mart reduced truck operating costs by 20 percent by using computers, GPS devices, and cell phones in trucks. Amoco's use of new seismic processes and computer analysis reduced the cost of finding oil from about $10 per barrel in 1991 to about $1 per barrel in 1999.[50] Weyerhaeuser's use of scanners and computers in log milling increased yields by 30 percent in less than a decade, and "precision farming" technology using computers, sensors on machinery, and GPS systems reduced agricultural costs and raised yields.[51] The list of such improvements seems endless, but living amid the change, we often do not see the forest for the trees.

There has always been potential profit in what is commonly viewed as waste. One of the first extensive works to document this was by business and technology journalist Peter Lund Simmonds, who, in a 400-page study published in 1862, noted that "[i]n every manufacturing process there is more or less waste of the raw material, which it is the province of others following after the original manufacturer to collect and utilize."[52] He reported on such work involving cotton, wool, silk, leather, and iron. Even Karl Marx grudgingly acknowledged this productive feature of competition:

> With the advance of capitalist production the utilization of the excrements of production and consumption is extended. . . . The general requirements for the re-employment of these excrements are: A great quantity of such excrements, such as is

only the result of production on a large scale; improvements in machinery by which substances formerly useless in their prevailing form are given another useful in reproduction; progress of science, especially of chemistry, which discovers the useful qualities of such waste.[53]

Other, less earthy, economists of that era discussed the wonders of the Chicago meat packing industry, where there were developments "of tallow, glue, soap, felt, bone meal, glycerin, knife handles, buttons and countless other articles whose main inputs were previously wasted blood, feet, heads and other non-edible animal parts."[54] Later, Henry Ford built his River Rouge complex in Dearborn, Michigan, with waste reduction in mind. Among many innovations, a cement plant was built next to the car factory to dispose of tons of blast furnace slag. Some of the cement was used in Ford construction activities; the rest was sold.[55] The process of technological innovation is continuous and usually so gradual that we do not appreciate the extent of improvements.

Over the long term, market forces in conjunction with technological change have increased the efficiency of energy processes remarkably.[56] Table 2.1 shows the technological progress in delivering energy for heating, stationary power, electricity, transportation, and lighting since the start of the Industrial Revolution around 1750. Although most of the data are from the United Kingdom, they are qualitatively applicable to the United States. The table shows that, compared to 1900, each unit of energy input in 2000 could provide four times as much useful heat, move a person 550 times farther, provide 50 times more illumination, and produce 12 times as much electricity. Much of the improvements occurred prior to 1950 (i.e., before the advent of the regulatory era in either the United Kingdom or the United States).

More importantly, after taking into consideration the changes in fuels, fuel mixes, and energy conversion technologies, these forces have decreased the cost of energy services—namely, the provision of heat, stationary power, transport, and lighting—to the consumer by an order of magnitude or more (see Table 2.2). As Fouquet and Pearson note:

> In [the] last two hundred and fifty years, the cost of generating useful heat has fallen more than 10-fold. To generate a unit of power costs 50 times less. To travel one kilometre is 150 times cheaper. To produce the same quantity of light, it costs us 8,000 times less.[57]

Table 2.1

LONG-RUN TRENDS IN THE ENERGY TECHNOLOGIES, U.K. OR U.S., 1750–2000

Energy Service	Area	Year						
		1750	1800	1850	1900	1950	2000
Heating (% energy converted to heat)	U.K.	11	11	13.5	21	41	86
Stationary power (% thermal efficiency converted to power; includes power derived from electricity)	U.K.	0.5	4.6	10	15	20	
Thermal power plant (watt-hours of electricity produced per thousand BTU of heat input)[1]	U.S.				8.3	71.3	98.0
Transport (passenger-kilometer per ton of oil equivalent)	U.K.		10	24	36	11,700	20,000
Lighting (lumen-hours per kWh)	U.K.	29	36	190	500	11,600	25,000

SOURCE: Indur M. Goklany, *The Improving State of the World: Why We're Living Longer, Healthier, More Comfortable Lives on a Cleaner Planet* (Washington: Cato Institute, 2007), p. 144; EIA, *Annual Review 2008*, p. 364, Table A6; Fouquet and Pearson.

[1]The figure for 1900 is taken from 1899. Goklany, p. 144; 1950 and 2000 figures are from EIA, *Annual Review 2008*, pp. 68–71.

Table 2.2
LONG-RUN TRENDS IN THE PRICE OF ENERGY SERVICES, U.K. OR U.S., 1750–2000

Energy Service	Area	Year					
		1750	1800	1850	1900	1950	2000
Heating (constant (2000) pounds sterling per ton of coal equivalent of *effective* heat)	U.K.	1,400	700	500	460	380	130
Stationary Power (constant (2000) pence/kWh)	U.K.	140	35	35	20	4	2.5
Electricity, residential (constant (2000) cents/kWh)[1]	U.S.				267	17.4	8.2
Transport (constant (2000) pence per passenger-kilometer)	U.K.	15	5	1	0.38	0.16	0.1
Lighting (constant (2000) pounds sterling/millions of lumen-hours)	U.K.	13,690	6,630	1,175	276	10	1.7

SOURCE: Bureau of the Census, *Historical Statistics of the United States: Colonial Times to 1970* (Washington: Bureau of the Census, 1976); EIA, *Annual Review 2008*; Fouquet and Pearson; Bureau of Economic Affairs, "All NIPA Tables," http://www.bea.gov/national/nipaweb/SelectTable.asp (follow "Table 1.2.4. Price Indexes for Gross Domestic Product by Major Type of Product (A) (Q)" hyperlink).

[1] 1900 figure is taken from 1902 data and calculated from Bureau of the Census, pp. 211, 827; EIA, *Annual Review 2008*; Bureau of Economic Affairs., "All NIPA Tables."

These improvements occurred when there was an upward trend in average energy prices during the latter half of the 19th century and much of the 20th century, a period that witnessed massive changes in energy systems and substitutions toward more expensive but higher quality fuels, such as petroleum for transport and natural gas and electricity for other uses.[58]

In the following subsections, we examine U.S. energy consumption trends in some specific energy-intensive sectors and, with respect to some specific energy-consuming technologies, demonstrate both how this process operates and its importance in energy consumption.

1. Iron and Steel

The iron and steel industries are crucial industrial sectors, therefore "greening" jobs in these areas is a high priority for green jobs advocates.[59] The green jobs literature gives a sense that these are remarkably energy inefficient, noncompetitive industries. The UNEP report states that "making steel mills greener and more competitive is a must for job retention."[60] The reality is that iron and steel production has become much more energy-efficient in the absence of programs advocated by green jobs proponents, who have no apparent expertise in steel manufacturing. For example, as Figure 2.1 shows, the amount of energy consumed per ton of U.S.-produced steel declined by more than 60 percent from 1980 to 2006, and by 29 percent from 1990 to 2006.[61] These improvements were driven by the need to stay competitive in a tough business environment, which led to restructuring of the industry through the bankruptcies in the 1990s and early 2000s, closure of older and inefficient operations, and increases in the proportion of scrap iron and steel recycled via electric arc furnaces.[62] Not reflected in Figure 2.1 is the fact that today's steels are thinner and stronger, which means that for the average application, the decline in energy intensity is even greater than reflected on the figure.

2. Aluminum

Based on data for 2000, it takes 44,700 BTU to produce one pound of primary aluminum in the United States, which makes it the most energy intensive major material manufactured.[63] On the other hand, secondary aluminum (i.e., recycled aluminum)

Figure 2.1
Energy Intensity in Steel Production (MBtu/Ton)

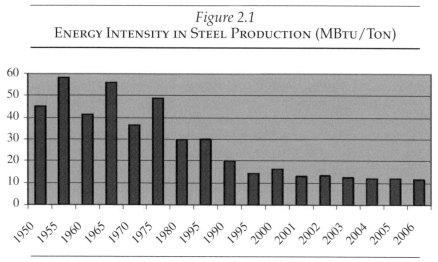

Source: Table 16, p. 27, John Stubbles, *Energy Use in the U.S. Steel Industry: An Historical Perspective and Future Opportunities* (U.S. Dept. of Energy, 2000).

requires only 6 percent of the energy necessary to manufacture primary aluminum.[64] Between 1960 and 2000, secondary aluminum as a share of total aluminum production increased from 18 percent to 47 percent. As noted earlier, the UNEP report expresses concern that more metals should be recycled; the trend has been in that direction already.

In addition to reduced energy consumption from recycling, primary aluminum production also became more efficient. Between 1960 and 2000, the energy required for smelting a kilogram of the primary ore, a key energy-intensive operation necessary to produce the primary metal, declined by 35 percent. As a consequence, the total energy intensity of aluminum production in the United States declined by more than 58 percent over this period (see Figure 2.2).[65]

3. Ammonia

Ammonia production is the third most energy intensive production process, after aluminum and pulp and paper production (12,200 BTU per pound).[67] As was the case with iron, steel, and aluminum, ammonia production became steadily more efficient during the 20th century. Newer ammonia factories use 30 percent less energy than plants from the 1970s[68] and are approaching the theoretical minimum based on the

Figure 2.2
ENERGY INTENSITY FOR U.S. ALUMINUM PRODUCTION, 1960–2000[66]

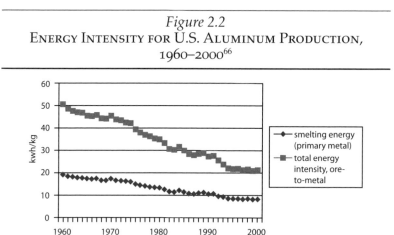

SOURCE: William T. Choate and John A.S. Green, *U.S. Energy Requirements for Aluminum Production: Historical Perspective, Theoretical Limits, and New Opportunities* (U.S. Dept. of Energy, 2003), Appendix L.

processes that are in use today (see Figure 2.3). Note that most of the efficiency gains preceeded the modern regulatory era and so were the result of competition, not government mandates.

Figure 2.3
TECHNOLOGY CHANGES AND ENERGY CONSUMPTION IN AMMONIA PLANTS, 1910–2000[69]

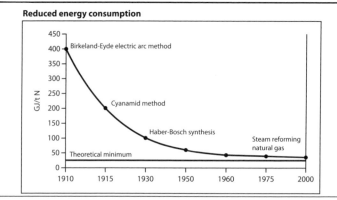

SOURCE: Adapted from A. Anundskas, Technical Improvements in Mineral Nitrogen Fertilizer Production, in Harvesting Energy with Fertilizers (European Fertilizer Manufacturers Assn., 2000).

4. Pulp and Paper

The second most energy-intensive industry after aluminum is production of paper and paper board (15,100 BTU per pound).[70] Typically, two-thirds of the energy used by this industry is in the form of heat, with the remainder being consumed as electricity.[71] Unfortunately, the energy efficiency story in this industry is not as positive. The International Energy Agency notes that the United States is the largest chemical pulp producer in the world and has one of the world's most energy-intensive pulp and paper industries, "at least partly due to the old age of [its] pulp and paper mills."[72]

Why has the pulp and paper industry not modernized its equipment and adopted more energy-efficient production methods? A major part of the problem is that U.S. environmental regulations applicable to new sources act as a deterrent to replacing old plants and equipment. That is, a regulatory bias against new sources ("new source bias") leads to an "old plant effect," whereby companies would rather retain old, inefficient plants by patching them up occasionally instead of replacing them with more efficient, but more capital-intensive, new plants that are made even more expensive because of the need to meet tighter regulatory standards.[73]

5. Appliances

The preceding sections describe both increasing energy efficiency in production of important goods and how regulatory barriers sometimes impede market forces pushing firms to adopt more efficient methods of production. We now turn to consumer goods, where increasing energy efficiency has been an important policy goal for decades.

California began setting energy efficiency standards for appliances as early as 1978.[74] Beginning in 1980, a federal labeling program for major household appliances ("EnergyGuide"), enacted into law in 1975, went into effect. In 1988, the Department of Energy started imposing federal standards under the National Appliance Energy Conservation Act of 1987,[75] which was enacted in large part to preempt a multiplicity of state standards.[76] NAECA established minimum efficiency standards for many household appliances, such as refrigerators, refrigerator-freezers, and freezers; room air conditioners; fluorescent lamp ballasts; clothes washers and dryers; dishwashers; kitchen ranges and ovens; pool heaters; television sets (withdrawn in 1995);[77] and water heaters.[78] Congress set initial federal energy efficiency standards and established schedules for DOE to review these standards.[79] The Energy Policy Act of 1992 (EPAct) added standards for additional devices and systems, such as some fluorescent and incandescent reflector lamps; plumbing products; electric motors; commercial water heaters; and heating, ventilation, and air conditioning (HVAC) systems, and allowed the future development of standards for several other products.[80] It also provided for voluntary testing and consumer information programs for office equipment, luminaries, and windows.[81] The existence of a federal standard for energy or water conservation products generally preempts state standards, unless the state standard is identical to the federal standard. "Any State regulation providing for any energy conservation standard, or water conservation standard . . . or other requirement with respect to the energy efficiency, energy use, or water use. . . of a covered product that is not identical to a Federal standard in effect under this subpart is preempted by that standard. . . ."[82] These standards provide an opportunity to test the efficacy of the sort of mandates for energy efficiency proposed by green jobs advocates.

Among home appliances, refrigerators are among the largest energy consumers (see Figure 2.4). The U.S. experience with refrigerators is a way to test the home appliance standards' effectiveness.

The first thing we notice in examining refrigerator energy efficiency is that the efficiency of household refrigerators has been in-

Figure 2.4
BREAKDOWN OF ENERGY CONSUMPTION FOR
HOME APPLIANCES FOR 2010

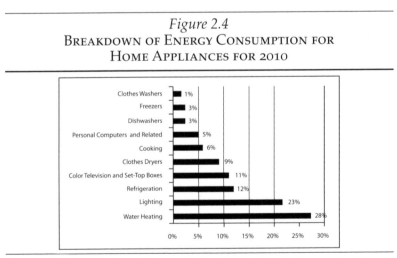

SOURCE: EIA (2010), *Annual Energy Outlook 2010*. Note that space heating, air conditioning, fans, pumps, and "other" are excluded.[83]

creasing steadily at least since the mid-1970s (see Figure 2.5). Several analysts claim that "the majority of efficiency gains have been driven by the introduction of regulatory policies."[84] If true, this would support the introduction of the sort of mandate policies advocated by green jobs proponents.

There are a number of reasons to believe that the improvements in refrigeration efficiency have not been due to the mandates. First, as Figure 2.5 shows, more than half the improvements preceded the imposition of federal standards. Instead, the change in slope of the line in Figure 2.5 appears in response to the first oil shock of 1973, which was reinforced by the run-up in energy prices from 1979 to 1985.[86] Since the slope reverses prior to the policies, the policies cannot be the cause of the change. Second, even the post–federal policy efficiency improvements in the early- to mid-1980s can be ascribed to high energy prices reinforced by the ready availability of information to the consumer, via labeling requirements (i.e., the Energy Guides available for each appliance) rather than the efficiency guidelines. Third, a portion of these improvements, particularly since the 1980s, can be attributed to broader use of microchips and

Figure 2.5
AVERAGE ENERGY USE PER REFRIGERATOR, 1947–2000[85]

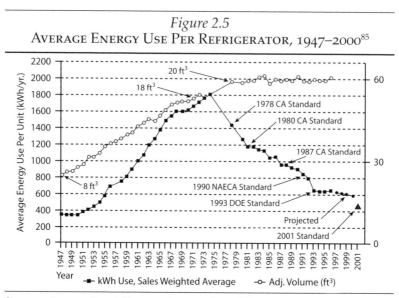

SOURCE: International Energy Agency, http://www.iea.org/publications/free_new_Desc.asp?PUBS_ID=1127.

electronic controls and the drop in in the price of such controls.[87] These factors were probably driven as much, if not more, by consumer desires and increased competition in the marketplace heightened by globalization and trade than by mandates. This was an era in which made-in-America goods were under increasing pressure from made-in-Asia goods, first from Japan, then Taiwan and Korea, and currently China, Thailand, and Malaysia. Appliance manufacturing was part of this general trend. This led to greater pressures to improve the quality of products and reduce prices for customers.

Moreover, the increase in the energy use per unit prior to the mid-1970s was not due to increased energy inefficiency in home refrigerators. Rather, it was caused by increases in the sizes of refrigerators (see Figures 2.5 and 2.6) and progressive improvements in their features over time. These features include increases in the relative size of freezer sections, the advent and greater penetration of frost-free/frost-proof units, and icemakers.[88] In short, consumers were getting more and better re-

Figure 2.6
NEW U.S. REFRIGERATORS: AVERAGE ANNUAL ENERGY USE AND RETAIL PRICES, 1947–2002

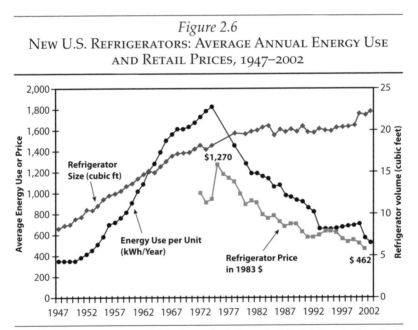

SOURCE: Arthur H. Rosenfeld, *From the Lab to the Marketplace to Standards* (Presentation to Berkeley Energy Resource Collaborative, University of California, Berkeley, March 21, 2007), Slide 22, http://www.energy.ca.gov/2007publications/CEC-999-2007-014/CEC-999-2007-014.ppt.

frigerators for their money, which, however, required greater energy to maintain and use. At a time of cheap energy prices, it is unsurprising that the market provided consumer goods that used energy to eliminate unpleasant chores such as defrosting freezers or enabled consumers to economize by storing food in larger freezer units.

Moreover, national refrigerator sales data indicate that following the introduction of refrigerator standards, real prices decreased, even after adjusting for changes in refrigerator size and amenities (see Figure 2.6). Normalized to food and freezer volumes, real refrigerator prices declined 8 percent from 1987 to 1993.[89] It has been argued, therefore, that energy standards have little or no effect on appliance prices. This, of course, is probably a testament to the price-lowering effects of competition. It is possible that the price may have dropped further but for the standards. Alternatively, the price may not have been much different because reduced energy consumption is an amenity that the manufacturers would, in a competitive free market system, have provided of their own volition to consumers sooner or later regardless of the existence of any standards.

Our analysis is consistent with the findings of the IEA examination of similar data across countries:

> Analysis . . . for 16 IEA countries shows that improved energy efficiency has been the main reason why final energy use has been decoupled from economic growth. Without the energy efficiency improvements that occurred between 1973 and 2005 in 11 of those countries, energy use would have been 58%, or . . . higher in 2005 than it actually was. However, since 1990 the rate of energy efficiency improvement has been much lower than in previous decades.

> These findings provide an important policy conclusion—that the changes caused by the oil price shocks in the 1970s and the resulting energy policies did considerably more to control growth in energy demand and reduce CO_2 emissions than the energy efficiency and climate policies implemented in the 1990s.[90]

Conclusion

The UNEP study, like other green jobs reports discussed in this book, recommends an array of governmental mandates to reduce energy usage and force adoption of alternative energy sources such as solar power. Such reports repeat a drumbeat of literature forecasting the economic doom that will occur if society relies on market prices and entrepreneurial innovations to generate effective use of energy sources.[91]

Our examination of energy consumption across both producer and consumer goods demonstrates important lessons relevant to the evaluation of the claims of green jobs advocates. Market forces provide a powerful incentive that drives greater efficiency with respect to costly inputs. This suggests that the net gains from green jobs policies mandating conservation are likely to produce fewer gains than the advocates claim since some, all, or even most of the efficiency gains claimed would occur even in the absence of mandates due to rising energy prices. Adopting mandates is not risk-free with respect to energy efficiency. The green jobs literature does not discuss the extensive data, including that summarized here, on increases in energy efficiency over time in the very industries they propose to regulate. This ahistorical approach casts serious doubt on the credibility of the green jobs literature. The authors of this book are not experts on aluminum or refrigerators. Yet we were able to find from widely distributed, publicly available sources, extensive data on a crucial issue in the green jobs literature that is completely ignored by that literature. Such gaps suggest a need for great skepticism in evaluating the claims of those who profess to know how energy markets and our future should be controlled.

3. The Challenge of Green Energy

Green energy is at the heart of green economy efforts. Advocates tout sources of green employment in building, operating, and maintaining approved energy facilities, such as windmills and solar photovoltaic (PV) panels, both as sources of employment and as a means of greening energy-using industries. In their enthusiasm for a radical change in energy production, green energy advocates have ignored important issues about greening the energy sources we use.

Electricity production must meet electricity demand. Wind and solar electricity production differs significantly from energy production using coal, natural gas, or nuclear power. Coal, natural gas, and nuclear power plants can work almost continuously, providing power day or night, on windy days and still days, and when it is sunny or raining. Neither wind nor solar is produced continuously or at the flick of a switch—the wind must blow or the sun must shine. As a result, they add significant technical complexity to managing the power supply. Wind- and solar-produced electricity is likely to be generated far from the existing grid that distributes electric power throughout the country. Any strategy that relies on dramatic increases in wind or solar production of electricity must take these problems into account—and green energy advocates largely do not, except to claim as a benefit the billions of dollars necessary to rebuild the grid to accommodate such facilities.

All forms of energy involve trade-offs. As economists often like to remind non-economists, there is no free lunch. Producing energy has costs, no matter how it happens. Even energy facilities that green energy proponents are most fond of—wind farms and solar (PV) fields—are not uncontroversial once there are plans to build one in someone's backyard. Windmills can cause "shadow flicker" for neighbors, slice and dice birds, and create visual and noise pollution that annoys those living nearby. The American Bar Association's *Jour-*

nal—hardly a bastion of anti-green energy propaganda—reported on complaints about wind farms by neighbors, quoting a couple who had leased land next to a wind farm: "We can't sleep. We can't watch TV. This has been a disaster for us and our neighbors."[1] The most famous example is the Cape Wind project off Nantucket, where the prominent green energy advocate Sen. Edward Kennedy fought to prevent an offshore wind farm because of its impact on his view of Nantucket Sound. Similarly, solar PV fields can interfere with endangered species' habitats.[2] As a result, building such facilities is often much harder than green energy advocates suggest—in early 2010, more than 70 wind farm proposals were "bogged down by moratoriums, restrictive ordinances, environmental challenges and lawsuits filed by community groups."[3] Growing crops for biofuels can cause environmental damage, including significant water pollution. Diverting existing food crops to biofuel production can raise food prices, thereby harming the poor. The point is not that we can never change anything but that the choices before us involve complex trade-offs among competing priorities.

Green is in the eye of the beholder. Defining what energy counts as "green" symbolizes the problems in reconciling the interest groups within the green coalition. For example, is nuclear power "green"? It is almost impossible to imagine meeting the ambitious greenhouse gas (GHG) emission reduction targets proposed by those concerned with climate change without a dramatic increase in the use of nuclear power. An Oxford research team, for instance, concluded that it would be necessary to maximize nuclear plant construction to meet GHG emission reduction targets.[4] Despite this, green energy proponents are, at best, ambivalent about new nuclear plants. For example, the U.S. Council of Mayors report suggests counting jobs at existing nuclear plants, but not at new ones. Other green groups oppose nuclear energy and do not count any nuclear power plant or construction jobs as "green." In general, nuclear power confronts green energy advocates with a difficult question about trade-offs—more nuclear power plants would undoubtedly reduce CO_2 emissions, a key goal for most green interests. But nuclear power also has environmental downsides, most notably in the disposal of long-lived radioactive waste products. Such trade-offs are not particular to nuclear power. Producing solar PV panels often involves the production of hazardous waste products, and the land footprint of solar panel farms increases their environmental impact.

48

The sunny regions best suited for solar power are often among the most fragile environmentally. There are similar trade-offs in the use of biofuels and hydro power.

You can't eat your cake and have it too. The major trend in hydropower in the United States has been the dismantling of existing dams under pressure from environmentalists, many of whom have also now discovered the virtues of "green power."[5] U.S. hydro power capacity declined by about 5 percent from 1980 to 2006.[6] Environmentalists vociferously oppose new large dam projects both in the United States and abroad. In many cases, environmentalists are right to oppose dams. Many were or will be built with extensive public subsidies and so are a transfer of wealth from taxpayers to the special interests that get access to the power the dams generate. But the suggestion by green energy advocates that "small scale" and "micro" hydro power projects—whose names suggest the problem with relying on them as a major source of energy—will play a significant role in the future is unrealistic. For example, small hydro advocates tout the approval of permits for 104 small hydro projects with a combined capacity of 2,400 MW, or an average of 23 MW. (Small hydro plants are generally defined as between 1 MW and 30 MW.) The Rampart Canyon Dam, a U.S. project canceled in the late 1970s, would have had a capacity of 4,500 MW; even larger hydro projects being built in China, such as the Xiangjiaba Dam, rated at 6,400 MW.

This chapter looks at two of the most important issues involved in the dramatic changes in our electricity supply and transportation fuels proposed by green jobs advocates. First, we look at green energy proponents' selective technological optimism, which drives their view of how to change electric power generation. Second, through a close examination of biofuels and the environmental trade-offs involved in their production and use, we look at the problems raised by shifting the power to choose technologies from individuals to governments.

Selective Technological Optimism

Figure 3.1, from the U.S. Department of Energy's Energy Information Administration, shows the sources and uses of energy in the U.S. economy for 2008.

This diagram reveals several important things about U.S. energy consumption that any effort to change how we use or where we get

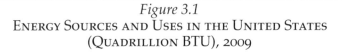

Figure 3.1
ENERGY SOURCES AND USES IN THE UNITED STATES
(QUADRILLION BTU), 2009

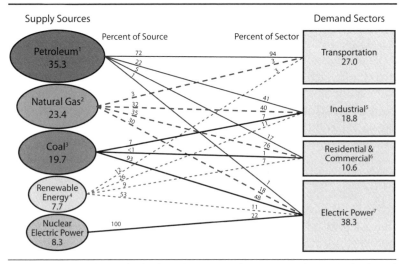

[1] Does not include the fuel ethanol portion of motor gasoline—fuel ethanol is included in Renewable Energy.
[2] Excludes supplemental gaseous fuels.
[3] Includes less than 0.1 quadrillion BTU of coal coke net imports.
[4] Conventional hydroelectric power, geothermal, solar PV, wind, and biomass.
[5] Includes industrial combined-heat-and-power (CHP) and industrial electricity-only plants.
[6] Includes commercial CHP and commercial electricity-only plants.
[7] Electricity-only and CHP plants whose primary business is to sell electricity, or electricity and heat, to the public.

NOTE: Sum of components may not equal total due to independent rounding.
SOURCE: U.S. Energy Information Administration, *Annual Energy Review 2009*, Tables 1.3, 2.1b–2.1f, 10.3, and 10.4.

our energy must take into account. First, different uses depend on quite different types of energy. Transportation is almost entirely dependent on petroleum: 95 percent of transportation energy comes from petroleum and only 3 percent from renewable sources. Electricity, on the other hand, is largely produced by coal (51 percent), nuclear (21 percent), and natural gas (17 percent).

Second, "nongreen" energy sources (petroleum, natural gas, and coal) provide 97 percent of transportation energy, 91 percent of industrial energy, 93 percent of residential and commercial energy, and 69 percent of electrical energy. If we include nuclear energy as "non-green" as most green energy proponents do, the percentage of nongreen electrical energy rises to 91 percent. Given the overwhelming proportion of nongreen energy in all these areas, even shifting a modest amount of energy consumption to "green energy" will require massive investments in new infrastructure. And since half of current renewable energy (almost entirely hydro power) goes into generating electricity, altering the mix in the other three sectors is an even more daunting task.

Third, 59.6 percent of our current energy supply comes from the two least green sources, coal and petroleum, and those sources are concentrated in transportation (95 percent) and electric power (52 percent). These areas, which green energy proponents frequently cite as ready for radical transformation, are among the hardest to change because both require massive infrastructure. Distributing transportation fuels requires a massive network of pipelines, barges, tankers, terminals, storage tanks, and filling stations to get fuel from oil refineries to our vehicles. Because ethanol, the primary biofuel in use, cannot be blended into gasoline until the last stages of distribution or be transported in existing pipelines, and because it is largely refined in different places from where oil is refined, expanding ethanol use requires creating new distribution infrastructure. Because wind, solar, and new hydro locations are not served by transmission lines, connecting them to the electrical distribution system will require huge investments in new lines. The Department of Energy estimated the cost of transmission lines in the "wind corridor" from Texas to Canada, where T. Boone Pickens proposed building $150 billion of turbines, at $60 billion.[7] Pickens abandoned his own planned 4,000 MW wind farm in the Texas panhandle in part because he was unable to persuade the state to fund the necessary transmission lines.

Moreover, energy use is complex. Once you drill down into the details, it becomes apparent that we can't simply plug a wind farm or solar PV array into the transmission grid and disconnect a corresponding amount from coal power plants. The transmission grid is a complex system, and adding a large number of new power sources would be tricky regardless of the type of energy, in part because the U.S. grid is aging and needs modernization. But wind's variability and the location of high quality wind sites far from where power is used make things even more complex. For example, on February 26, 2008, reduced winds in west Texas meant that output from wind farms there fell 1,500 MW (75 percent) over the course of three hours, just as demand spiked. As an article in *Science* reported:

> At 6:30 p.m., the alternating current in the state's transmission lines started to alternate more sluggishly, an ominous signal that the system was approaching collapse. Fortunately, managers of the state's power network had struck a set of agreements with large industrial customers allowing them to cut off power temporarily in exchange for lower rates. Within 10 minutes, about 1200 MW of load was sliced from the sagging electrical grid, and the system stabilized.[8]

Coping with such events would need to become routine if our electric supply became more dependent on wind-generated power. In Denmark, where wind energy is in widespread use, the capacity to generate 19 percent of electricity has resulted in actual generation of only an average of 9.7 percent from 2004–2009 and as little as 5 percent in one year. As a review of the Danish experience noted, even that degree of wind power was possible only because "Norway and Sweden provide . . . access to significant amounts of fast, short term balancing reserve, via interconnectors. They effectively act as Denmark's 'electric storage batteries.'"[9]

Integrating wind into the electricity grid requires more than additional transmission lines—it will take contracts with large users allowing transmission grid operators to shut off their power quickly, backup power systems capable of being switched on rapidly, and more sophisticated electric grid management techniques and equipment. Even renewable power advocates in Great Britain cautioned that wind facilities require massive backup—noting an industry rule of thumb that credited wind facilities with only the square root of their total capacity due to intermittency.[10] Moreover, renewable sources of electricity are not necessarily aligned with use patterns (wind power comes mostly at night), requiring development of storage techniques (e.g., pumped hydro) that raise their own questions about environmental impact (more dams and reservoirs, restrictions on water flow) or shifts in use patterns to accommodate power availability (e.g., night shifts at factories).

Similarly, introducing ethanol as a major transportation fuel is not just a matter of mixing it with existing petroleum-based fuels. Leaving aside issues about ethanol's environmental impact and energy content for now, there are significant problems caused by ethanol's propensity to attract water, which gasoline does not share. That means that ethanol storage and transportation networks must be more resistant to water intrusion than our existing gasoline networks. Moreover, in part because it attracts water, ethanol is more corrosive than gasoline, requiring significant differences in everything from gas station pumps to car fuel systems to accommodate levels above the E10 blends sold today and the new E15 blends the EPA has mandated. Blending and distribution mistakes have led to reported problems with fuel pumps when ethanol levels above the level for which nonflex fuel vehicles are rated was accidentally used.

These problems are complex but not impossible to solve, of course. The point is that the energy issues facing us are both simpler (transportation energy is almost entirely from petroleum) and more complex (integrating wind power into the electric grid is trickier than it appears) than green energy proponents appear to understand. The question isn't simply where the billions of dollars to build transmission lines and ethanol plants will come from, and the answer isn't just to find someone to write a check. Rather, there are thousands, if not millions, of adaptations, innovations, and decisions necessary to successfully change the sources and uses of energy in our daily lives. Time and experience have repeatedly shown that decentralized markets are the best institution for coordinating those efforts, not decisionmaking by government bureaucracies wedded to favored technologies and existing special interests. We now turn to some specifics about wind, solar, and nuclear power to illustrate these issues.

Wind power

Partly because of subsidies, the contribution of wind to renewable electricity generation is expected to increase from 7 percent in 2006 to 16 percent in 2020 and 20 percent in 2030.[11] That will leave wind producing still less than 4 percent of U.S. electricity in 2030.[12] However, despite being heavily subsidized, its total contribution to "energy security" is slight and unlikely to rise to a significant level over the foreseeable future. Wind contributes less than 0.6 percent of total U.S. energy production, based on federal statistics through September

2008.[13] According to the DOE's latest projections, it will account for less than 0.9 percent of total energy consumption in 2020 and 1.1 percent in 2030.[14] Wind plays an increasing role in electricity generation, but electricity is only a fraction of energy production in the United States, which is why wind is such a tiny share of total energy produced.

Wind's contribution to energy security is diminished by its intermittent delivery of electricity. Wind turbines cannot produce when wind speed is too low or too high, or if the turbine blades or other critical components are iced up. In fact, the Electric Reliability Council of Texas assumes, based on historical experience, that only 8.7 percent of wind power's installed capacity would be available during summer peak hours, one of the times when electricity is most needed.[15]

A study of small (10 kW or less) wind projects funded by the Massachusetts Technology Collaborative, which admininisters the state's Renewable Energy Trust and has been funding small wind systems through the Small Renewables Initiative since 2005, indicates that, on average, such facilities are generating only 6.6 percent of the energy that they could generate had they been operating at full capacity for all the time during the year.[16] Because of this lack of reliability and the fact that wind energy cannot be stored to alleviate the reliability/availability problems, electricity generated by wind must be backed up by more reliable electric generation sources, which increases the cost of wind energy substantially.[17] So while wind is free, even if one ignores construction, installation, maintenance, and transmission costs, wind turbines by themselves cannot satisfy consumers' need for reliability and continuous, around-the-clock availability.

As we noted earlier, another problem associated with wind energy is that the most favorable locations for wind power are often not accessible by the existing electrical grid.[18] According to the DOE, it would require an additional 12,000 miles of high-voltage transmission lines costing $60 billion (undiscounted) to increase the potential contribution of wind to national electricity production to 20 percent by 2030.[19]

Wind power thus faces two key problems in increasing its share of electricity generation. First, it is unavailable at some times of peak power demand and so requires costly backup capacity. Second, current infrastructure is inadequate to support a rapid expansion of wind energy generation. Further, as we noted earlier, existing efforts to increase wind generation capacity have run into major hurdles with regulatory laws and NIMBY efforts.[20] Despite these widely known problems—which are never discussed in-depth in the green jobs literature—green energy policy proposals propose enormous increases in wind and solar capacity without detailing a strategy for how these problems will be solved.[21]

The wind story illustrates one of the most important problems with the green energy literature: selective technological optimism. Substitution of wind-generated electricity for existing coal and natural gas plants will require solving complex and costly technological questions, such as how to store the electricity generated at night during low demand times for use during the daytime peaks. It would also require designing and building substantial infrastructure to move the power generated from windy, but low population, areas such as the Texas panhandle to places where large populations demand power. And it will require doing all those things at the same time as figuring out how to make wind-generated electricity cost-competitive with existing alternatives. Even Texas' State Energy Conservation Office, which is generally a promoter of wind technology, concedes, "For wind farms being installed today, the production tax credit is still the main driver of economic viability."[22] Some wind producers even pay users to take their energy; that is, the price is negative, because they receive the federal production tax credit only if the energy they produce is sold.[23]

It is one thing to be optimistic that technological progress will make wind energy economically viable, independent of subsidies, when investing your own money. An investor with a hunch about wind could make a fortune if he were right, or lose everything if he were wrong. But it's an entirely different thing to build such optimism into government programs spending other people's money.

Solar power

Solar power is another technology about which the green energy literature is resolutely optimistic. As with wind energy, substantial—and largely unacknowledged—hurdles to a significant expansion exist in solar electric generation. First, despite decades of effort and high subsidies,[24] the current contribution of solar to meeting the nation's energy needs is only 0.05 percent.[25] Most of this (95 percent) is from solar thermal and hot water production rather than electricity generation; the remainder is from solar PV.[26] By 2030, the contribution of solar to energy consumption is projected by the EIA to rise to just 0.13 percent, with only half of that from solar PV.[27]

55

Although solar PV is projected to grow faster than other forms of solar energy, current technical analyses suggest that the costs of current solar PV installations far exceed their benefits. Indeed, no reasonable valuation of the benefits of GHG reductions would result in positive estimates for the total net benefits from solar PV.[28] Now, it's certainly true that, in California and in most U.S. locations, solar electric power is produced disproportionately during summer peak demand hours. It is also true that energy losses from electricity transmission and distribution from PV sources is low because it is primarily generated on-site. But even so, University of California-Berkeley Professor Severin Borenstein found that:

> the net present cost of installing solar PV technology today far exceeds the net present benefit under a wide range of assumptions about levels of real interest rates and real increases in the cost of electricity. Lower interest rates and faster increases in the cost of electricity obviously benefit solar PV, but even under the extreme assumption of a 1% real interest rate and 5% annual increase in the real cost of electricity, the cost of solar PV is about 80% greater than the value of the electricity that it will produce. It is worth noting that even without further technological progress in energy generation from wind, geothermal, biomass, and central station solar thermal, with a 5% annual increase in the real cost of electricity, all of these technologies would be economical (without subsidies or recognition of environmental externalities from fossil fuels) well before the 25-year life of the solar panels was over. Under more moderate assumptions about the real interest rate and the escalation in the cost of electricity, the net present cost of a solar PV installation built today is three to four times greater than the net present benefits of the electricity it will produce.[29]

Borenstein estimated that the market costs of solar PV exceed market benefits by \$148/mWh to \$492/mWh, in 2007 dollars.[30] This cost-benefit gap is, he notes, "much greater than plausible estimates of the value of greenhouse gas reduction."[31] In a meta-analysis of more than 200 estimates of GHG reduction, economist Richard Tol concludes that there is a 1 percent probability that the social cost of carbon exceeds \$78 per ton of carbon in 1995 dollars, based on a 3 percent pure discount rate of time preference.[32] Such calculations are not popular. In a response to critiques of his analysis, Borentein concludes that:

> the current cost of solar PV, as it is being installed in California and the rest of the U.S. today, is extremely high not just compared to fossil fuel generation, but also compared to generation from wind, central station solar thermal, geothermal and other renewable resources.[33]

Solar PV proponents argue that costs will decline in the future, as occurs with most new technologies. Declining costs argue in favor of delay, not immediate action, however. As Borenstein notes:

> if solar PV costs are coming down very rapidly for reasons exogenous to the solar PV subsidy policy, then it is more likely to make sense to delay investment. If solar PV costs are declining by 20% per year, for instance, the same amount of investment (in present value terms) made 5 years from now will yield much more renewable energy than today. Given that the damage from GhGs is cumulative over time, it makes almost no difference whether the gasses are released in 2007 or 2012.[34]

As with wind power, the green energy literature's treatment of the technical challenges facing solar power suffers from selective technological optimism. Economically viable solar PV depends on significant improvements in cost-effectiveness; as a result, insisting on substantial increases in solar power generation without a serious discussion of the hurdles is irresponsible.

Nuclear power

In contrast to how the favored technologies are treated, the green energy literature shuns the alternative of expanding nuclear power generation. This illustrates the inconsistency of green energy advocates about technology. Unproven technologies that raise serious technical problems, such as wind and solar PV, are assumed to be minor issues; an existing technology with widespread commercial use producing 8 percent of U.S. energy consumption is ignored. Nuclear power raises its own environmental issues; our point is merely that these issues are no different in kind than those facing wind and solar PV, yet they are treated dramatically differently. Moreover, this difference is barely discussed in the green energy literature, revealing important embedded assumptions about technology.

The United States currently gets 21 percent of its electricity from nuclear reactors.[35] This power is essentially carbon-free to generate, just like solar and wind, and does not require blanketing huge areas of land with wind turbines or solar panels.[36] In Europe, 15 nations produce an even greater share of their electricity from nuclear power. Japan and South Korea also get a larger share of electricity from nuclear power than does the United States.[37] The widespread use of nuclear power across nations—something likely to increase as European nations formerly skeptical of the environmental impact of nuclear power turn to it to reduce GHG emissions and to reduce their reliance on shaky Russian natural gas supplies[38]—is a striking contrast to the tiny shares of electricity generated by wind and solar. It ought to produce a serious discussion of the relative merits of nuclear power and other alternatives. That it does not suggests that politics has trumped economics and science within the green energy movement.

An important reason for the failure of the green energy literature to assign a role to nuclear power appears to be its political unpopularity among green energy proponents' constituents. In the United States, nuclear power became unpopular after the Three Mile Island incident in 1979, during which a small amount of radiation was released.[39] That, combined with falling energy prices in the 1980s, reduced interest in and political support for nuclear power.[40] Politically, nuclear power is controversial and the U.S. environmental groups oppose it, as a survey of their websites indicates:[41]

- Sierra Club: "The Sierra Club opposes the licensing, construction and operation of new nuclear reactors. . . ."[42]
- Greenpeace USA: "Dangerous. High-Risk. Meltdown. Catastrophe. . . See why these words accurately describe nuclear energy and join us as we push for no new nukes."[43]
- National Audubon Society and National Wildlife Federation: "Clean, renewable energy like solar and wind power currently produces about 2 percent of our electricity nationwide. In contrast, nearly 90 percent of our electricity still comes from polluting sources of energy like coal and nuclear power."[44]

- World Wildlife Fund: "But among currently deployed commercial technologies, scaling up nuclear power is not an effective course to avert carbon emissions."[45]
- Environmental Defense Fund: "Serious questions of safety, security, waste and proliferation surround the issue of nuclear power. Until these questions are resolved satisfactorily, Environmental Defense cannot support an expansion of nuclear generating capacity."[46]

This skepticism is incorporated into the green energy literature. For example, as noted previously, the United Nations Environment Programme report states that "nuclear power is not considered an environmentally acceptable alternative to fossil fuels, given unresolved safety, health, and environmental issues with regard to the operations of power plants and the dangerous, long-lived waste products that result."[47] In the United States, John Wellington, chairman of the Federal Energy Regulatory Commission, asserts that the country does not need any new nuclear power plants, "ever."[48]

The overt opposition to nuclear power, or simply ignoring it, raises questions about the real concern of advocates of "green power" with effective strategies to reduce carbon. Nuclear power represents proven technology that is moving ahead rapidly in the rest of the world. Plants in operation today in the United States were licensed in the 1960s and early 1970s and so represent technology about 40 years old; 23 new plants were under consideration in 2007 and 2008.[49] In an extreme case of the selective technological pessimism in the literature, opponents of nuclear power, despite the lack of problems in the United States even with the old technology, still talk as if 40-year-old technology was the norm today.

While the experts at assorted environmental groups claim to know that nuclear power should be off the table and that limited options, such as wind and solar, are desirable, the same is not true among experts outside these groups. The National Research Council issued a report in 2008 recommending that, to help deal with carbon emissions, a concerted effort should be under way to enhance research in nuclear energy and to streamline the process to get the approvals for new plants, as they take years to construct.[50] And in 2003, a group of experts at MIT issued a major report on addressing GHGs and urged that nuclear power generation be taken seriously as an option,[51] a call they repeated when they updated the study in 2009.[52] The MIT study concluded that, for the foreseeable future, only four major "realistic options" existed for reducing carbon dioxide emissions in electricity production, including nuclear. Crucially, the authors state that it is not possible to know, looking decades ahead, which strategy is best; rather, "it is likely that we shall need all of these options and accordingly it would be a mistake at this time to exclude any of these four options from an overall carbon emissions management strategy."[53] The MIT study discusses, in-depth, the key issues of cost, safety, proliferation, and waste. None of the issues involved are simple, and the experts in nuclear power do not pretend they are matters to be taken lightly.

The MIT study illustrates how technology consistently advances and that there are strategies to deal with real problems inherent in any complex process. The best technologists cannot predict what technology will dominate years from now, as they know technology changes. A policy that eliminates major possible options, assuming that the technology we know today is what will exist in decades to come, will have us locked into costly, economically destructive policies.

Even more profound changes could be in the offing. The National Ignition Facility, dedicated in 2009, will soon begin experiments to generate useful fusion. As its website explains, the Laser Inertial Fusion Engine "is an advanced energy concept under development at Lawrence Livermore National Laboratory. Based on physics and technology developed for the National Ignition Facility, LIFE has the potential to meet future worldwide energy needs in a safe, sustainable manner without carbon dioxide emissions."[54] This is a publicly funded research project. The environmental and economic implications are huge and all on the upside. That does not mean it will work, but why do the green energy advocates talk about spending $100 billion here and there on run-of-the-mill projects of highly dubious value, when it is possible that a few billion dollars invested in this project could produce profound technological leaps? We are not capable of commenting on the likely success of this project, but spending federal tax dollars on potentially path-breaking research seems worthy of consideration as an alternative to windmills on the plains.

There are serious technological issues that must be addressed if nuclear power use is to be expanded. The crucial point is that the failure of the green power advocates to deal in a straightforward manner with alternatives such as nuclear power indicates a bias. The prospects for technological change should be treated consistently across technologies.

Who Chooses Technologies?

Green energy programs are built on the idea that government officials can make better choices about energy technology than consumers and firms in the marketplace. By besting our choices, green energy proponents contend they can shift us to a different mix of energy technologies that will yield benefits for everyone: less pollution, lower energy costs, more jobs. Individuals make bad choices, they argue, because they don't experience all of the costs of their choices. The driver filling her car with gasoline doesn't pay the price for environmental problems caused by oil production, refining, and use. The consumer turning on a light doesn't pay the cost of increased power plant emissions. The home owner rejecting adding insulation to his house on cost grounds doesn't pay the full costs of using more natural gas to heat it. Armed with better information about these broader costs, they argue, governments can make those choices better.

Thus, central to the green energy agenda is the claim that governments can and will make the right choices. As we noted in the previous section, one problem with this claim is that it depends on a selective optimism about favored technologies and an equally problematic pessimism about disfavored technologies. There are additional problems with taking choices away from individuals and firms. Consumers and firms don't perceive all the costs of their actions in the marketplace, although prices convey a great deal more information to them than green energy proponents generally concede. Governments don't have all that information either, however. Most important, governments make decisions in a political environment. In that realm, the information that consumers and firms have is often treated as irrelevant, thereby subordinating consumer preferences, cost information, and the like to politics. In this section, we explore why it is a mistake to entrust such choices to governments, rather than the marketplace, through an examination of the government's record of choices relating to biofuels.

61

Corn in Your Gas Tank

Green energy proponents put a great deal of emphasis on developing biofuels to replace petroleum, although they are often careful to hedge their statements about the dominant biofuel in use today, ethanol. For example, the Center for American Progress report calls for the "investing" of huge sums of (next-generation) taxpayers' money in "next-generation biofuels," "advanced biofuels," and "low-carbon" and "cellulosic biofuels," in an effort to avoid the problems of corn-based ethanol.[55] Corn-based ethanol is problematic as a fuel, and our heavy investment in it as a result of politics should make us hesitant to allow politics to determine which fuels we will use.

Indeed, as the UNEP report notes, "There is vigorous and contentious debate over the economic and environmental merits of biofuels, including the question of direct competition with food production."[56] There are important issues revealed by the history of the efforts to develop biofuels. These problems are particularly evident with biofuels because we already know a great deal about how government programs to expand biofuel production operate. In general, however, while green energy advocates admit there are problems with corn-based fuels, for the most part they presume biofuels are the wave of the future. This technological optimism about "advanced" biofuels contrasts sharply with their technological pessimism about fossil fuels.

In fiscal year 2007, ethanol and biofuels received federal subsidies and support of at least $3.25 billion in the United States alone, as Table 3.1 shows.[57] Note that this estimate does not include the value associated with the Renewable Fuel Standard (discussed below) mandate and so underestimates the total subsidy. Since then, Congress, with one minor downward adjustment, has greatly expanded the scope and level of biofuel subsidies. Under the 2008 farm bill, gasoline suppliers receive 45 cents per gallon of ethanol, down from 51 cents per gallon. However, it provided special subsidies for cellulosic ethanol, which at the time of passage of the farm bill had yet to be manufactured commercially.[58] Under it, refiners will get $1.01 per gallon of ethanol, and growers will get $45 per ton of biomass.[59] In addition, domestic suppliers of ethanol continue to be protected from imports via an import duty of 54 cents per gallon that blocks imports of cheaper Brazilian sugar-based ethanol.[60]

Table 3.1
ENERGY SUBSIDIES NOT RELATED TO ELECTRICITY PRODUCTION

Fuel category	Fuel consumption (quadrillion BTU)	FY 2007 subsidy and support (millions 2007 $)	Subsidy per million BTU (2007 $)
Coal	1.93	78	0.04
Refined coal	0.16	214	1.35
Natural gas and petroleum liquids	55.78	1,921	0.03
Ethanol/Biofuels	0.57	3,249	5.72
Geothermal	0.04	1	0.02
Solar	0.07	184	2.82
Other renewable	2.50	360	0.14
Hydrogen	n.a.	230	NM
Total fuel specific	60.95	6,237	NM
Total non-fuel specific	NM	3,597	NM
Total end-use & non-electric energy	NM	9,834	NM

NOTE: NM = not meaningful.
SOURCE: U.S. Energy Information Administration, "Federal Financial Interventions and Subsidies in Energy Markets 2007," Report #:SR/ CNEAF/2008-01,2008,http://www.eia.doe.gov/oiaf/servicerpt/subsidy2/ index.html.

The changes in the farm bill followed the upward revision of the RFS under the Energy Independence and Security Act of 2007.[61] Under the Energy Policy Act of 2005, the RFS required the amount of renewable fuel in gasoline to increase from 4 billion gallons in 2006 to 7.5 billion gallons in 2012. The 2007 EISA increased this from 9 billion in 2008 to 36 billion gallons by 2022.[62] The percent of America's corn crop that goes to ethanol has been rising rapidly, to an estimated 37 percent in 2010.[63] The EISA also specifically mandates the use of 16 billion gallons of cellulosic biofuel by 2022 and 1 billion gallons of biomass-based diesel fuel annually by 2012, although the EPA administrator has the authority under certain conditions to waive these requirements in whole or part.[64] In 2008, a request for a waiver from the governor of Texas to reduce the effect of the RFS on food and feed prices (and the Texas economy) was denied by the administrator.[65]

Green energy advocates' support for subsidizing biofuels (including ethanol) is based on one fact and many oversights. The fact is that biofuels are the products of photosynthesis; that is, they are derived from vegetation that takes carbon dioxide from the atmosphere and converts it into biomass which then may be processed into liquid or gaseous biofuels (such as ethanol) that, when burned, provide energy to meet human needs while returning the carbon dioxide to the atmosphere. Thus, in theory, the production and consumption of a biofuel should be part of a closed loop system, with no net emissions of CO_2, the primary anthropogenic GHG in the atmosphere.[66] As will be shown below, however, reality is much more complex because of some unintended consequences associated with biofuel use.[67] Belated recognition of these consequences has led to the current emphasis on cellulosic ethanol, which biofuel supporters believe can reduce, if not avoid, some of them.[68]

Assuming that the biomass is grown as part or all of a crop, as opposed to being scavenged off the landscape, it takes extra energy to grow the biomass. This energy is provided, in part, from fertilizers and pesticides needed to increase crop yields, and from fuels used to operate the machinery needed to cultivate, seed, and harvest the crop. If the energy is not needed in concentrated—and preferably liquid—form, it is probably more efficient overall to burn the biomass as wood without further processing. Otherwise, extra energy will be required to convert the biomass into more concentrated liquid forms such as methanol, ethanol, or biodiesel. Consequently, the net energy obtained from such biofuels is significantly less than the gross energy produced when it is finally consumed.

The uncertainties related to the net energy balance associated with the life cycle of biofuel production and use has led to a cottage industry in estimating whether the production of particular liquid biofuels produces any net energy benefit.[69] The answers vary with assumptions regarding, among other things, the specific crops used to grow the biomass; crop yields; cultivation practices; the amount of energy consumed at the farm and in ethanol processing; whether the byproducts and residues can be used to supplement food or feed; and the amount of GHG or energy credit that should be given for that. Currently, the accepted wisdom is that substituting at least some biofuels for gasoline does indeed produce net energy savings.[70] However, a European Union study concluded that "the cost disadvantage of biofuels is so great with respect to conventional fuels (at least in the mix foreseen in the scenarios analyzed), that even in the best of cases, they exceed the value of the external benefits that can be achieved" and estimated the net discounted cost of the EU's efforts to substitute biofuels for gasoline and diesel to be 33–65 billion euros through 2020.[71]

Even if biofuels produce net usable energy, it does not follow that their use would necessarily reduce GHG emissions. First, nitrogenous fertilizers, which are used as inputs to grow energy crops, are a primary source of nitrous oxides, a GHG that is pound-for-pound 300 times more damaging as a GHG than is carbon dioxide.[72] Second, cultivation of any crop generally involves disturbing the soil. Globally, there is more carbon stored in the soil than in the atmosphere. Disturbing the soil leads to decomposition or oxidation of the stored carbon. That results in carbon dioxide emissions to the atmosphere.[73] Accordingly, clearing any vegetated land (such as forests and grasslands) to raise energy crops adds to the atmospheric concentration of GHGs, which some have labeled as a "carbon debt" that would have to be "repaid" by the net reductions in carbon dioxide emissions resulting from the subsequent use of any biofuels produced from that land.[74] Fargione et al. estimate that it would take 93 years to repay the carbon debt if central U.S. grassland is converted to cropland for corn (for ethanol), and 48 years if land enrolled in the Conservation Reserve Program for 15 years was converted for corn ethanol.[75] However, if biofuels were made from waste biomass or from biomass grown using perennials on CRP lands, then the carbon debt, if any, could be repaid in as little as a year.[76]

Searchinger et al. used a worldwide agricultural model to estimate emissions from the conversion of habitat to cropland as farmers worldwide respond to higher prices for food commodities set in motion with the artificially created demand for biofuels.[77] This increased demand would result in greater conversion of forest and grassland to new cropland to replace the grain (or cropland) diverted to biofuels. Specifically, they found that:

> corn-based ethanol, instead of producing a 20% savings, nearly doubles greenhouse emissions over 30 years and increases greenhouse gases for 167 years. Biofuels from switchgrass, if grown on U.S. corn lands, increase emissions by 50%. This result raises concerns about large biofuel mandates and highlights the value of using waste products.[78]

Neither the Searchinger or Fargione papers are definitive, and both have come under criticism.[79] Alternative assumptions regarding the type of tilling system or other agronomic practices, for instance, may change the results dramatically.[80] The key point is that there is active scientific controversy about the net impact of biofuels, a controversy that is barely acknowledged in the green energy literature. The green energy reports simply assert that "next-generation biofuels" deserve massive public support.[81] Ignoring an ongoing debate over whether the policies in question actually produce a net benefit is not just a serious analytical problem but raises ethical issues as well.

An even larger environmental problem for biofuels than whether they actually reduce GHGs is that the biomass used for feedstock is generally harvested as part of a crop. If grown as a crop, it is plagued by all the environmental problems associated with agriculture; namely, it contributes to soil erosion, pesticide residues, and nutrient runoff from the fertilizers, all of which worsens water quality. Even more important, biofuel crops divert land and freshwater from other uses.[82] In fact, conversion of land and freshwater to agriculture is the single largest threat to the conservation of terrestrial and freshwater species and biodiversity in the United States and worldwide,[83] and growing energy crops to produce biofuels only adds to these pressures.

Scharlemann and Laurance reported in *Science* on a Swiss study by Zah et al.[84] that compared the net GHG emissions and "total" environmental impacts based on life cycle analysis for 29 kinds of fossil fuels and biofuels.[85] The total environmental impacts are estimated by aggregating estimates of natural resource depletion and damage to human health and ecosystems into a single indicator. While the results no doubt are sensitive to the specific impacts included in the study, the methodologies used to estimate these impacts; the aggregation methodology; the weights employed in reducing the different types of impacts to a common metric; the fact that the study was based on 2004-vintage technologies; and a host of other assumptions, the results indicate that when broader environmental factors are considered, many biofuels may create substantially greater environmental problems than the fossil fuels they would replace. Furthermore, these environmental problems may not be offset by reductions in GHG emissions. Contrary to popular belief, soy- and corn-based biofuels grown in the United States have substantially higher environmental impacts than natural gas, diesel, and gasoline despite reductions in GHG emissions. This brings into question one of the central premises for subsidizing or mandating biofuels.[86]

These are not just theoretical concerns. In 2007, 25 percent of the U.S. corn crop ended up as ethanol (see Figure 3.2). This has increased the pressure to take land out of the Conservation Reserve Program and cultivate it.[87] In South Dakota alone, about 425 square miles of grassland were turned into farmland between 2002 and 2007. This was partly because of the demand for corn to be used in ethanol, stimulated by subsidies and mandates against a backdrop of higher oil prices due to the petroleum demand from China, India, and other economies that were then firing on all cylinders.[88] In fact,

Figure 3.2
GROWTH IN U.S. ETHANOL PRODUCTION (IN BILLIONS OF GALLONS)
AND THE SHARE OF CORN PRODUCTION GOING TO ETHANOL

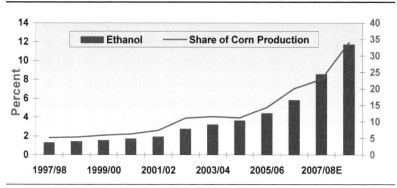

SOURCE: Hunter H. Moorehead, "U.S. Farm Bill and Beyond" (presentation to HarvestFest Global Food and Agriculture Conference, September 25, 2008).

Figure 3.3
U.S. CROPLAND (MILLIONS OF ACRES), 1996–2008

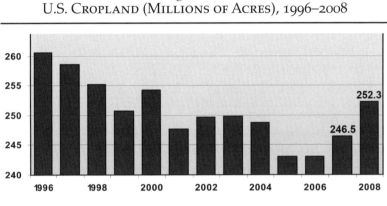

NOTES: 2008 planted area based on September 12, 2008, *Crop Production* report; includes wheat, feed grains, soybeans, upland cotton, and rice.

SOURCE: Hunter H. Moorehead, "U.S. Farm Bill and Beyond" (presentation to HarvestFest Global Food and Agriculture Conference, September 25, 2008).

cropland devoted to corn and soybean, which is used for biodiesel, has increased sharply in the United States over the past few years, as indicated by Figure 3.3.

Not surprisingly, the total amount of U.S. cropland devoted to grains has increased over the last few years, with crops now being planted on land that would otherwise not have been cultivated without the help of biofuel subsidies and mandates (see Figure 3.3, which also confirms Searchinger et al.'s basic approach).

One Man's Fuel Is Some Child's Meal

In addition to questions about the net environmental benefits of biofuels, scientists and others have raised serious issues relating to the impacts of biofuels on the world's poor. As environmentalists regularly express concern for these populations, it is surprising that this problem receives so little attention. The UNEP report is the only one to address this issue, noting that the UN Food and Agricultural Organization is concerned about the percent of cropland that could be turned from feeding people to producing fuel, but the report comes down in favor of more biofuels so long as done in a labor-intensive manner with respect for water supplies and such.[89] The analysis represented in Figure 3.3, as well as the analyses of Fargione et al.[90] and Searchinger et al.,[91] do not consider these impacts of biofuel subsidies and mandates on global food production and any resulting consequences for global hunger and malnutrition. Consideration of these factors further reduces the attractiveness of biofuels and associated subsidies and mandates.

The increased demand for corn for ethanol has additional "multiplier" effects on other food and feed commodities by increasing the price of all corn-based products, including feed for animals and many foods consumed by human beings. Ethanol-related demand for corn has been linked to increases in the price of eggs, milk, meat, cereal, candy bars, and any product containing corn-based sugars or starches, to name a few.[92]

The food price increases are clearly linked to corn-based ethanol. Although commodity prices have declined more than 50 percent since the middle of 2008, the FAO's Food Price Index was 28 percent higher in October 2008 than two years previously.[93] These price increases, fueled in part by the diversion of cropland to produce energy rather than food (and feed) and in part by energy subsidies and mandates in the United States and the EU, reduced the availability of food for millions in the developing world.[94]

The FAO estimates that 963 million people worldwide were suffering from chronic hunger in 2008, an increase of 115 million compared to the 2003–2005 period despite economic growth during that time.[95] This marks a reversal of one of mankind's signal achievements of the 20th century—the reduction of hunger in developing countries. The proportion of the developing world's population suffering from chronic hunger, which had declined from around 30–35 percent in 1969–1971[96] to 16 percent in 2003–2005, has now increased to about 18 percent.[97] As the FAO's *State of Food and Agriculture* report notes, biofuel production would have a significant negative impact on hunger globally but provide relatively modest energy gains.[98]

Many have argued that the problems associated with using crops and cropland for producing biofuels can be avoided by using cellulose as feedstock.[99] However, tilting the field to help cellulosic ethanol, whether directly through subsidies or indirectly through mandates, will inevitably make it more attractive for farmers to divert land and water to grow fuel rather than food.[100] As a result, some portion of the resources that would otherwise be used for food production would go toward fuel production. This is exactly what is indicated by Searchinger et al.'s research.[101] Specifically, their results indicate that "biofuels from switchgrass, if grown on U.S. corn lands, increase emissions by 50%." If switchgrass is grown on CRP land, its GHG impacts would be worse.[102]

It is also claimed that using crop wastes would increase the effective yield of biofuel production, and therefore mitigate some negative environmental impacts of crop-based biofuels. However, this argument overlooks the fact that so-called crop "wastes" are often utilized to conserve both soil and moisture (i.e., water) on many farms, and they are frequently cycled back into the soil to replenish its nutrient content; in other words, "crop waste" is frequently a misnomer.

From this brief survey of the biofuels debate we can draw two important conclusions. First, biofuels are not necessarily environmentally preferable to fossil fuels, particularly in their present forms. Requiring billions of dollars of investment in biofuels infrastructure and production *before* we know enough to choose the right technologies will require politicians and government planners to have a greater degree of insight into future technological developments than is humanly possible. Policies that require large, early bets on specific technologies are less desirable than ones that spur innovation such as prize competitions and profits. Second, the record of ethanol's development thus far is not encouraging, as it reveals an extraordinary degree of special-interest activity from the start.[103] The UNEP report summarized the matter well: "Many studies that lay out pathways toward a sustainable economy declaim a future of green jobs—but few present specifics. This is no accident. There are still huge gaps in our knowledge and available data."[104]

Conclusion

In this chapter, we made two major criticisms of the green energy literature. First, we showed how green energy proponents base their proposals on a selective technological optimism that assumes the answer they desire: favored technologies with serious problems today are assumed to have solutions just around the corner, ready to be discovered if funding were just available, while disfavored ones that are cost-effective today are assumed to be incapable of improvement. Second, the green energy vision is built on a substitution of government choices for those of individuals and firms in the marketplace. Such a change presumes that governments can make better choices about energy technologies. Unfortunately, the record of government choices about ethanol suggests that substituting political decisions for market decisions leads to more political decisions, not better ones.

4. Defining Green Jobs

While green jobs have been talked about for years, it was only in late 2010 that the Bureau of Labor Statistics pinned down how such jobs could be counted: "Green jobs are either: A. Jobs in businesses that produce goods or provide services that benefit the environment or conserve natural resources. B. Jobs in which workers' duties involve making their establishment's production processes more environmentally friendly or use fewer natural resources."[1]

Before we can evaluate the claims of green jobs proponents, we must understand what is being discussed when the term is used. Unfortunately, on close examination, green jobs estimates turn out to depend on highly contested definitions of "green," which vary from study to study. These differences not only render most comparisons among green jobs claims meaningless but also threaten to turn green jobs efforts into a fight over claiming resources by fiddling with definitions. Before we can have a coherent policy debate about green jobs, we must have clarity about what a green job is.

Most of us are likely to think of green jobs along the lines of jobs in renewable energy production and environmental engineering.[2] But green jobs advocates often have something much broader in mind. Their varying definitions incorporate important, but often unstated, assumptions about environmental policy, economics, and related standards of living. These assumptions have the potential to produce counterproductive policies that lead to a worsening of environmental quality, reduced economic efficiency, and a lower standard of living. We'll first explore what it means to be "green" and then turn to the definition of a "job."

What Counts as "Green"?

As the United Nations Environment Programme report notes, "not all green jobs are equally green"; some actions and related jobs are "lighter shades of green" than others.[3] The authors of that report insist that the "bar needs to be set high" in defining green jobs to prevent the term from becoming diluted because of a "low threshold" that might call many jobs green but would only "yield an illusion of progress."[4] Having said that, the report then goes on to use multiple criteria about green jobs that make counting highly impractical. Employment measures are slippery unless one is versed in the assumptions. For example, even in unemployment, which has been studied for decades, different countries have different rules to count who is employed and who is unemployed, so comparing unemployment rates across countries, as is often done, is an apples-to-oranges problem. Similarly, measures within a single country can change over time because of definitional issues of who may be considered unemployed.[5]

The definitional issue is critical. If the widespread subsidies proposed by many for green jobs are implemented, classifying a job as "green" will be valuable. Special interest groups and employers will assert many activities to be green where the jobs in question are not green in any meaningful sense. For an analogy, consider how the federal financial bailout program grew from a focus on repairing financial institutions to include subsidies for wooden arrow makers and tax breaks for rum producers.[6] So too, a massive green jobs program will attract its own set of interest groups looking to ensure that their companies' jobs are labeled "green" so that they can benefit from tax credits, spending programs, and set-asides. Economists refer to this process as "rent-seeking," or the use of the political process to obtain rewards for a factor of production in excess of the market rate.[7] It often occurs when individuals or groups invest in the political process to create barriers to entry or capture public resources for private gains. Any efforts to develop a public program to promote green jobs must therefore include a carefully drafted definition of "green" to limit special interest rent-seeking.

Differing Definitions

In the literature, being green differs significantly depending on who is doing the classification. For example, the Conference of Mayors report defines a "green" job as:

> Any activity that generates electricity using renewable or nuclear fuels, agriculture jobs supplying corn or soy for

transportation fuels, manufacturing jobs producing goods used in renewable power generation, equipment dealers and wholesalers specializing in renewable energy or energy-efficiency products, construction and installation of energy and pollution management systems, government adminis-tration of environmental programs, and supporting jobs in the engineering, legal, research and consulting fields.[8]

Somewhat inexplicably, the Mayors report counts *current* nuclear power generation jobs as green jobs but not *future* jobs in nuclear power.[9] In contrast, the UNEP report defines "green jobs" both more restrictively, excluding all nuclear-power-related jobs and many recycling jobs, but more expansively in other areas, including all jobs asserted to "contribute substantially to preserving or restoring envi-ronmental quality."[10] The UNEP report defines a green job as:

Work in agricultural, manufacturing, research and devel-opment (R&D), administrative, and service activities that contribute substantially to preserving or restoring environ-mental quality. Specifically, but not exclusively, this includes jobs that help to protect ecosystems and biodiversity; reduce energy, materials, and water consumption through high-efficiency strategies; de-carbonize the economy; and mini-mize or altogether avoid generation of all forms of waste and pollution.[11]

The differences between these definitions are substantial. The more expansive supply chain claims included in the UNEP report allow the authors to claim credit for a considerable number of jobs in supplier industries. For example, wind turbine towers involve "large amounts of steel" and so the supply chain for the wind power indus-try involves jobs extending back into the steel industry. These jobs are declared to be green so long as the steel being created ends up in a wind turbine.[12] (Creating a "sustainable" steel industry itself is also expected to produce green jobs.[13]) Crucially, the steel jobs themselves are not required to be "green," only the use of the steel made by the employees in question. Comparing these two definitions illustrates the significant hurdles to establishing a consistent, workable defini-tion of a "green job." Important value judgments, which are often not explained, are embedded in the definitions.

One important issue is illustrated by the Mayors and UNEP reports' respective treatments of nuclear-power-generation jobs and their comparison with the broader debate over the future role of nuclear power. Besides an environmental objection to nuclear power, the UNEP report explains that since nuclear power is capital-intensive, it is not a major employer compared to more labor-intensive methods of energy production; hence, it is similarly ill-suited as a solution to the world's employment challenges.[14] While the UNEP report explains (briefly) the basis for the total exclusion of nuclear jobs from the green category, the Mayors report says little about its reasons for including the nuclear jobs of today but not those in the future. One possible explanation for the difference is that Worldwatch, a major contributor to the UNEP report, opposes nuclear power, like many environmental advocacy groups.[15] On the other hand, the Mayors report is produced by a group that represents local government figures, including those who benefit from nuclear power plants' roles as taxpayers, employers, and a source of energy. Similarly, the Mayors report is careful to stress that all regions of the United States should benefit from a focus on green jobs, ensuring it offers something to local government officials everywhere.[16]

The point is not whether nuclear power is green or not. There is room for disagreement over that, and both advocates and opponents of increasing nuclear generation include governments often viewed as green. For example, a major reason that France has lower carbon emissions per capita than does the United States is that France obtains nearly 80 percent of its electricity from nuclear power.[17] Sweden, which gets about half its electricity from nuclear power, had planned to phase out nuclear plants, but the government has been considering building new plants.[18] Some environmentalists have warmed to nuclear power due to its low emissions, while others have not.[19] As we discuss in detail later, nuclear power is seen by many as an important component of a strategy to address greenhouse gas (GHG) emissions by fossil-fuel-based power plants,[20] yet the environmental impact of waste disposal issues could be the basis for a principled exclusion, as it appears to be in the UNEP report. The lack of consensus across reports is significant not simply because it reflects a major difference among those calculating green jobs numbers but because it mirrors a wider debate over the appropriate role of nuclear power created by the growing concern with GHG emissions.[21]

Nuclear power is not the only technology—or even the only energy technology—that requires trading off one environmental problem for another. As an illustration, consider that producing renewable energy equipment creates pollution. As the UNEP report notes, producers of solar photovoltaic (PV) cells often produce long-lived hazardous byproducts that are frequently disposed of improperly. Using "environmentally responsible" methods raises the cost of producing polysilicon for solar PV cells from between $21,000/ton and $56,000/ton to $84,000/ton.[22] This is a problem conceptually similar to the waste disposal problems of the nuclear power industry. Unlike nuclear power jobs, however, the UNEP report does not exclude all PV-related jobs, even as the lower-cost PV production allowed by improper disposal has played a role in the rapid expansion of the use of PVs by reducing their costs.

Inconsistencies Produce Rent-Seeking

The failure to treat technologies consistently—such as excluding products that pose environmental threats when disposed of improperly—is emblematic of an important problem in the green jobs literature. When winners and losers are selected according to nontransparent and inconsistent application of selection criteria, the potential for rent-seeking is enormous. Before billions in taxpayer money are committed to promoting what are classified as green jobs, proponents need to make clear the criteria used to select those who qualify for access to those resources.

A different version of this problem can be seen in the way some analyses consider almost anything green if the technology does not use petroleum, without considering the alternative's environmental impact. For example, the Mayors report touts biomass as a "group of technologies where additional investment and jobs will help to develop the nation's alternative energy infrastructure."[23] Most of the green jobs literature extols the virtues of generating energy using "wood waste and other byproducts, including agricultural byproducts, ethanol, paper pellets, used railroad ties, sludge wood, solid byproducts, and old utility poles. Several waste products are also used in biomass, including landfill gas, digester gas, municipal solid waste, and methane."[24] Unfortunately, because biomass includes burning wood, "perhaps the oldest form of human energy production,"[25] it is a means of energy production associated with smog, air pollution, and massive release of carbon.[26]

Wood burning, despite its status as a renewable source, can be a major source of fine particulate matter air pollution. As noted by Michael Faust of the Sacramento Metro Chamber:

> Wood burning has been identified as the largest single source of wintertime PM 2.5 [very small particulate matter] in the Sacramento region. The 2005 emission inventory for Sacramento County shows that wood smoke accounts for 45% of wintertime PM 2.5 emissions and is the largest single category. Prohibiting wood burning on days when particulate levels are projected to exceed a set threshold has been identified as the most cost effective way to reduce PM 2.5. By prohibiting the release of particulate matter from wood smoke on specific days, the Sacramento region can prevent particulate matter levels from reaching unhealthy levels, and avoid being designated a nonattainment for the federal 24-hour PM 2.5 standard.[27]

Areas that have been declared nonattainment of federal primary (health-related) ambient air quality standards for particulate matter pollution at one time or another partly due to wood burning include Tacoma and Spokane, Washington; Eugene, Oregon; Sandpoint and Pinehurst, Idaho; and Kalispell and Missoula, Montana.[28]

Yet biomass is included "because of the short time needed to re-grow the energy source relative to fossil fuels."[29] In other words, biomass counts as green because it is not petroleum, even though biomass causes environmental problems. Similarly, the Mayors report counts biodiesel and ethanol as green "because of their ability to reduce reliance on fossil fuels."[30] This report overlooks arguments that growing corn or soy for ethanol or biodiesel requires agricultural practices that increase air and water pollution.[31] It also ignores the fact that bringing marginal land into production for biomass reduces wildlife habitat,[32] increases emissions of carbon dioxide and nitrous oxides,[33] and increases the amount of nitrogen and pesticides in the environment. The UNEP report took a more skeptical approach to biofuels, perhaps because it was less concerned with the political calculation necessary to build support for green energy initiatives within the United States.[34]

Even if we focus on the one environmental issue that the green jobs literature generally puts at the top of the list of reasons to develop green jobs—preventing GHG emissions—there are significant problems with the definitions. It is not surprising that "not all fuels derived from biomass necessarily offer meaningful carbon emission advantages over fossil fuels, and some may even impose new environmental costs," UNEP concedes.[35] Even if we ignore the costs of heavily subsidized programs such as ethanol before embarking on large-scale burning of used railroad ties and corn extracts (which may not be so environmentally friendly), it would be wise to know more about the specifics of the science underlying the claim that all the things labeled "biomass" do in fact produce a net environmental gain when used as an energy source.

While we do not claim to know how to scientifically make a final judgment on how green particular biomass and biofuel programs are, the enthusiastic advocates of the green jobs programs do not appear to have considered whether they need to be able to do so. Instead, they make simplistic assertions about what energy can be counted on to substitute for current supplies and offer only vague cost and environmental impact estimates in justifying the creation of these products by people who will be declared to hold green jobs. Policies designed to have major impacts on the economy and environment should be better researched and understood before massive resources are committed to them.

Playing Politics with Definitions

Calculations of green jobs often incorporate criteria unrelated to the environmental impact of the job or production process. For example, recycling is generally touted as a major source of green employment.[36] But in the UNEP report, many current jobs in recycling industries are excluded[37] because those jobs are "characterized by extremely poor practices, exposing workers to hazardous substances or denying them the freedom of association."[38] Furthermore, "While recycling offers the benefit of recovering resources that otherwise would have to be mined and processed at considerable environmental expense, the procedures prevalent in most of China's recycling sector themselves impose considerable human and environmental costs. Particularly the manual disassembly jobs cannot be described as green jobs."[39] Even today's symbol of environmental consciousness, the hybrid car, is not necessarily "green" in the eyes of all green jobs proponents. The UNEP report cautions that "only under certain conditions" can hybrids "be seen as unambiguous proxies for a greener auto industry."[40] What is "green" is not always so straightforward, as in the claim by a controversial report that contended that the net environmental impact of a Toyota Prius is greater than that of a Hummer H1.[41]

There may be good reasons to exclude public support from jobs that fail to meet various criteria related to the ability to form labor unions or employers' records in workplace safety. However, those reasons have nothing to do with the environmental impact of the job, and including such criteria in a definition of a "green" job obscures the issues. Moreover, those criteria are themselves contested—for example, whether governments should promote, hinder, or remain neutral in labor disputes is not something on which there is a consensus.

What these examples demonstrate is that the green jobs literature does not engage in serious analysis of whether a particular job is "green" but instead simply labels jobs as green if they are found within a favored industry. The Bureau of Labor Statistics publication *Occupational Outlook Quarterly* quoted Ann Randazzo of the Center for Energy Workforce Development in Washington, D.C., that "jobs in renewable energy are not all that different from jobs in traditional energy sources. . . . For example, a person who is trained to work on power lines also has many of the skills to work on wind turbines."[42] Similarly, the Mayors report suggests that existing manufacturing operations will simply switch from making other things to making wind turbines. The report states:

> The technology of wind electricity is relatively new, but the manufacturing base for its production is very similar to past products. Every state in the country has firms and a labor force with experience making products similar to the blades, gearboxes, brakes, hubs, cooling fans, couplings, drivers, cases, bearings, generators, towers and sensors that make up a wind tower. These jobs fall into the familiar durable manufacturing sectors of plastics and rubber, primary metals, fabricated metal products, machinery, computer and electronic products, and electrical equipment.[43]

Likewise, the Center for American Progress report states that "the vast majority" of the green jobs its program would create are "in the same areas of employment that people already work in today . . . ."[44] And the UNEP study noted that job creation in "sheet metal work, semiconductors, electronic equipment, and others" would be "a welcome antidote to the loss of manufacturing jobs in recent years."[45] Industries learn to get in on the act. An HVAC trade association notes that jobs involving taping ductwork to reduce air loss are considered green jobs that might be eligible for federal stimulus funds.[46] Taping ductwork is hardly an innovation, but *now* it can be called green work. Previously it was just HVAC or construction work.

Are these jobs truly green? The only criteria used by any of these analyses to exclude a job within a favored industry is UNEP's insistence on job characteristics unrelated to environmental quality, such as "decent work, i.e. good jobs which offer adequate wages, safe working conditions, job security, reasonable career prospects, and worker rights."[47] Hence, some jobs that generally might be thought of as green, such as working on biofuel feedstock in Latin America, are not qualified to be called green jobs because of "poor practices" in the work process.[48] It is unlikely that the vast majority of jobs around the world, green or not, would meet that criteria as it would be understood by most Americans. These are wonderful characteristics of any job, but their inclusion seems to be motivated more by a desire to build a coalition with labor groups than by any interest in improving the environment.

The matter is further complicated by issues of equity and international reality. Workers in only a fraction of the world enjoy the wealth of American workers. But global warming is a global issue, so international issues are highly relevant. While ignored in the domestic reports, the UNEP report expresses considerations that have little to do with the environment but will be raised in the global debate. This includes developing nations: "Just as vulnerable workers should not be asked to incur the costs of solving a problem they did not cause, the same principle should apply to resource-starved countries that today face major problems due to climate change caused by the emissions of the richer countries."[49] This also includes women and ethnic minorities: "There are important equity issues with regard to minorities as well as gender."[50] One may argue for transfer payments to developing nations or employment quotas or other programs for favored groups; the troubling aspect is the inclusion of such advocacy in a green jobs strategy.

These issues are not simply inconveniences to the analysis of green jobs claims; they make it impossible to compare the different reports' claims. The UNEP study concedes that existing green jobs literature consists of studies using quite different methodologies and assumptions. "One problem with the array of existing studies is that they employ a wide range of methodologies, assumptions, and reporting formats, which makes a direct comparison of their job findings—or any aggregation and extrapolation—very difficult or impossible."[51] They represent fundamental confusions about the very idea of a "green job," a confusion that ought to be resolved before committing billions of taxpayer dollars and compelling even larger sums of private resources to generate "green jobs."

Obscuring Policy Choices

Because there is no agreement on what it means to be a "green" job, and little transparency in making clear the differences in assumptions underlying the various definitions, the literature obscures fundamental public policy choices that require thorough debate. Green jobs advocates create incentives for interest groups to work the political system to have their own industries or jobs designated as "green" and their rivals' excluded. Such rent-seeking not only wastes resources but is likely to entrench inferior technologies in the marketplace, as has occurred with ethanol.[52] "Technology-based emission limits and discharge standards, which are embedded in most of our pollution laws, play a key role in discouraging innovation."[53] The heavy weight put on nonenvironmental criteria suggests that the "green" label is already a vehicle for rent-seeking.

Consider the much-touted Leadership in Energy and Environmental Design building certification that is promoted by the U.S. Green Building Council as a way to reduce energy usage and provide other environmental benefits. Many green jobs advocates recommend LEED certification (certified, silver, gold, or platinum) as a policy. Portland, Oregon, has adopted gold LEED as the standard for all new city-owned construction.[54] Contractors have an incentive to push LEED because it increases construction costs. LEED certification sounds good, but a study sponsored by the National Research Council of Canada found that while, on average, LEED-certified buildings use less energy than non-LEED-certified buildings, about a third of the LEED buildings used *more* energy than conventional counterparts.

Further, higher levels of certification did not produce greater levels of energy savings.[55] The study concluded: "The weak relationship between energy performance and energy credits achieved extended to commissioning, and measurement and verification credits. These credits might be expected to have a relationship to energy performance, but we found no such relationship in practice."[56] We must carefully consider the value of green jobs' bang-for-the-buck rather than presume that the vaunted green standards must be worth the extra cost. Developing an open, clear definition of "green" is a critical prerequisite to public policy measures to promote green jobs if such efforts are not to turn into rent-seeking extravaganzas with little impact on the environment. Thus far such a definition has not appeared.

There is some overlap—every report thinks weatherizing public buildings is a good idea, for example. If there are unemployed people, why not put them to work replacing windows in public schools? There are undoubtedly less productive uses of public funds—such as the classical Keynesian suggestion of having one group dig holes and another fill the holes in[57]—but that is hardly a positive recommendation. The question is not whether weatherization is a good thing generally but whether the weatherization that occurs only when subsidized is a good thing.

What Counts as a "Job"?

The second major problem with the green jobs literature is that it consistently counts jobs that do not produce final outputs as a benefit of spending programs. These jobs should be counted as a cost rather than a benefit. For example, the Mayors report includes as green jobs those jobs involved in "government administration of environmental programs, and supporting jobs in the engineering, legal, research and consulting fields."[58] The UNEP report also includes such jobs in its definition.[59] Another estimate of green jobs, by the primary consultant on the American Solar Energy Society report, Management Information Services, finds that the single biggest increase is in secretarial positions; next are management analysts, then bookkeepers, followed by janitors. MIS estimated that there were fewer environmental scientists than of the other jobs just listed.[60] Similarly, looking at green jobs created in Michigan in 2003, MIS found that the largest number of jobs created were for garbage collectors; next were water and sewage treatment workers, then office clerks, followed by janitors, secretaries, customer service representatives, and truck drivers.[61]

The impact of including nonproduction employees within the definition of green jobs can be seen in the Mayors list of the top metropolitan areas for current green jobs, which is led by New York City (25,021) and Washington, D.C. (24,287).[62] As there is little manufacturing or biomass farming in such locations, this suggests that most of the green jobs in those locations are likely to be in the overhead categories. The report claims that "engineering, legal, research and consulting positions play a major role in the Green Economy, as they account for 56% of current Green Jobs. They have also grown faster than direct Green Jobs since 1990, expanding 52%, compared with 38% growth in direct jobs."[63] Note that this lumps engineers and scientists, who may be inventing new green technologies, in with lawyers and consultants who are seeking government subsidies, lobbying, or engaging in other forms of unproductive rent-seeking. For example, the Pew Foundation reported that environmental law should grow rapidly because lawyers "help clients determine whether their projects qualify for environment-related funding through [the federal stimulus program] and other programs."[64] Regardless of who is included in such counts, the Mayors claim that most jobs will be green-collar professional positions does not square with MIS's findings that most existing green jobs are the more typical customer service representatives, janitors, and other positions normally not considered in the professional category. There is a considerable disparity between the claims of high-end green positions in the Mayors report and the nitty-gritty of picking up trash that MIS found in its counts of existing green jobs.

The Mayors report made a "conservative" estimate of one new indirect job for every two direct jobs, conceding that "we do not expect that each marginal electricity generating job will require another environmental lawyer . . . and not every retrofitting position will require commensurate growth in research or consulting."[65] UNEP also noted a high range of indirect jobs from energy efficiency measures, finding estimates from 66 percent to 90 percent indirect job creation.[66] That it could be seen as a positive benefit if policies required more lawyers or consultants demonstrates the fundamental incoherence of green jobs definitions. This problem is widespread in the green jobs literature, with the focus almost entirely on the hypothesized economic impact of increased public spending on favored projects. For example, CAP touted retrofits of public buildings because they "have the most potential for operating at a large scale within a short time period."[67] CAP's proposal is for a $26 billion program to retrofit all 20 billion square feet of education, government office, and hospital space. The average payback for these expenditures would be "about five years" because they would save "about $5 billion per year" in energy costs. And CAP promises that spending $20 billion on "mass transit and light rail and smart grid electric transmission systems" would "reap similar macroeconomic returns over time as these investments stabilized oil prices through transportation diversification and energy efficiency gains."[68]

These numbers illustrate an important point. The purpose of a business, green or not, is not to use resources (whether labor, energy, raw materials, or capital). The purpose of a business is to produce a good or service desired by consumers that can be sold in the marketplace for more than the cost of production. For a given level of output, businesses that use more resources are less efficient—have higher costs—than those using fewer resources. Moreover, it is crucial to recognize that many jobs created in response to government mandates are not a benefit of environmental measures but rather represent a cost of such programs. Such costs may be worth incurring for the benefits the program produces, but they must be counted as costs, not benefits.[69]

A simple example comparing two hypothetical energy policies illustrates the point. Both policies require power companies—whenever possible—to use renewable energy plants rather than their fossil fuel power plants to generate the energy they sell. Policy A requires the power companies to install a data recorder that measures how much power comes from each type of plant in real time and transmit the information to the Environmental Protection Agency, where a computer program analyzes the data. When the program detects underuse of renewable energy plants, it alerts an EPA official, who can then initiate enforcement action against the power company for violating the rules. Aside from the initial work in installing the monitor and programming the computer, and whatever maintenance is required on the monitors and computer program, this policy requires only the occasional attention of the EPA official.

Policy B requires the same monitor, software, and EPA headquarters staff. However, it also requires an EPA employee be stationed in the power companies' control rooms 24 hours a day, 7 days a week, 365 days a year to ensure that no one tampers with the monitoring unit. Policy B produces many more "green" jobs under both the Mayors and UNEP definitions. Yet these additional employees add nothing to the actual greening of energy production. At most they deter some fraudulent tampering with the monitors. For our purposes, we can assume this is zero. Of course, much tampering can be detected ex post rather than prevented ex ante, and so the marginal amount of fraud deterred will be less than the total amount of fraud possible.

It is not just bureaucrats who get counted as a benefit rather than a cost under these definitions but repair personnel as well. For example, UNEP forecasts that there will be "tremendous job growth" in installing and maintaining solar systems.[70] This ignores the fact that a system that requires more labor to install or maintain is less efficient than one that requires less labor.

Conclusion

The inclusion of consultants, lawyers, and administrators as benefits of green jobs spending illustrates a major problem with the definition of green jobs. This is the same logic as declaring that a benefit of the war on drugs is an increase in the number of prison guards. By making increased labor use the end, rather than treating labor inputs as a means to production of environmentally friendly goods and services, the literature makes a foundational error in analyzing the economy. By promoting inefficient use of labor resources, green jobs and green energy policies will steer resources toward technologies, firms, and industries that will be unable to compete in the marketplace without permanent subsidies.[71] Dooming the environmentally friendly economic sector to an unending regime of subsidies is both fiscally irresponsible and harmful to efforts to continue to build a competitive and environmentally friendly economy. As we discuss later, this is a seriously underappreciated feature of economic progress.

5. Forecasting Green Jobs

Forecasts of potential growth in green jobs—however they are defined—depend on extrapolating from recent growth rates in the numbers of existing green jobs, which raises issues about the calculation of growth rates. As a result of low base numbers for many categories of jobs, green jobs forecasts are likely to be overoptimistic about the potential for green employment.

These calculations are based largely on surveys by interest groups and conjecture rather than on hard numbers from comprehensive research. Former Obama administration green jobs czar Van Jones, for example, agreed in an interview that "we have a lot of anecdotal evidence because the concrete numbers aren't ready." The *Newsweek* article that included the interview also provided some context:

> In large part, the very idea behind a green job ensures there will never be a full definition, but the Bureau of Labor Statistics agreed in April [2009] to start measuring data on them. (Critics, in response, quickly suspected that the BLS, an agency supposed to measure objective data, could soon help carry water for an administration eager to show the stimulus is working.) Several environmental advocates polled by *Newsweek* defined green jobs the way Supreme Court Justice Potter Stewart famously defined obscenity: I'll know it when I see it.[1]

As a result, policy debates over green jobs measures cannot be reasonably conducted without ensuring that those advocating particular green jobs strategies include technical appendices that disclose the basis for the extrapolations central to their claims. They have largely failed to do so. Given the scale of the investments proposed, much better data is needed to justify the gamble that such growth rates can be sustained.

Forecasting

Forecasts of green jobs are universally optimistic. For example, *Occupational Outlook Quarterly*'s forecast for green jobs notes that renewable power "is one of the fastest growing segments of the electric power industry."[2] The U.S. Conference of Mayors report asserts that "wind energy is currently the fastest growing alternative energy source in the country,"[3] and "solar power is an alternative energy source providing opportunity for massive job growth" [4] Similarly, the United Nations Environment Programme report claims that "[a] long with expanding investment flows and growing production capacities, employment in renewable energy is growing at a rapid pace, and this growth seems likely to accelerate in the years ahead."[5]

We found five major problems with these optimistic forecasts.

First, many of the sectors declared to be green are extremely small. Hence, even minor changes in capacity produce large *percentage* increases in growth. Whether such large percentage increases will continue, or whether the progressively larger denominator from prior periods' growth will result in a slower rate of growth, is thus an important question that must be answered before extrapolating from current growth rates. Ironically, for an area of study so concerned with sustainability issues, the authors of these reports generally assume that these rapid rates of growth can continue even as the denominator grows.

Second, the growth rates forecast are huge by any standard, thus raising questions regarding their reliability. In the energy field in particular, the projections in green jobs reports yield astonishingly fast spreads of new technologies, some of which do not even exist yet in economically viable forms. Such assumptions are inconsistent with past experience with other technologies.

Third, the green jobs literature exhibits a selective technological optimism. It assumes away any problems that might slow adoption of favored technologies while ignoring the likelihood of technological improvements of disfavored ones. This selective optimism about technological change biases the forecasts in favor of the favored technologies, but it is unsupported by evidence of systematically faster growth in favored technologies over their competitors.

Fourth, because many industries discussed as major drivers of green jobs are small and new, no official, vetted statistics are available. This means that many assumptions are necessary about the distribution of green, and less green, employment within the larger categories for which data are collected. As a result, the underlying basis for many forecasts is not statistics collected by neutral, skilled analysts, such as those at the U.S. Energy Information Administration, but assertions made by green jobs proponents and interest groups with a vested interest in the outcomes.

For example, the Department of Energy estimated that if the United States attempted to achieve 20 percent wind power by 2030 (which would be an incredible undertaking given its small market share at present), there would be 500,000 jobs at that time in the wind-related field, of which 150,000 would be manufacturing, construction, and maintenance.[6] That contrasts to the American Solar Energy Society claim that to achieve a goal of 15 percent renewable energy (wind, solar, etc.) by 2030 would mean 3.1 million jobs by then; a goal of 30 percent would mean 7.9 million new jobs in that sector of the economy by 2030.[7] The ASES numbers are not broken down by energy source, but they are vastly higher than the jobs numbers projected by the DOE, which looked only at wind. Even more optimistically, Van Jones recommended (before joining and then being dismissed from the Obama administration) that the president should enact policies that will "create 5 million green jobs as part of a plan to conserve 20 percent of our energy by 2015."[8] Political bias by green jobs enthusiasts means that caution must be exercised in making policy decisions based on such numbers.

Finally, the reports often assert results that appear precise, giving the illusion of scientific certainty. Yet these apparently detailed results vary widely from estimate to estimate of the same issue, thereby illustrating the inappropriateness of reliance on the results. We will now walk through the specific details of each of these areas.

Small Base Numbers

Rapid growth on a small base produces an absolute number that is still small. This is concealed in the presentation in green jobs reports by emphasizing growth rates and using misleading base numbers. For example, the Mayors report states:

> Wind energy is currently the fastest growing alternative energy source in the country.... The rapid pace of investment has continued, leading to a 45% increase in capacity, and net

generation from wind energy is expected to increase significantly in 2008. This rapid investment has led to an increased
share of electricity generation, and it now accounts for 10%
of renewable electricity generation. In terms of total energy
generation for the U.S., though, it maintains an extremely
low share, generating just 0.8% of the total in 2007.[9]

If one focused on the "rapid pace of investment," the "45% increase in capacity," and "significantly" increased share of electricity
generation, it would appear that shifting a large share of electricity
production to wind generators would be feasible in the short term.
When we look at the base on which these increases are calculated,
however, it becomes clear how small even a much larger wind energy
sector would be. For example, even the Mayors note that solar power
provided just "0.2% of [U.S.] alternative-based energy in 2007." The
reason for the small contribution is "high generation costs relative to
fossil fuel-based power."[10]

Let us be clear what this means. Wind power constituted 0.3 percent of total energy consumption in the United States and solar
PV only 0.08 percent—eight one-hundredths of 1 percent—of total
energy consumption in the United States in 2007.[11] The Mayors report
is right that massive job growth would accompany any significant
increase in use of solar power to generate electricity. Just to install
the PV panels necessary to reach even 1 percent of total electricity
demand would take an extraordinary number of installers.

The consequence of the tiny level of production is ignored in the
emphasis on rapid growth: electricity generated from PV and thermal
devices rose 23 percent between 2000 and 2007, and investment in
solar "surged 21% in 2007."[12] The absolute numbers are much less
impressive than the percentages. The Mayors report concedes that
production of PV cells increased only from 46,354 peak kilowatts of
capacity to 337,268 peak kilowatts from 1997 to 2006, with employment in manufacturing growing from 1,700 to 4,000.[13]

Extrapolating from the growth over such a small base is unreliable,
since random factors can have an immense impact due to the small
base size. Indeed, wind power generation has run into significant
problems, as the quality of equipment has proven problematic in a
number of instances.[14] Moreover, given the subsidies for expanding
these technologies, their expansion has been driven to an unknown
extent by the subsidies rather than by technological promise alone.

This appears to be the case for solar PV[15] and the U.S. corn-based ethanol industry, for example.[16]

Because the expansion of many green industries has occurred from such a small base, and because of the degree of policy-driven behavior, rather than market-driven behavior, the reported large percentage increases are unreliable indicators of the future potential of these green technologies. Until these industries have developed a track record of production of a significant share of electricity generation, it would be unwise to assume that they can readily scale up without encountering problems.

Huge Growth Rates

The spread of new green technologies is forecast by all green jobs proponents to proceed at remarkable rates. For example, the Mayors report assumes a 17-fold increase in wind power and a 621-fold increase in solar power between 2008 and 2038.[17] The report predicts a 59-fold increase in solar by 2018 alone. Yet the report contains no references to the massive solar-generation equipment and sites that would have to be under construction already for this to occur. The report, published in October 2008, estimated wind power generation in 2008 to be at 38,850 million Kilowatt hours (MW). That conflicts with the wind industry estimated operating capacity at the end of 2008 of 25,170 MW, which represented an increase of 8,359 MW capacity over 2007, almost a 50 percent increase. Why the Mayors report would presume more than a doubling of wind from 2007 to 2008 is not known. The report presumes an increase averaging over 18,000 MW per year from 2008 to 2018, which is way beyond the optimistic assumption of the wind trade association. The American Wind Energy Association claims 85,000 people were employed in the wind industry in 2008. However, the AWEA noted that in 2009, employment would fall as production and construction were slowing due to financial problems.[18] These reports exemplify the problems described by Vaclav Smil with most forecasts, which display "excessive confidence in the potential of particular technical fixes that are seen to hold (often near-magical) solutions to our problems and whose early commercialization is forecast to bring prosperous futures."[19]

Overall, the Mayors report proposes that the share of "renewable" energy of our total electricity use to rise from 3 percent in 2008 to

40 percent by 2038, which is a transformation of more than 1 percent of the total each year. Yet, according to the Energy Information Administration, renewable energy sources accounted for 7 percent of power in 2007. How Mayors got the number down to 3 percent is not clear, but it deletes most large hydroelectric sources. The only hydropower it reports for 2008 and beyond is "[i]ncremental Hydropower added since January 1, 2001." [20] Apparently, the Mayors report does not wish to include big hydro, such as the Grand Coulee Dam, as such items are on the no-no list for some environmentalists. As we discuss later, the only hydro to be counted are new little hydro projects. Removing big hydro drops renewable source energy substantially, making the renewable energy development battle even more daunting. Similarly, an ASES report projects an increase in wind energy employment of 1 million persons by 2030, up from the 39,600 people employed in 2007, about a 25-fold increase, based on a "push the envelope" policy to move to significant renewable energy by 2030.[21] The figures are based on a multiplier of base employment in the industry, which in the case of wind was 17,300 direct jobs in 2007.

The Mayors report forecasts a 16-fold increase by 2038 in hydro production, with a 4-fold increase by 2018.[22] In contrast, the 2009 ASES study, apparently seeing little future for hydro, barely registers it as a bump on the employment chart for 2030.[23] The rapid hydro growth predicted by the Mayors report is implausible. We are unaware of a single major new dam/hydropower project under way in the United States, and the major hydropower-related activity in the United States is the removal of existing electricity-generating dams to improve water quality and fish habitat.[24] That "minor" detail of a decline in existing hydro power sources is ignored.

Despite the rapid growth estimates for hydropower, the Mayors report implies that big hydro (such as the Hoover Dam), which accounts for most hydropower generation, may decrease. Instead, "small hydro" is asserted to be the wave of the future. Citing a DOE study, the Mayors report states that if every state ramped up construction on "all potential" little hydro projects, most could double their hydro power.[25] But a doubling of hydro power is not remotely close to a 16-fold increase.

It is not just hydropower where such rapid growth rates are assumed. Geothermal power is to increase more than 14-fold by 2038 (5-fold by 2018).[26] Once again, no details are provided about when and where this massive power increase is supposed to occur. Biomass energy is to increase 12-fold—again with no explanation.[27] While some marginal land can be converted to agricultural use, and land can be converted to biomass production, the current policies have already driven corn prices to record highs in 2008. And green jobs proponents are not looking to import biomass; all this energy must be produced domestically since the Mayors report asserts that importing energy "is worse than a tax—for the money flows out of the country."[28]

The UNEP report has similarly optimistic assessments of the potential for growth among its favored technologies:

- Spending on wind power installations is expected to expand from $8 billion in 2003 and $17.9 billion in 2006 to $60.8 billion in 2016. (The asserted expansion is in doubt. One large project, a multibillion dollar 2,700-wind-turbine project in West Texas, had to put plans on hold because of the decline in oil and natural gas prices.[29])
- Markets for the manufacturing and installation of solar PV modules and components are slated to grow from $4.7 billion in 2003 and $15.6 billion in 2006 to $69.3 billion by 2016.[30] (In fact, as with wind power, many solar projects were canceled in 2008 and 2009.[31])
- The biofuels market of $20.5 billion in 2006 is projected to grow to more than $80 billion by 2016.[32]
- The markets for fuel cells and distributed hydrogen "might" grow from $1.4 billion in 2006 to $15.6 billion over the next decade, according to Clean Edge; Roland Berger Strategy Consultants project a $103 billion market for fuel cells by 2020.[33]
- Geothermal power "might" become a $35 billion industry by 2020.[34]
- Ocean wave power "could" become a $10 billion per year industry by 2012.[35]

These are astonishingly rapid expansions of a set of technologies of dubious technical practicality, let alone economic viability.

No doubt, assorted renewable energy sources can do more, but much of this is purely speculative. Hydropower is not going to come from dammed up rivers; that is as politically off-the-table as drilling for oil near Santa Barbara. As the UNEP report notes, even in other parts of the world, large-scale hydro projects are "problematic."[36] Some hope that new technologies that capture ocean and tidal energy might be developed.[37] This contrasts with a statement at the World Economic Forum in Davos in 2009 by Lord Turner of the U.K.'s Committee on Climate Change. He said there was "mounting skepticism over the Government's plans for a huge expansion of wind and tidal power."[38] Despite interest in this new area of hydropower, the UNEP report, like the Mayors report, asserts that "small-scale hydro" will dominate.[39]

The point is that the renewable energy advocates who make renewable energy a key part of green jobs programs appear to have little appreciation for or knowledge of the technical realities of renewable alternatives. For example, a significant increase in geothermal energy is a vague claim. It can happen, at unknowable costs, only after basic research is started, since little is admittedly known of how it could work on the massive scale envisioned.[40] The Gigaton Throwdown Initiative, a collaborative effort of scientists and entrepreneurs, concluded that "[d]espite geothermal's great potential, scaling the industry up in such a short time frame presents a number of challenges."[41] Nevertheless, the CAP report claims that geothermal is an "obvious option for rapid green investment."[42] To assert that geothermal and other renewable power sources output will increase significantly in the next decade and beyond is simply wishful thinking, unless it is backed by a careful inventory of where such projects might actually be constructed and assessment of the technologies they might use (cost considerations aside).

As the Cape Wind project in Nantucket Sound illustrates well, our existing regulatory structure is not designed to facilitate bringing alternative energy projects online quickly, and politically powerful opponents are often able to block or significantly delay alternative energy programs. The Cape Wind farm was proposed in 2001, but by 2010, it still had only some permits in place.[43] Even an April 28, 2010, announcement from the secretary of the interior approving the project notes that the developer will still need to submit to additional requirements before completing the facility.[44] If there is to be a massive increase in wind, hydro, solar, and other energy sources, will permit requirements be swept aside so there are not long, costly delays as at Cape Wind?

The rapid expansion rates for new technologies in green jobs estimates are also often based on unrealistic assessments of potential.

For example, the Mayors report asserts that four states with the most potential for wind power—North Dakota, Texas, Kansas, and South Dakota—have the potential to generate 4,500 billion kWh of electricity, "enough to power the entire country."[45] Perhaps so, but wind power is unable to provide base load generation capacity because winds do not blow consistently when power is needed, even in North Dakota.[46]

Even a proposal by Stanford scientists for integrated wind farms capable of providing baseline electrical power would require more than one mWh of installed capacity per mWh of baseload capacity.[47] A recent major technology effort by GE, the largest turbine producer in the United States, to reduce wind power generation costs fell short.[48] This is of little concern to the lawyer who chairs the Federal Regulatory Energy Commission. He has stated, "I think baseload capacity is going to become an anachronism."[49] Wind and other "renewable" sources can do the job to constantly provide the electricity needed. Jay Apt, a professor at Carnegie Mellon University who specializes in electricity, was not as sure: "You need firm power to fill in when the wind doesn't blow. There is just no getting around that."[50]

Policies that rely on wishful thinking about rapid rollout of new technologies are inherently prone to error. We understand how long it takes to build railroad tracks, highways, and oil refineries because many have been built. But much less is known about building wind farms, solar panel arrays, and biomass generators, especially on the scale the reports discuss—a scale never before attempted. We have considerable experience with the reliability of coal-, nuclear-, and natural gas–fired power plants, but much less experience with alternatives. The growth rates assumed in these reports do not take into account the uncertainties and difficulties in ramping up new technologies on massive scales.

Selective Technological Optimism

The green jobs literature exhibits a selective technological optimism about favored technologies but assumes no technological progress in disfavored ones. For example, the Mayors study asserted that "[t]he basic technology [for solar powered electricity generation] has existed for decades," while conceding that "widespread adoption has not occurred mostly because of high generation costs relative to fossil fuel-based power."[51] Astonishingly, just after conceding that photo-voltaics are not yet in widespread use because of cost, the Mayors report asserts that "most areas receive enough sunlight for solar power to be economically viable."[52] Similarly, one might note that the "basic technology" of landing people on the moon has existed for decades, but that commercial lunar tourism has failed to materialize because of high costs. What matters is technology at an affordable price.

While estimates about favored energy technologies are resolutely sunny or windy, predictions for conventional energy sources are dark and dreary. For example, the Mayors report estimates oil costs will be an average of $240 billion per year based on the consulting firm Global Insight's cost forecasts and "expectations for crude oil prices."[53] It asserts that this cost "acts very much as a tax on the U.S. economy. Indeed, it is worse than a tax," the report explains, "for the money flows out of the country—not to be re-invested in areas such as health care, education, or infrastructure."[54] This is incorrect on multiple grounds. Not only is the form of fuel used to generate energy irrelevant to the buyer after controlling for cost, but making payments for solar energy is just as much a "tax" as oil.[55] In addition, predicting oil prices has proved difficult. The Mayors report was published in October 2008, in the midst of a fall in gas prices from over $4 per gallon in July 2008 to under $2 per gallon in February 2009.[56]

Even if one wanted to use promoting green energy as a way to alter the country's current account balance, a recent think tank report suggests that just the opposite result is likely.[57] The author finds a large and growing green trade deficit, including a deficit of $6.4 billion in 2008 in the renewable energy sector that has been an important component of the Obama administration's agenda.

There is also a track record of pessimistic bias in forecasting energy efficiency even when there is no political axe to grind. In 1980, the National Academy of Sciences issued a report predicting economic growth and energy use from 1985 through 2010.[58] Two scenarios yielded an expected increase in annual energy use from 80 quads (quadrillion BTU) to 130 quads. The first scenario was average annual growth in GDP of 2 percent combined with roughly constant energy prices, while the second scenario increased GDP growth to 3 percent and doubled energy prices. In fact, average GDP growth was close to 3 percent, and energy prices stayed roughly constant. Under that combination, the prediction would be that annual energy consumption in the United States would be well over 130 quads. In fact, energy consumption is currently at about 98 quads, at least 25 percent lower than the best scientific forecast.

Selective technological optimism in the green jobs literature is so omnipresent that there is almost no bad news anywhere except related to fossil fuels. But it will mean major restructuring on many fronts not generally acknowledged. For example, air travel will be greatly reduced by proposed environmental restrictions, reducing employment in the airline industry. "A climate-sensitive transportation policy will need to reduce the number of such short haul flights and encourage passengers to switch to high speed rail instead, which produces only a fraction of the emissions [of air travel]."[59] Yet the report does not see this as a problem because we will have an increase in employment in the virtual conferencing services: "Business travelers account for a substantial share of flights. In addition to making considered choices as to the mode of transportation when traveling to conferences and business meetings, they may be able to shift to increasingly capable virtual-conferencing services when face-to-face meetings are not essential. Such services also offer business and employment opportunities in their own right."[60] New farming techniques are needed—not a cost, but an opportunity for more USDA extension agents to teach farmers how to grow crops with fewer capital inputs:

> High-input farming has reduced both biological and genetic diversity, but farmers could be encouraged to rotate and diversify their crops—thus reducing the need for pesticides and fertilizers. Here, the employment implications are also positive. This kind of farming is knowledge intensive and requires research and extension systems "that can generate and transfer knowledge and decision-making skills to farmers rather than provide blanket recommendations over large areas." Developing the ecological literacy of farmers could, therefore, create significant employment.[61]

Not Just Jobs: Good Jobs!

The optimism of the policy proponents, which may be greeted with dismay by participants in industries forced to undergo wrenching changes, extends to the quality of the jobs these policies will produce—despite the dominance of existing green jobs growth by green secretarial and janitorial positions[62]—green jobs advocates are quick to assure the public that green jobs are not just jobs, but good jobs that pay high wages. "Green investments generate . . . significant numbers of well-paying jobs."[63] Indeed, the jobs are better than what we have now. "The average pay of the green investment program is about 14 percent higher than that for the industries associated with household consumption."[64] Even the lower-paying green jobs are good ones because they "offer career ladders that can move low-paid workers into better employment positions over time."[65]

Where green means fewer jobs, green jobs proponents punt. For example, the UNEP report notes that data limitations prevent accurate calculations for the steel industry: "Steel industry employment data are incomplete and data collection for many aspects of this industry are still in its infancy in many developing countries. This limits the extent to which even rough green jobs calculations can be undertaken beyond the numbers suggested here."[66]

Wind power is greatly touted for green energy expansion, as technology exists. However, the position of the United States in wind power is much like, but the reverse of, the position of China with respect to the United States. Consider the iPod. The United States captures most of the economic value from iPods, but China gets the assembly work, which is little more than 1 percent of its retail value.[67] The same is true of many "Made in China" products. Chinese firms capture a fraction of the market value for doing assembly work; the firms do not have the high-value technology.

Wind turbines are much the same. The technology and patents are largely European. The United States imports most high-valued turbine parts. The largest maker, Vestas, is Danish, at about a quarter of the market. Gamesa from Spain and Enercon from Germany are next at about 15 percent each of the market. GE and Suzlon from India are next, but most of GE's components come from Europe. GE is not considered a strong player in the market but is the only U.S. firm of significance in the production market.[68] Turbine technology is highly technical and not easy to replicate. Hence, most wind energy work in the United States consists of importing the key technology and performing the assembly work.[69] Importing wind turbines is like importing oil; U.S. dollars go overseas.[70] While we have no problem with free trade, this fact belies the claim of many wind advocates who celebrate the possible reduction in imported oil. Oil and wind turbines both require imports.

We do have some evidence about how technology is changing. Hybrid electric–internal combustion vehicles are darlings of the environmental movement, and their sales are growing, from 353,000 this year to a projected 578,000 in 2014.[71] But "auto executives are concerned that unless the government offers more subsidies, electric-car sales could stall because consumers won't have enough places to charge their cars, or will balk at the relatively high cost of the new technology."[72] A more efficient gasoline engine, using direct injection, will likely sell 5.1 million vehicles that same year, according to the same forecasting firm, up from 585,000 this year.[73] These engines can get up to 10 percent improved mileage at a fraction of the cost of a hybrid's 20 percent improvement.[74] Yet the green jobs forecasts rarely discuss the impact of such incremental improvements in existing technologies, relying instead on unknowable technological revolutions that will need to happen rapidly to expand the technologies they favor.

The selective technological optimism exhibited by the green jobs literature is evidence of important embedded assumptions within the literature. Before public resources are committed to promoting an economic vision based on these unstated assumptions, we must carefully explore how realistic these assumptions are and how desirable policies based on them would be.

Unreliable Underlying Statistics

Estimates of future green jobs begin with estimates of existing green jobs. These estimates are problematic because they are based on opaquely calculated estimates by parties with an interest in the results, rather than more objectively and transparently calculated sources. For example, ASES estimates 16,000 jobs in wind turbine construction and maintenance in 2006 and 7,600 jobs in solar PV and solar thermal energy industries.[75] These numbers are derived from Bureau of Labor Statistics data using ASES's assumptions about how BLS categories could be subdivided, as BLS does not separately collect data on these industries.[76] The method of derivation is unclear.

A similar problem lurks in the UNEP estimates of worldwide green jobs—2.3 million in renewables, 300,000 in wind, 170,000 in solar PVs, and 600,000 in solar thermal.[77] These are not numbers collected by a neutral statistical agency but are estimates by the Worldwatch Institute, which has a vested interest in the outcome.[78]

A more recent report by The Pew Charitable Trusts provides a relatively transparent data appendix regarding its use of establishment-level data to calculate employment by state.[79] Despite using an expansive definition of green jobs that goes beyond energy generation to include employees of companies involved in training, conservation and pollution mitigation, resource management, and recycling, they find a total of only 770,000 green jobs in the United States in 2007, with almost two-thirds of the jobs estimated to be in conservation and pollution mitigation.

Although all reports attempt to use official statistics, virtually every calculation depends at some point on assumptions and estimates made by organizations interested in the outcome and are simply not objective, verified numbers on which to base an analysis.

Moreover, the calculations are not transparent, with little detail provided about how the estimates were created, the assumptions of any models used, or the review process that checked the results. Since there are internal consistency problems for at least some of the calculations visible from the estimates themselves, this omission is particularly serious.

For example, the Mayors report notes that electricity generation in the United States in 2008 is likely to be 4.1 trillion kilowatt hours (TKW) and should rise to 5.4 TKW by 2038.[80] More electricity will be needed for millions of new homes and business operations, among other things. While all the new energy sources are being developed and constructed, the report also predicts enhanced efficiency in residential and commercial buildings that will produce a decline from 2.7 TKW power use in 2008 to 1.8 TKW use in 2038 (a 35 percent decline in use over 30 years).[81] Hence, in 2008, 66 percent of total power use is residential and commercial (2.7 out of 4.1 TKW); by 2038, only 33 percent will be residential and commercial (1.8 out of 5.4 TKW). That means a doubling of total electricity usage, as a share of the total, in nonresidential and noncommercial sectors by 2038. Trillions of kilowatt-hours are missing from its analysis of the 2038 estimates, yet there is no explanation of where those kilowatt-hours are going.

Further, existing green jobs are often the result of subsidy programs, not success in the marketplace. For example, the "success" of ethanol and biodiesel programs in the United States is presented as an indication of the potential for green jobs. The Mayors report notes

Table 5.1
SUBSIDIES AND SUPPORT TO ELECTRICITY PRODUCTION

Fuel/End Use	FY 2007 Net Generation (billion kWh)	FY 2007 Subsidy and support (million 2007 $)	Subsidy and support per unit of production (2007 $/mWh)
Coal	1,946	854	0.44
Refined Coal	72	2,156	29.81
Natural Gas and Petroleum Liquids	919	227	0.25
Nuclear	794	1,267	1.59
Biomass and biofuels	40	36	0.89
Geothermal	15	14	0.92
Hydroelectric	258	174	0.67
Solar	1	14	24.34
Wind	31	724	23.37
Landfill Gas	6	8	1.37
Municipal Solid Waste	9	1	0.13
Unallocated Renewals	NM	37	NM
Renewables (subtotal)	360	1,008	2.8
Transmission and distribution	NM	1,235	NM
Total	4,091	6,747	1.65

NOTES: Unallocated renewables include projects funded under Clean Renewable Energy Bonds and the Renewable Energy Production Incentive. NM = not meaningful. The average U.S. electricity price was about $53 per mWh at the wholesale level in 2006 and about $92 per mWh to end users in all sectors in fiscal year 2007.

SOURCE: Energy Information Administration, U.S. Department of Energy, Report no. SR/CNEAF/2008-01, *Federal Financial Interventions and Subsidies in Energy Markets 2007*, p. xvi, Table ES5 (2008), http://www.eia.doe.gov/oiaf/servicerpt/subsidy2/pdf/subsidy08.pdf.

that "[b]oth ethanol and biodiesel production are growing rapidly in the United States, with heavy investment in both types of facilities in recent years."[82] Similarly, renewable energy sources are currently heavily subsidized by the federal government. This is particularly true in terms of the amount of subsidy per unit of production for wind and solar, as Table 5.1 indicates.

The response to subsidies is not indicative of the response to actual market conditions, making these numbers suspect as a basis for predicting market behavior. Furthermore, the information available from the subsidized firms is itself questionable, since these firms have an incentive to report success to ensure their subsidies continue.[83]

Bias toward large numbers is embedded in the sources cited by the reports as well. For example, the UNEP report cites as the basis for its calculations:

- forecasts from Clean Edge, which it describes as a "U.S.-based research and advocacy group";[84]
- a study by the "Blue-Green Alliance (a joint effort of the Sierra Club and the United Steelworkers Union)" showing 820,000 jobs possible from renewable energy investments;[85]
- a study by the California Public Interest Group that suggests demand in California could support 5,900 MW of renewable energy producing 28,000 person-years of work in construction jobs, 3,000 permanent operations jobs, and 120,000 person-years of maintenance work;[86]
- Environment California Research and Policy Center's estimate of creating 200,000 person-years of work, with more than a third from exports;[87]
- the Solar Initiative of New York estimates of 3,000 direct installation jobs and 10,000 "manufacturing and integration jobs" in New York from 2,000 MW of solar power;[88] and
- a Union of Concerned Scientists study showing 185,000 jobs by mandating 20 percent of demand be satisfied by renewables.[89]

In a similar vein is a report by the Apollo Alliance—which bills itself as "a coalition of business, labor, environmental, and community leaders working to catalyze a clean energy revolution in America to reduce our nation's dependence on foreign oil, cut the carbon emissions that are destabilizing our climate, and expand opportunities for American businesses and workers"[90]—claims 420,000 new jobs from a 10-year, $36 billion investment.[91] All of these sources are from organizations with strong interests in the outcomes. Such interests do not mean that these groups necessarily do bad work but that such estimates must be treated with caution.

These flaws are difficult to detect because the studies generally do not address alternatives to their proposals. For example, CAP compared spending $100 billion on "new oil and gas subsidies and subsidizing gasoline and oil prices" to green investments.[92] But what CAP has done is convert a positive (the high efficiency of the domestic oil and gas industries) into a negative. "Relative to spending within the oil industry, the green investment program utilizes far more of its overall $100 billion in spending on hiring people, and less on purchasing machines and supplies."[93] The expenditure also produces less power, which will have a negative effect on consumers. CAP concedes that labor-intensive production is "the primary reason" why its proposal creates more jobs than the artificial alternatives it uses as benchmarks. Of course, any program that spends more on labor will hire more labor than will a program that spends less on labor. Dressing this up in a "model" is merely engaging in pseudoscientific mumbo-jumbo.

The Pew report is more transparent about counting jobs but similarly flawed in analyzing the implications of its job counts. Pew estimates that about 53,000 people are employed in producing clean energy.[94] They find that the bulk of the jobs (about 32,000) are in solar power generation, while about 5,000 are in wind power. However, the relative amount of electricity available from these two sources is reversed, with solar accounting for 0.05 percent of electrical capacity in 2007 and wind 1.5 percent, according to the DOE's Energy Information Administration.[95] Solar combined with wind makes for hot air—a valuable resource when lobbying for subsidies but not so effective in meeting the needs of consumers.

The report estimates that 1.27 million people are employed in the traditional energy sector of coal mining, oil and gas extraction, and utilities. Coal, petroleum, and natural gas combined to account for about 77 percent of electrical capacity in 2007, more than 50 times the contribution of solar and wind. If coal and natural gas electricity were produced at the labor productivity found in solar and wind, over 1.8 million people would have been needed. A green jobs advocate would point to that difference as a problem with traditional energy sources. However, the higher productivity keeps prices lower, which benefits consumers in two ways. First, they directly benefit when purchasing less expensive electricity. Second, they benefit indirectly as the prices for other products—made using electricity—are lower.

If all that mattered were the number of jobs, then we could hire thousands of people to blow on the windmills when it was calm. Counting the number of people employed is hardly a useful measure of the contribution of an industry to national well-being.

Also troubling is the tendency to assume results by using highly controversial assumptions to drive up the numbers of green jobs. For example, the Mayors report simply states that "we assume 40% of electricity generated in the United States [in 2030] must come from alternative resources. Qualifying alternative resources are wind, solar, geothermal, biomass and incremental hydropower."[96] The Mayors report's predicted percentages, based on linear projections,[97] differ dramatically from the EIA's reference case for power sources, as Table 5.2 illustrates.[98] To take just one example, the Conference of Mayors' estimate of wind power's predicted share is 500 percent larger than the

Table 5.2
VARIATIONS IN ENERGY PROJECTIONS

	Mayors	EIA	Difference: Mayors/EIA
Solar	8%	<1%[100]	>800%
Wind	12%	2.4%	+500%
Biomass	12%	3.2%	+275%
Geothermal	4%	0.6%	+667%
Incremental Hydropower	4%	−1.3%[101]	+>500%
Coal		54%	
Natural Gas	60%	14%	−30%
Nuclear		18%	

SOURCE: U.S. Energy Information Administration, *Annual Energy Review 2008* (Washington: Energy Information Administration, 2009), pp. 68–71, http://www.eia.doe.gov/aer/pdf/aer.pdf.

EIA's prediction. EIA projects that "Solar technologies in general remain too costly for grid-connected applications, but demonstration programs and State policies support some growth in central-station solar PV, and small-scale customer sited PV applications grow rapidly."[99]

Similarly, the Mayors report simply assumes that ethanol and biodiesel will provide 29 percent of transportation fuels for cars and light trucks by 2029.[102] Compare this assumption to the EIA's estimate of 11 percent for light duty vehicles in 2030.[103]

The data used as the basis for green jobs estimates are thus of questionable value. Some come from interest groups, some are derived by opaque methods, and some are simply of unclear origin. Before undertaking billions in public spending on green jobs initiatives, we need better data.

False Precision Masking Large Variations Across Estimates

How many green jobs are there or could there be? The estimates vary considerably. The ASES report claims that they are not something simply on the horizon but here now, claiming that in 2006, there were 8.5 million direct and indirect jobs in renewable energy and energy efficiency.[104] Even more green jobs are on the horizon. With no change in policy, by 2030, ASES asserts that 16.3 million jobs will be attributed to renewable energy and energy efficiency. With ASES's favored policies, it claims 40.1 million jobs (one in four in the nation) will be attributable to those categories by 2030.[105]

The CAP report contends that a "green economic recovery program"—which should be kicked off with $100 billion in new federal spending for solar and wind power, biofuels, smart electric grid, mass transit, and building retrofitting—will lower unemployment around the country by more than 1 percentage point by creating 2 million jobs.[106] The asserted result will be lower energy costs and more jobs. Each state will get its share of these new green jobs, according to CAP. For example, under the plan envisioned by CAP, Missouri would receive $1.8 billion and New Mexico would receive $599.9 million. The unemployment rate in Oregon would fall 1.4 percentage points and 1.1 percentage points in North Dakota.[107]

Not to be outdone, the Mayors report provides even more job details. However, while the ASES report claims 8.5 million green jobs exist already, the Mayors report finds only 751,051 to exist.[108] Give or take 7.75 million existing green jobs, the Mayors want to force development of renewable energy sources and energy-efficiency programs that would add 2.5 million new green jobs by 2018 and greater numbers in the years after that.[109] According to the Mayors report, everyone will share in the new green jobs. By 2038, Santa Barbara, California, will have 6,145 new jobs; Vero Beach, Florida, will have 719 new jobs; Portland, Maine, will have 6,145 new jobs; and Corpus Christi, Texas, will have 5,178 new jobs. The numbers are provided city by city.[110] This is, of course, impossible unless Congress is going to order a freeze in the location of workers and economic activity, something the report does not mention. The notion that green jobs will be spread evenly in proportion to the existing population is rhetoric to generate political support for the agenda from every burg in the country. Americans are highly mobile; some locations are shrinking and others are growing.[111]

The UNEP report does not provide estimates of green jobs specifically for the United States, and UNEP acknowledges that green job counts differ significantly. "Different methodologies in tallying employment, plus different approaches and diverging labor intensities in materials collection and recovery, make it almost impossible to compare countries across the world or to compute a reliable global total" in recycling.[112] But it estimates that by 2030, worldwide there could be 2.1 million new jobs in wind energy, 6.3 million in solar, and 12 million in biofuels.[113]

As demonstrated here, despite the seeming precision of each of the estimates, the total green jobs count varies a great deal across the literature. Compare just the different estimates of the impact of a 20 percent renewable energy production mandate by 2020 made by different sources. The Union of Concerned Scientists estimated in 2004 that 355,390 jobs would be created by 2020 by such a requirement.[114] Such production would eliminate 197,910 jobs in the fossil fuel sector, for a net increase of 157,480 jobs.[115] Not only would net employment be created, but electricity and natural gas prices would drop, saving consumers $49.1 billion a year by 2020.[116] But things change quickly; three years later, the same group estimated that the 20 percent renewable energy standard for 2020 would create a net increase of 120,000 jobs and result in annual consumer savings of $10.5 billion by 2020.[117]

In contrast, a 2004 study from the University of California at Berkeley estimated that a 20 percent renewable energy policy for 2020 would produce a net increase in employment between 77,300 and 101,649 jobs, depending on the mix of biomass, wind, and solar sources.[118] The authors of that study noted that a 2001 study published by the World Wide Fund for Nature estimated a net increase in employment from a 15-percent-renewable-energy-by-2020 policy would result in a net increase in energy employment of 1,314,000.[119] A 2002 paper from the University of Illinois estimated that 200,000 new jobs would be created in a 10-state Midwest region by 2020 if there was a push for wind and biomass energy. Another 2002 study estimated that steady increases in energy efficiency and reductions in carbon emissions would produce an additional 660,000 net jobs by 2010 and 1.4 million net new jobs by 2020. A 2004 study estimated that annual investments of $30 billion a year for 10 years in renewable energy, energy-efficient buildings, and other infrastructure improvements would produce more than 3.3 million jobs and stimulate a $1.4 trillion increase in GDP.[120]

A DOE report estimated that, should the United States adopt a policy of achieving 20 percent electricity from wind generation, the result would be the creation of an average of 73,000 jobs per year between 2007 and 2030. The job measurement technique used in the report is the standard input-output analysis using multipliers, which will be critically reviewed in Chapter 8. The "direct impact" jobs would be in construction and manufacturing. Those jobs would support 66,000 more jobs by "indirect impacts" and 120,000 jobs by "induced impacts," for a total of 259,000 jobs per year. The cumulative impact over 23 years is estimated to be $944 billion, with a net present value of $358 billion.[121] That is, each job created in the production and construction of wind turbines and related equipment would result in an additional 2.5 jobs. The indirect-impact jobs result from payments made to supporting businesses, such as bankers financing the construction, contractors, and equipment suppliers"; induced impact jobs "result from the spending by people directly and indirectly supported by the project, including benefits to grocery store clerks, retail salespeople, and child care providers."[122] This estimate is similar to the job multiplier of 2.5 presumed for geothermal energy projects.[123]

These varying estimates—a range from 77,300 to 1,314,000—suggest that the calculation of green jobs estimates has a long way to go before the figures are reliable and thus replicable. This is an immensely complex matter oversimplified by assertions such as the Mayors report's prediction of 291 new green jobs in Pine Bluff, Arkansas, by 2038.[124] The difficulty in making such detailed projections is magnified by the ongoing creation and destruction of jobs as part of the normal evolution of the economy. For example, a study of 34 metropolitan areas found that during a three-year period, the average job loss was 20.5 percent, with a minimum of 13.3 percent. The net employment change over that period ranged from a low of −8.2 percent to a high of 19.4 percent, with an average of 6.0 percent.[125]

Summary: Unreliable Forecasts

As political literature, the green jobs reports are masterpieces. They provide what on the surface appears to be scientific statistical backing for their recommendations, add an impressive array of tables and charts, and throw out remarkably precise numbers in their forecasts. The most egregious in this regard is the Conference of Mayors report, which provides detailed breakdowns of potential green employment for every town in the United States. The problems with the numbers underlying this seeming precision are immense. What jobs will be considered "green" and why? Who will decide which jobs are green "enough"? Decisionmakers need to be skeptical about projections based on small base numbers and rapid expansion of technologies not well developed. Taken as a whole, they make the forecasts in the green jobs literature an unreliable basis for policymaking.

6. The Green War on Trade[1]

Trade has been part of human society since prehistoric times.[2] Changes in energy production and usage are not likely to change this fundamental characteristic of human civilization that predates modern energy sources. However, in the debate about environmental improvements resulting from a shift in the major sources of energy production, emphasis is often placed on preventing trade. For example, a report from the Apollo Alliance, a self-described "coalition of labor, business, environmental, and community leaders," includes the recommendation that funding to support green energy investments should be available only if the components are produced in the United States. This recommendation is intended to promote self-sufficiency and reduce the extent of international trade.[3] It is fundamentally flawed because the assumption that autarky is preferable to trade is faulty. This chapter introduces some economic concepts about trade in order to critically assess some of the "green jobs" advocacy literature.

A Conceptual Discussion about Trade

Trade is not remote; rather it is a key part of modern society and our economy. However, the logic of trade can be difficult to grasp and frequently falls prey to nationalist chest-thumping by domestic special interests who garner political benefits by deriding trade with foreigners. Trade is often called free trade to recognize the fact that it occurs voluntarily—parties engage in trade because it is to their mutual benefit. Hence, restrictions on trade are limits on the decisions of free actors attempting to make their lives better.

An economy imports when its consumption of a good or service exceeds its production. An economy exports when its production exceeds consumption. This is true whether the economy is a nation, a state, a city, or even a person. When you use money earned as an attorney to hire a plumber, it is trade. You have exported legal services and imported plumbing services. Similarly, a city that produces solar panels and sells them to other cities is engaged in export, and the proceeds from selling the solar panels can be used to purchase goods and services not produced locally. Whether trade is regional or international often depends on accidents of history. Trade between a California homeowner installing solar panels and an Iowa firm manufacturing them is trade within a nation; trade between a French homeowner installing solar panels and a German manufacturer manufacturing them is called international trade, even if the goods move a shorter distance.

Trade entails costs. Most obviously, there are the costs of transporting the goods and services from one location to another. The plumber has to drive to your house, continuing the example from above. Trade will occur only if the benefits to the participants exceed the costs. Because transport requires energy, an increase in energy costs will tend to reduce the extent of trade, all else being equal.

Energy is a good desired not for its own sake but because of the benefits from goods and services it helps to produce. Its widespread role in production of virtually all goods and services led energy economist Robert Bradley to term it "the master resource."[4]

There are two ways in which energy can be traded. First, it can be transmitted directly. There are high costs to current methods of transmission over long distances, although high-voltage direct current may be promising for future applications. Second, the energy can be incorporated into a good or service that is more easily traded. This fundamental insight is part of the Hecksher-Ohlin model of trade.[5] Aluminum production, for example, requires large amounts of energy. The energy is more difficult to transmit than aluminum. Thus, aluminum production tends to occur close to large quantities of energy; for example, U.S. aluminum production was traditionally located near hydropower resources in the northwestern and southeastern United States. A more recent example is the growth of server farms, which consume considerable energy powering and cooling large numbers of computers. The output of these operations consists of digital signals transmitted via fiber-optic lines, which can be moved at lower cost than electricity. Because of trade, inexpensive aluminum and cloud computing services are available even in areas that lack large quantities of cheap electrical generating capacity.

Economies in any location export goods and services that they can produce inexpensively relative to other economies. This is known as *comparative advantage,* and it is the fundamental concept used to analyze trade. Comparative advantage is based on a given set of resources, prices, and technologies, and can change if any of those factors change. A carbon tax, for example, will make carbon-based energy-intensive production less advantageous relative to other energy sources. Similarly, a change in technology that makes backyard steel mills economically viable would change the pattern of trade.[6]

The United States as a Free Trade Zone

Much of the discussion of trade focuses on goods and services that cross national borders. This is an interesting issue, but it can obscure the even larger amount of trade that occurs within the United States on a daily basis. The United States is an economy the size of Western Europe without national borders.[7] Thus, trade that is measured in Europe is not captured in the United States. The diversity of the U.S. economy is reflected in the pattern of production, with various cities specializing in different products and then trading them.[8]

No city is completely specialized in producing one good or service. Generally, larger cities are less specialized, and larger cities are also where new technologies tend to be first developed. However, those technologies are often placed into full production in locations away from their initial invention, so that an export of large, diversified cities is new ideas and technology. Because the green jobs literature relies on significant technological progress, it implicitly relies on this pattern of trade and economic development. Barriers to trade, whether within the United States or between the United States and other countries, are therefore counterproductive in improving the technological possibilities for energy production and consumption.[9]

A change in technology (or other factor affecting comparative advantage) will not affect all metropolitan areas equally. Harvard economist Edward Glaeser, in a study of how Boston has continued to thrive despite multiple changes in its economic base, emphasizes the role of a flexible and well-educated workforce in promoting resilience.[10] Because most production requires a minimum scale to be efficient, cities do not produce every good but instead engage in trade.

A policy-driven (carbon tax) or technology-driven (continued development of alternative energy sources) change in energy production will not revoke this fundamental economic truth.

It is possible to alter the prices of inputs through government policy, which will in turn have implications for the pattern of production in an economy. For example, encouraging energy to be produced at higher prices (through renewable portfolio standards or feed-in tariffs, for example) will reduce an economy's comparative advantage in energy-intensive goods, all else being equal. In turn, this will attract sellers of energy to the economy while discouraging users of energy from locating or increasing activity there. This is the fundamental logic of Gabriel Calzada's critique[11] of Spanish policy to encourage the use of wind power. He found, using data from 2000 to 2008, that the high cost of energy resulting from various subsidy policies such as feed-in tariffs drove the most energy-intensive companies and industries away from Spain. However, there is nothing inherently Spanish or wind-related about this critique. It is a logical implication of standard economic models of trade.

A more subtle implication harkens back to the discussion of the green jobs advocacy for labor-intensive production of energy. Because energy is an intermediate good, a move to labor-intensive production is implicitly an increase in the labor intensity of all goods and services that use energy. If the price of labor is artificially constrained, for example by a requirement that employment be unionized at high wages, then there are further implications. The high price of labor will induce migration toward these high-wage places and encourage capital to leave. Some of the most energy-efficient cities in the United States have policies that discourage or prevent people from moving there. In particular, cities in California are both energy-efficient and restrictive toward development. Because the restrictive policies tend to be justified on the basis of minimizing environmental impact, the effect is somewhat ironic.[12]

Rejecting Comparative Advantage

Nobel laureate Paul Samuelson once described the theory of comparative advantage that underlies the economic analysis of trade as an insight from economic theory that was both "nontrivial and nonobvious."[13] It is certainly not obvious in the green jobs literature, since green jobs reports routinely treat comparative advantage as false and view trade as a harm, rather than a benefit, to trade partners.[14] This is problematic for two reasons. First, voluntary trade produces net benefits or it would not occur. This does not mean that every exchange that is made is "optimal" in a global sense or even in a personal sense. We have all made decisions we later regretted, but when we made the decision to engage in an exchange, we believed it to be the best decision based on our preferences at that time. Measures to restrict trade will thus be costly.

Second, the assumption that trade is a net loss to an economy is hidden within the green jobs literature, not stated openly. As a result, the policies stated as intended to promote environmental and employment goals are also policies designed to reverse long-standing public policies in favor of increasing trade without openly debating the issue.

The green jobs literature often simply asserts that green jobs are not subject to comparative advantage and will be distributed abundantly everywhere. For example, the Center for American Progress reports that green jobs will be created "in every region and state of the country,"[15] while the U.S. Conference of Mayors takes pains to describe with an illusory precision in a 14-page appendix how the green jobs will be distributed among all metropolitan areas (Farmington, New Mexico, will get 726 green jobs and Sheboygan, Wisconsin, will get 1,267) and "are not restricted to any specific location, so cities and their metropolitan areas across the country can and are expected to compete to attract this job growth."[16]

Even looking only at the reports' internal descriptions of green industries, it is questionable whether or not these predictions of uniform benefits could be accurate, since these reports do recognize at times that green industries are not currently uniformly distributed. For example, a third of world production of solar PV cells and wind turbines is located in Germany.[17] The UNEP report notes disapprovingly that this has come about in part because Germany has followed "low-wage strategies" in producing solar equipment.[18] The assertion of "low" wages in Germany would come as a shock to employers in Germany and to most employees around the world, as Germany is one of the higher-labor-cost economies. One report estimated average manufacturing compensation in Germany in 2004 at $32.53 per hour as compared to $23.17 per hour in the United States.[19] In

113

any event, as a result of this market dominance, any effort to cause a rapid increase in PV installations will have to involve German firms if it is to succeed.

A look at the wind power industry may be instructive. Supported by subsidies and renewable energy mandates, net wind power generation grew 35 percent from 2008 to 2009 (January–April).[20] In the absence of a "Buy American" law, a company investing in wind turbines should seek either to maximize profits for shareholders (publicly traded energy companies) or at least minimize costs (municipal utilities or coops). Only one, admittedly very important, U.S. firm (General Electric Wind) was listed among the top 10 manufacturers of wind turbines from 1995–2004. Other countries represented include Germany (three companies), Spain and Denmark (two each), India, and Japan.[21] The top four firms (Vestas, Gamesa, Enercon, and GE Wind) remain major players today.[22] In 2008, Steve Sawyer, secretary general of the Global Wind Energy Council, ominously predicted: "One of the big issues is to prepare for the onslaught of relatively inexpensive Chinese turbines onto the world market."[23] When investing in a major wind energy purchase, an energy company may be hard-pressed to pick GE Wind turbines versus turbines manufactured by foreign competitors. While we applaud efforts to turn rust-belt locations, such as abandoned steel mills, into wind farms in order to create jobs,[24] foreign companies are well-positioned to control a significant portion of the market for large wind turbines. Assembly of foreign turbines in the United States would provide jobs, but most of the profits and patent royalties likely would go to the foreign companies.[25] (See the discussion in Chapter 5 of this issue.)

Regardless of whether local content strategies are attainable, however, the green jobs literature uniformly regards them as desirable. For example, CAP touts the domestic content aspects of its program as a plus:

> In general, about 22 percent of total household expenditures will go to imports. With the green infrastructure investment program, only about 9 percent purchases imports. This is a critical benefit of a green economic recovery program: Investments are focused primarily on improving domestic infrastructure and making both local markets and the national economy more efficient over the long term.[26]

Similarly, the UNEP report concludes that green jobs' high local content is desirable, as local content means "a more equitable distribution of wealth since the money saved is invested back into the local economy."[27] Where a purely local strategy cannot be followed, the green jobs literature is critical of the role of trade. An example is the UNEP report's discussion of biofuels, where the main flaw is the potential sacrifice of "the interests of local communities" because "human needs, especially of the poor and marginalized, all too easily lose out to profit interests."[28]

The UNEP report argues that comparative advantage should not apply: "Public policy can and should seek to minimize disparities among putative winners and losers that arise in the transition to a green economy, and avoid these distinctions becoming permanent features."[29] That is, trade is winning and losing, despite the fact that voluntary trade is understood to be a winning strategy for both or it would not occur. Bananas from Guatemala are traded for wheat from Kansas; both parties gain, since comparative advantage is exploited through the market mechanism. The cost efficiency of bananas from Guatemala and wheat from Kansas is at the heart of the problem for the green advocates who wish to direct economic activity. The green jobs and economy strategy is "diametrically opposite to one where companies compete on price."[30] Comparative advantage must be suppressed for the green strategy to work. Price is an irritant that must not be allowed to distract consumers from the choices they would be allowed to make.

Even if the United States were to be purely self-sufficient, there would still be trade because of the differences in comparative advantage across the country. Changes in the price or technology of energy production will have effects that vary depending on how energy is currently produced. A review of current patterns of electrical generation in the United States by economists Michael Cragg and Matthew Kahn confirms the substantial variation within the country.[31] Consider, for example, the difference between Idaho and Indiana. In Idaho, 78 percent of electricity is generated using hydropower, 15 percent using natural gas, and only 1 percent using coal. Indiana generates 95 percent of its electricity using coal and 1 percent using natural gas. Thus, the two states have very different levels of carbon emissions, and their economies would fare quite differently under a move toward using less coal. Even states that are neighbors can have very different situations. Vermont, according to Cragg and Kahn, has the lowest carbon emissions of any state, as it generates over 90 percent of its electricity using nuclear power (71 percent) and hydropower (20 percent). New Hampshire, with only about half of its power coming from those two sources, is a higher emitter of carbon. There are political consequences to these differences. A study by Andrew Morriss found a pattern of low-carbon-emitting, high-renewable-energy-producing states supporting greater federal regulation of carbon dioxide emissions.[32]

The anti-trade attitude embedded throughout the green jobs literature is part of a larger criticism of the global economy. The UNEP report is among the most explicit in stating its overall anti-trade agenda. The report argues:

> Particularly with regard to trucking services, however, there is a need to reassess the way in which the global economy is developing. So called "just in time" production systems are biased toward frequent, precisely timed deliveries of materials and parts to factories instead of warehousing of supplies. And both production and consumption now depend on shipments of raw materials, intermediate goods, and final products over ever longer distances. Highly complex production, shipping, and retailing networks have emerged on an increasingly global scale, with varied impacts on employment, wage levels, and the economic viability of communities and regions.
>
> The onslaught of ever-growing transportation volumes threatens to overwhelm gains from improving fuel efficiency and limiting pollutants on a per-vehicle basis. Companies like Wal-Mart (with its policy of global sourcing and especially its policy of searching for cheap products, with potential negative impacts for labor and the environment) are major drivers and symptoms of this phenomenon. When products are shipped around the world in "sending coals to Newcastle" fashion, improving the efficiency of vehicles or planes—or improving the energy efficiency of stores, as Wal-Mart has pledged to do—can only have limited impact. Ultimately a more sustainable economic system will have to be based on shorter distances and thus reduced transportation needs. This is not so much a technical challenge as a fundamental systemic challenge.[33]

The UNEP report goes on to argue that globalization is a particular problem with respect to food production, claiming that "there are many farmers' organizations, NGOs, and others in civil society who regard the existing global food system as fundamentally unsustainable and who propose a more radical change of course—a course that recognizes that traditional knowledge and skills of farmers are the key to solving the major problems of the existing food system and to meet the challenges of increasing demand."[34] The report contrasts this with the vision of the World Bank and World Trade Organization, "who view the present liberalized and increasingly global food system as providing a path from poverty for hundreds of millions of rural dwellers, but who nonetheless recognize that it is a system that needs to do much more in order to become truly environmentally and socially sustainable."[35]

The romantic view of traditional knowledge and happy peasants does not square with the historical record. Prior to 1800, most of the world lived in what economic historian Gregory Clark termed "the Malthusian Economy," in which standards of living barely changed over millennia.[36] Much of the developing world still does.[37] Indeed, by the 1950s and 1960s, traditional agriculture even in the developed world seemed destined to lose the battle to feed the masses in many parts of the developing world. This led to dire predictions about coming famines that would inevitably decimate populations.[38] However, it was the Green Revolution—a distinctly nontraditional form of agriculture—that saved the day. Not only has the Green Revolution helped reduce hunger and malnutrition in developing countries, it has also saved more land from conversion in the developing world than has been set aside in all the areas that have been fully or partly set aside for conservation.[39] A major part of the Green Revolution was the application of more energy, embodied in fertilizers and improved seeds, to agriculture.[40]

Despite citing UN statistics that show that per capita food production has increased by 25 percent while real food prices have fallen by 40 percent over the last 40 years, the UNEP report nonetheless sees an equivalence in the two perspectives, warning that as population increases and diets move toward more meat and processed foods, global food production will need to triple by 2050 without using more land or water.[41] Moreover, as noted earlier, it sees the increased labor efficiency of agriculture as a problem, concluding:

> The industrial model of agriculture, along with rich country subsidies to agribusiness, has been identified as one of the primary drivers of urbanization globally, which then spurs a cycle of urban unemployment or underemployment when economic development does not keep up with the growing urban labor supply. Policies that keep farmers on their land, and facilitating green production practices, could generate employment and income both in agriculture and in non-farm occupations.[42]

This assertion does not square with historical experience. All countries that have enjoyed rising standards of living have seen a shift in their economies such that they are less dependent on the agricultural sector in terms of its contribution to the economy and total employment.[43]

A prominent example of the economic illiteracy of the green literature is in the concept of "food miles." This concept focuses on a part of the energy cost of producing and distributing food, specifically the part involved in moving the food. The intuition is that minimizing food miles by consuming locally produced food is optimal. However, this intuition fails to account for all of the costs and benefits of trade as compared to autarky. In an argument so familiar as to be clichéd, Adam Smith[44] observed that Scotland could grow its own grapes rather than importing wine, but that the cost would be so high as to dwarf any benefits. To take the example of reducing food miles to its logical extreme would be to return to subsistence farming or hunter-gatherer societies. Desrochers and Shimizu, in a comprehensive critique of the food miles approach, conclude that this logical extreme is not the goal. This is clear because the food miles minimizers are willing to partake of other benefits of trade, such as high-quality medical services, that are only possible because of the specialization facilitated by food surpluses.[45] Desrochers and Shimizu also compare "buy local" practices to the naval blockade of Germany during WWI.[46] While extreme, the economic analogy is appropriate.

The anti-trade agenda also works at cross purposes with the purported goal in the green jobs literature of improving the living conditions of low-income individuals. A standard target of opprobrium is Wal-Mart, with its global supply chain and nonunionized workforce.[47] However, the low prices that Wal-Mart delivers to its customers have a substantial impact on the standard of living possible at a given income. Because the reported government price indices do not include the effect of Wal-Mart and other discount retailers, there is a bias toward finding a decline in the standard of living.[48] Wal-Mart is also assailed for its negative impact on local labor markets. However, the evidence from the most careful research indicates the opposite to be true. Professor Emek Basker concludes, after a review of the scholarly literature, "Media reports often portray Wal-Mart as a 'job destroyer'and a force that levels Main Streets, but there is little evidence to support this view. Wal-Mart's impact on jobs is modest, and probably positive. . . ." Wal-Mart's success is the result of rapid adoption of new technology and taking advantage of economies of scale.[49] This is the recipe for success that the green jobs literature claims to support, so perhaps it should focus more on emulating Wal-Mart than attacking it.

'Cash for Clunkers' as a Substitute for Trade

An interesting recent government policy was the Car Allowance Rebate System, generally known as "cash for clunkers."[50] The program provided a subsidy to individuals to exchange older, less fuel-efficient cars and trucks for new cars and trucks that met certain standards. It also required that the older vehicles be scrapped rather than resold. The CARS program was acclaimed as a success because of the number of participants in the program. By construction, the average gas mileage for the newly purchased cars exceeded that of the destroyed cars and trucks. According to the CARS site, the fuel economy for the destroyed vehicles was 15.8 miles per gallon (mpg) while that for the new vehicles was 24.8 mpg. Almost 700,000 sales were submitted for the program, with a variety of claimed benefits, including job creation and environmental cleanup.

There are a variety of criticisms of CARS, as developed more fully in Chapter 9. For example, the carbon emissions from construction of new cars exceeds the reduced emissions from replacing old with new cars; the lower marginal cost per mile could increase the miles driven, reducing the net emissions benefit; there is deadweight loss because of the subsidization of car purchases; there are timing effects that make the net impact of the policy on sales smaller than the gross impact; and there is the loss to charities of formerly donated clunkers.

Lost from much of the discussion of CARS was the fact that it was also an anti-trade policy. This criticism of CARS was developed by Lucas Davis and Matthew Kahn.[51] Between 2005 and 2008, an export market of more than 2.5 million used cars from the United States to Mexico developed following the deregulation of such trade in accordance with the North American Free Trade Agreement. Davis and Kahn's analysis shows that the average emissions per mile from the exported cars are higher than the typical American car but lower than the typical Mexican car. Thus, the trade improves the efficiency of both fleets of cars, all else being equal. In addition, it provides a source of relatively low cost automobiles to poor consumers in Mexico, providing them with transportation options not previously available. The requirement that vehicles acquired as part of the CARS program be scrapped is sure to reduce the supply of used cars for this export trade. An ironic potential impact could be to hinder the improvement in vehicle emissions in Mexico, reducing the net benefit of the CARS program even beyond the direct costs to American taxpayers. The myopia of allegedly green proponents to the benefits of trade is counterproductive in accomplishing the goal of a cleaner fleet of automobiles.

Conclusion

Our point is not simply that trade is beneficial to human welfare, a point on which the economic evidence is considerable. The problem is that the green jobs literature fails to acknowledge that its anti-trade assumptions are contested.[52] By burying critical assumptions on which exists considerable contradictory evidence and which are inconsistent with existing economic and trade policies (e.g., countries' commitments to the World Trade Organization),[53] the green jobs and green energy literature is smuggling in an economic policy in the guise of an environmental policy.

The anti-trade agenda is a fundamental tenet shared by many environmental organizations.

> It is widely accepted among critics of market-driven global-
> ization that it is inherently inimical to protection of the envi-
> ronment. To the extent that it is not inherently inimical, they
> argue, it is so *de facto* because of the way the World Trade Or-
> ganization operates. These propositions, though frequently
> repeated, suffer from a simple drawback: they are, where
> not altogether wrong, at least greatly exaggerated.[54]

The green jobs literature has embedded in it many of these strong
anti-trade assumptions, which are contradicted by both economic
theory and the experience of the world economy. Environmental
quality, like other desirable goods and services, is in higher demand
when incomes increase, and free trade increases incomes. Recent
scholarship on the link between trade, economic growth, and environmental quality illustrates that simply reducing trade will not
necessarily have positive environmental effects and can in fact be
harmful to the environment.[55] The collapse of long distance trade is
one of the main indicators of the dramatic decline in the quality of
life resulting from the end of the Western Roman Empire.[56] As the
World Bank staff explains, "trade spurs growth and growth spurs
trade." The economic success stories of countries emerging from
poverty, such as China and Vietnam, come from exploiting comparative advantage via world trade, not remaining inward-looking.[57]
Success in achieving benign autarky is an article of faith among the
policy advocates we analyze. This central assumption needs to be
clearly debated before accepting the green jobs literature's policy
recommendations.

7. Economic Fallacies of the Green Economy

The policy implications that fall under the "green jobs" rubric are much greater than creating so-called green jobs. As we discussed in the previous chapter, most green jobs advocates directly or indirectly favor restrictions on international trade. The green jobs literature contains other problematic assumptions about fundamental economics, especially how it will impact the labor market. Job creation is a sensible way for advocates of many policy initiatives to attempt to increase the appeal of proposals. In this chapter, we examine some of fundamental flaws about economics in general, especially about the use of labor.

First, the literature makes inappropriate calculations of consumer surplus, giving misleading results with respect to the benefits of proposed, favored policies.

Second, the green jobs literature frequently confuses responses to government mandates with market responses, improperly extrapolating from the former to predict the latter. In particular, green jobs analyses do not take into account how market incentives operate with respect to energy efficiency, instead using an incorrect model of market action in which energy efficiency results only from government mandates.

Third, the literature neglects consideration of the opportunity costs of the resources it proposes to devote to green jobs programs. The maxim that there is no such thing as a free lunch happens to be true—even if it is a lunch you like, paid for by someone else.

The rejection of fundamental principles of economics, such as the creation of wealth by exploitation of comparative advantage, as discussed in the previous chapter, and the fact that consumer surplus is a real benefit captured by consumers, means that many green jobs advocates ignore, or are ignorant of, foundational science. This is akin to ignoring the law of gravity when designing bridges. Similarly, opportunity costs must be considered, as they are critical to calculating the net benefit of a proposal. The value of the alternative uses of the resources must be deducted from the gains created by proposed green jobs policies. Further, by failing to take into account the incentive effects on energy consumption, green jobs analyses overstate the energy that is used in the absence of regulatory mandates and thereby overstate the benefits of their proposals. Using data on improved energy efficiency over past decades, as we reviewed in Chapter 2, we know that the market produces substantial increases in energy efficiency without the drastic measures proposed by the green jobs literature.

That the green jobs literature contains so many basic economic errors is not accidental but reveals that it is built on a thinly concealed hostility to market-ordered societies, a hostility that strongly influences its policy recommendations. Those who advocate central planning of economic activity because they believe markets to be deeply flawed have an intellectual and moral obligation to demonstrate that government planning can produce superior results. A century-plus of extensive literature on the topic produced a contrary result that cannot be dismissed merely by putting a green cloak on central economic planning and asserting that this time around it will produce a richer world. These flaws in economic reasoning reveal fatal flaws in the green jobs literature's analysis of the economics of green jobs policies.

Consumer surplus

The green jobs literature asserts benefits of green jobs policies using a flawed conception of improvements in human welfare. In economics, policies are evaluated by the calculation of the net social benefits based on both consumer and producer surplus. Consumer surplus is the difference between the price that consumers pay for a good and the value they place on a good (the highest price they would be willing to pay). Producer surplus is the difference between the price received by a producer when a good or service is sold and the lowest price the producer would have been willing to accept and still engage in the exchange. The existence of such surpluses is the reason exchange occurs—both parties gain.[1] Guatemalan farmers can grow bananas and transport them to rural Kansas so that farmers in Kansas find it cheaper to buy those bananas rather than grow their own.

The green jobs literature contains almost no mention of consumer surplus, focusing almost exclusively on costs and benefits to favored producers. For example, the United Nations Environment Programme report criticizes increased agricultural trade between the United States and Mexico because "cheap corn from the United States has hurt Mexican farmers who grow maize on small- to medium-sized plots in difficult environments using low levels of technology."[2] No mention is made of benefits of cheaper corn (or bananas) to consumers worldwide, only the costs to uncompetitive domestic producers are considered.

The benefits of trade are not just assertions from other-world economic theorizing. Trade has real-life consequences that affect the quality of life, such as by providing more food, and more varied food, at lower cost to billions of people. That is a huge consumer surplus. Nevertheless, the report criticizes expanded trade in foodstuffs:

> The growth of supermarkets in the global South is having a marked effect on farmers, and some maintain that this effect is bigger than that of trade liberalization. Leading supermarket chains have shifted away from wholesale markets where small farmers make their living, and toward procuring food through a few medium-to-large firms that can deliver a consistent quality product at large volumes.[3]

As a result, the UNEP report complains:

> The consolidation of retail has meant that farmers and producers often receive dwindling returns on their produce, as large retailers are in a position to lay down "take it or leave it" conditions. Retailers are also in a position to dictate terms to processors and distributors and even large food manufacturers, which results in manufacturers being more concerned to serve the interests of retailers and less concerned to maintain a good relationship with farmers.[4]

This evinces a lack of understanding that "the interests of retailers" is consistent with that of their customers. Wal-Mart has been a champion at cutting tough bargains with suppliers, thereby allowing consumers, especially lower-income consumers, to enjoy more value for their scarce dollars. Wal-Mart does not force farmers to sell to it—if anyone will offer more for their produce, obviously the farmers would sell to those buyers instead. Global Insight conducted a study that concluded that "the existence of Wal-Mart saves the average family $2,500 a year." The net increased purchasing power, however, is only $1,122 annually after taking Wal-Mart's depression of wages into account.[5]

These passages are typical of the results-driven nature of the green jobs literature's calculations of social costs and benefits. Economic concepts that the organizations sponsoring these reports do not like (e.g., markets, free trade, lower prices for many consumers) are simply assumed to produce net costs. Yet those economic concepts that the authors of the reports like (e.g., small agricultural holding, local production, and solar power) are assumed to produce net benefits. By counting only the benefits from favored technologies and activities, and only the costs from disfavored ones, the green jobs literature produces a distorted outcome.

There are other issues related to environmental policy and sustainability that are often ignored or danced around by green jobs advocates. Consider the case of ethanol. "Then there is the elephant in the room: ethanol. Most experts agree that the race among western countries to produce this grain-based alternative fuel is responsible, in significant part, for the rising costs. Their logic is simple: When countries put corn aside for energy, the amount available for food is in greater demand, and prices rise. If demand is already high, the effect is amplified."[6] The price increase in foodstuffs was partly due to the diversion of food crops such as corn, soy, and palm oil to meet the demand for ethanol created by subsidies and mandates in developed countries for biofuels to reduce dependence on foreign oil and greenhouse gas (GHG) emissions.[7]

Obviously, the benefits and the costs must be counted from both before an accurate comparison can be made. In particular, careful estimates of consumer surplus are necessary to compare the policies' impacts. This avoidance of the consideration of benefits from disfavored policies and costs of favored policies is not an oversight—the elimination of the benefits of market competition from the green jobs literature represents its sponsors' rejection of modern economics and, thus, the basis for the world's economy today.

The view taken by green jobs advocates harkens to a book that enthralled some members of an earlier generation at the time of a similar debate. E.F. Schumacher began with the "insight" that man is small, therefore small is beautiful.[8] He advocated an end to modern technology and production in favor of "Buddhist economics."[9] Much like the UNEP report, Schumacher imagined a world with "a multitude of vibrant, self-sufficient villages which, from their secure sense of community and place, work together in peace and cooperation."[10] If such a community were so desirable, more people would do it. There is nothing to prevent people in free countries from living that way. Either it simply does not work, or people find it more to their liking to participate in the modern economy. The Amish and Hutterites are communal organizations that do quite well, but their long-practiced model has not attracted legions of imitators. Schumacher's medieval world where people rely on a small number of other people in a village is a prescription simply not accepted, despite millions of people having read his or other authors' roadmap to a happy life. At least in the imagination, there continues to be a strong appeal to such a model, so let us consider that literature's claims about how a such an economy would work.

Mandates vs. Markets

Many green jobs programs are built around proposed government mandates to promote favored technologies over those chosen in a competitive marketplace. "On the basis of current experience in various areas—from vehicle fuel economy to carbon trading—it appears that a purely market-driven process will not be able to deliver the changes needed at a scale and speed demanded by the climate crisis."[11] That is, without green jobs mandates, market actors would not make the choice to use the green technology because they would not receive all of its benefits and/or would bear all the costs of using green alternatives. The argument is not just the usual one made concerning pollution—that the net social cost-benefit calculation is positive while the net private cost-benefit calculation is negative, requiring a subsidy or mandate to persuade private actors to adopt socially beneficial but privately costly measures. Rather, the green jobs literature asserts that mandates are necessary to encourage or force individuals, firms, and local governments to adopt policies that will provide a net private benefit as well as a net social benefit, such as weatherization. Why mandates are necessary to encourage economic actors to act in their own benefit is unexplained.

Moving from markets to mandates introduces a qualitative change that requires careful consideration in any analysis for three reasons. First, a competitive market disciplines firms that make mistakes. For example, a firm that chose an inefficient technology over an efficient one would have higher costs than a rival that adopted the efficient technology. However, no such pressures apply to political choices of technologies. Thus a policy that depends on a political process designating particular technologies as "green" and directing investment to them lacks an important check.[12]

Second, the shift of decisions about selecting technologies to a political process introduces new considerations unrelated to the merits. Does a firm that produces this technology have a plant in a key political figure's district?[13] Will a particular technology spoil the view from a senator's vacation home?[14] Choices made on political grounds are unlikely to maximize either economic efficiency or environmental benefits.[15]

Third, markets exert continual pressure for improvement. Mandates, on the other hand, tend to lock in technological choices. For all these reasons, mandates cannot be assumed to produce positive outcomes but must be carefully and regularly scrutinized. Mandating the use of particular technologies will certainly increase employment related to the mandated technology.[16] For example, it is true that requiring all public buildings to be retrofitted or offering "strong financial incentives" to private building owners to engage in retrofitting, as proposed in the report by the Center for American Progress, would create jobs.[17] Of course, so would requiring all public buildings to be painted purple or offering tax incentives to private building owners to paint their buildings purple. Painting jobs would increase, paint manufacturers would increase production of purple paint, paint stores would likely hire additional sales and delivery help, paint brush manufacturers would increase production, and so forth.

The question is not whether the mandate would spur some economic activity. The real question is: What would have happened to the resources used to meet the mandate or reap the incentive in the absence of the government program? The answer is that those resources would have been put to the building owners' highest and best use, and those uses would have also created demand for additional goods and services, even if not for purple paint. This is the same with the retrofitting mandates proposed in the green jobs reports.

Explanation of the costs of proposed green jobs strategies are vague, which is another key issue with the reports. The U.S. Council of Mayors and the American Solar Energy Society reports both say little more than that costs will be incurred. The CAP report primarily cites another study that contends that all educational buildings, government offices, and hospitals in the United States could be retrofitted for energy savings at a cost of about $26 billion, which would result in an annual energy cost saving of $5 billion per year.[18] The UNEP study notes that building retrofitting to improve energy usage "can be done on the basis of existing technology with little or no net cost."[19]

How could it be that a massive program such as retrofitting buildings is possible at no net cost but is not occurring in the absence of government mandates? The implication of the necessity of a mandate is that profit-seeking building (or home) owners are too foolish to make investments in energy saving despite the short-term paybacks. Consistently in the UNEP report, and at least assumed implicitly by the domestic reports, green jobs proponents assert that money could be made if only profit-seekers were smart enough to recognize the opportunities: "Green innovation helps businesses . . . hold down costs by reducing wasteful practices."[20] One study cited by the UNEP asserted that "green building" improvements are "paid back over 2–7 years."[21] Another claimed that a $9 billion investment in energy savings would generate $28 billion in savings over 17 years and generate 58,400 new jobs.[22] In short, the UNEP believes that one major profitable opportunity after another is missed by profit-seeking corporations. Similarly, the Union of Concerned Scientists claims that the auto makers could easily save themselves, if only they produced more fuel-efficient cars. Since they will not on their own, the UCS advocates a federally imposed 35-mpg fuel standard that it claims would generate 241,000 more jobs by 2020 and save consumers $37 billion per year.[23] If only GM, Ford, and Chrysler would take this path, their futures would be secure. Contrary evidence is ignored.[24]

Green jobs proponents argue not only that for-profit businesses are missing obvious opportunities to make money; they also contend that requiring or directing investment into their favored programs will yield a wide range of benefits beyond simply creating jobs. Green jobs proponents believe the required investments will change the direction of the economy. For example, CAP argues that mandating (public) and incentivizing (private) building retrofits will create:

> new markets for energy-saving technology, and could serve as a foundation for administering rapid federal investment. They could become the active starting point for constructing a more ambitious national program of public building retrofits that . . . could provide needed funds directly to cities and rural communities to invest in greater energy efficiency and reduced global warming pollution.[25]

That is, wise public policy and demonstration projects will show private firms the benefits of developing more energy-saving products and services that are not now understood.

Further, green jobs reports also allege that more jobs are created by green investments than by alternatives. Green jobs mandates are justified, at least in part, because they will produce higher employment than would alternative projects. For example, CAP claims that "[p]ublic spending directed toward a green recovery program . . . would result in more jobs than spending in many other areas, including, for example, within the oil industry or on increasing household consumption, which was the primary aim of the April 2008 stimulus program."[26] That is, CAP is asserting that public green jobs spending is more beneficial to the economy than is general, undirected government "stimulus" to the economy. Why is green public spending better? Because CAP's input-output model says it is. As we describe in Chapter 8, CAP's model (and others' models as well) rests on crucial assumptions that dictate the outcome. For example, in the appendix describing the model, CAP notes that it used a "synthetic representation" of green industries because the larger government input-output model on which it based its calculations did not include those industries as separate sectors.[27]

Moreover, CAP examined the impact of spending, rather than energy production, within each energy sector.[28] In other words, CAP's model focused on the number of jobs an additional $1 million spent on solar energy would produce compared to $1 million spent on oil. Yet, as CAP notes, $1 million spent on solar energy would produce considerably less energy than $1 million spent on oil,[29] precisely because of the relative inefficiency of alternative energy technologies. CAP considered using a constant energy output model, an approach it noted was "most consistent with the idea that we are attempting to proceed to a low-carbon economy without having to make significant sacrifices in the total amount of energy we consume."[30] Such an assumption would be a fantasy indeed. CAP rejected it because:

> under this approach our employment estimates become highly sensitive to the current state of technology and energy costs in each energy industry. This would have produced highly inflated employment figures for solar power and other forms of renewable energy, where, at present, the costs of generating a given supply of BTU is much more expensive than traditional energy sources.[31]

Solar and wind currently have capital costs per kWh generated that are sufficiently greater than costs of coal-fired and natural gas-fired power plants to make the cost of the electricity they produce uneconomical compared to conventional fuel-generated power. An investment in alternative energy would therefore produce less energy than a similar investment in fossil fuels. This is the equivalent of demanding increased banana production in the United States to improve diets. Jobs working in banana hot houses would be created at a high cost to produce expensive bananas.

More jobs per dollar might be created with alternative forms of energy, but there would not be as much energy, and what would be available will cost more, directly or indirectly, because of the subsidies and mandates embedded in their production. This would be true even if consumers are not presented with the bill for the subsidies and mandates at the gas pump or in their utility bills. The resulting loss in the quality of life of the American consumer, due to inefficient use of labor and other resources, is not accounted for in the CAP analysis.

In addition, CAP used a high multiplier for the indirect effects of the money paid to the individuals working as a result of the expenditures on alternative energy. Although CAP noted that estimates in the literature of such multipliers range from negative to 2,[32] it assumed a multiplier "closer to the high end estimates" because CAP's proposal "is designed specifically to generate a large induced expansion of jobs" by spending "focused on domestic industries rather than imports" and "stimulating private-sector investment rather than relying on government spending" and will "help control the upward movement in the price of oil."[33] CAP then adjusts its estimate downward to be "conservative," concluding that indirect job creation will be only one-third of direct job creation.[34] As explained in Chapter 8, job multipliers, especially based on government mandates for low-value goods and services, are largely bogus. The failure of the economic "stimulus" plan, funded by future generations, to have the promised multiplier effect to boost the economy, is an incredibly costly example of the bogus nature of that claim.[35]

Similarly, green jobs reports point to the growth of ethanol and biodiesel in the United States, in response to public mandates and subsidies, as evidence that properly targeted incentives and rules can produce green jobs. CAP reports that "public and private sector growth is already picking up pace, with renewable energy technology supporting sustained double digit rates of growth nationwide."[36] The Mayors report states: "National and state energy policies have encouraged increased usage of ethanol blended with gasoline in recent years. That, combined with rising petroleum prices making biofuels more economically palatable, has led to dramatic growth in their usage."[37] UNEP cited an estimate that the biofuels market could grow $80 billion by 2011, but it concludes that not enough spending is occurring.[38] CAP notes that "an unstable policy environment and the lack of long term incentives have hurt the investment climate for these technologies, preventing them from realizing even greater growth."[39] Hence, more investment is needed in "infrastructure for next-generation biofuels."[40]

While mentions of the costs of alternative energy sources are vague in the reports advocating their adoption, the advocacy groups do agree that the costs should be considered. For example, the UNEP report argues that to "the extent that government mandates that such alternatives [such as solar power] be given equal access to the [electricity] grid, higher costs will be passed on to the consumers," but "as renewables mature technologically . . . cost disadvantages disappear and may turn into a cost advantage."[41] Implicit in this discussion is that the utility companies are too short-sighted to make investments in renewable energy projects that would produce profits. That premise is seriously at odds with the desire of a number of utilities to be allowed to sink large amounts of capital into nuclear plants that take a decade or more to build and have a long recoupment period. If the people who make their living in the industry do not see the wisdom of investing in massive wind and solar farms unless they are heavily subsidized, then the economic feasibility of such green projects is much more dubious than the political promoters assert them to be.

Further, the premise that reorienting our economy in a "greener" direction by shifting to "sustainable" energy production will increase net employment in the economy is not true, because the bulk of jobs in renewable energy sectors are not self-sustaining without subsidies. In particular, most jobs in solar PV energy and wind energy rely heavily on direct subsidies (via favorable tax treatment) or mandates (e.g., renewable portfolio standards). A study done for the American Wind Energy Association and the Solar Energy Research and Education Foundation in early 2008 estimated that if the investment tax credit for solar PV projects and the production tax credit for wind energy were not to be renewed at the end of 2008, then together those industries could lose 77 percent of their jobs. Specifically, the study forecast in 2008 that without the subsidies, 57 percent of jobs in the solar industry (69,000 to 29,600) and 93 percent of jobs in the wind industry (82,300 to 5,700) would vanish by 2009.[42] Further, a report prepared for the Center for American Progress itself notes, "Lapses in federal production tax credits, occasional one- to two-year extensions, and uncertainty about the future of these credits have led to a 'boom and bust' cycle in the development of wind power."[43] (See Figure 7.1.) For example, the production tax credit (PTC) expired in 2003, and additions to wind power capacity fell from 1,687 megawatts in 2003 to 389 megawatts in 2004. The result: "when the tax credits were renewed in 2005, wind capacity rose sharply, by 2,431 megawatts."[44]

In fact, U.S. subsidies for renewable energy projects are so attractive that in 2008, BP announced that it had dropped all plans to build wind farms and other renewable projects in Britain; instead, it is shifted its renewables programs to the United States, where government incentives for clean energy projects provide "a convenient tax shelter for oil and gas revenues," and a BP spokesman said "the best place to get a strong rate of return for wind is the U.S."[45] Royal Dutch Shell announced that it was also abandoning wind energy projects in Britain in favor of the United States.[46] These developments lend support to the idea that renewable energy—including wind energy, the renewable source for electricity generation deemed most likely to become cost-competitive with fossil fuels—is viable only because of subsidies and mandates.

133

Figure 7.1
IMPACT OF PRODUCTION TAX CREDIT ON WIND CAPACITY
GROWTH, ANNUAL CAPACITY GROWTH

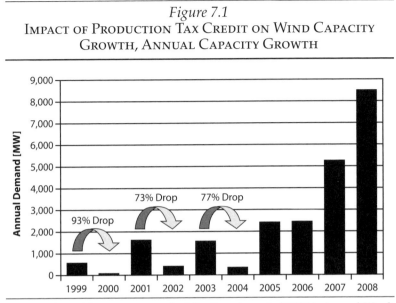

SOURCES: http://www.awea.org/publications/reports/AWEA-Annual-Wind-Report-2009.pdf, p. 4; Ryan Wiser et. al., "Using the Federal Production Tax Credit to Build a Durable Market for Wind Power in the United States," *Electricity Journal,* vol. 20, issue 8, pp. 77–88, Table 1.

Neglecting Opportunity Costs

As the above examples illustrate, a constant in the green jobs literature is the idea that maximizing employment, not attempting to maximize human welfare with the resources at hand, is the goal. Indeed, the UNEP study goes so far as to refer to the creation of jobs from spending on environmental projects as the "double dividend."[47] What is missing from these analyses is consideration of the opportunity cost of the public and private expenditures sought. CAP gives some consideration to the issue. It asserts that more jobs will be created by the "green investment" program than if the money was used in other ways. The report notes that if $100 billion were spent on domestic oil industry jobs, only 542,000 jobs would be created—far fewer than the 935,200 their proposal would generate. Why? The oil industry would spend a lot of money "purchasing machines and supplies."[48] Apparently, capital equipment is a bad, as are the jobs creating the equipment, compared to the more labor-intensive green jobs.

The CAP study's claim of 935,200 jobs created by spending $100 billion[49] implies a cost of $107,000 per new job created. This sum is very close to the Obama administration's claim that the economic stimulus program created jobs in 2009 at a claimed cost of $92,000 each.[50] Most people could go to a modestly priced college or university full time for four years for that sum.[51] The opportunity costs are real. Either the funds for these programs were taken from the pockets of people who have $100 billion less to spend on other things, causing an economic contraction in those other areas, or it means a bill passed on to the grandchildren of today's taxpayers through deficit spending, who will thus have less to spend.

The lack of consideration of opportunity costs can be seen in the UNEP report's consideration of a study of German tax-and-transit policy that recommended higher gasoline taxes, the revenue from which would be split evenly between "new infrastructure and financial support for public transport, and thus jobs in mass transit" and lowered taxes in other areas. The increased consumer spending from the tax cuts (financed by higher gasoline taxes) was predicted to produce three-quarters of the total net jobs produced by the policy. However, if that money were spent on reducing labor costs "by reducing employers' social security contributions" instead of being returned to taxpayers through tax cuts, "the net employment effects were thought to range as high as 400,000 new jobs."[52]

No consideration appears to have been given to the increase in the satisfaction of human needs and wants possible by leaving the tax revenues with taxpayers. This can also be seen in the negative attitude toward even environmental improvements that reduce demand for labor. "Making steel mills greener and more competitive is a must for job retention. At the same time, it must also be acknowledged that more energy-efficient mills do not necessarily employ many people. In the United States, electric arc furnaces (which require far less energy than blast furnaces) are characterized by a lean workforce."[53]

The UNEP report, unlike the domestic reports, notes that the push for green jobs means that some workers will move from declining areas such as fossil fuels to renewable fuels (substitute jobs). Some jobs will be eliminated as disfavored practices, such as certain packaging materials, are prohibited. Other traditional jobs will be transformed. Plumbers will become green job plumbers as "work methods . . . are greened."[54] Crucially, however, this estimate does not consider either the alternative use of nearly $1 trillion over that time period, nor does it estimate how many jobs would be destroyed. "The results do not reflect the net impacts of construction or operation of other types of electricity-generating power plants or replacement of existing power generation resources to meet growing needs."[55] In other words, no *net* job estimate was developed.

If $1 trillion is spent on wind energy generation projects, then there is $1 trillion less to spend on solar energy, education, health-related research and development, or any other activity. Jobs that could have been created in alternative sectors will not be created. Further, since the goal is to replace a portion of existing power generation with wind energy, fewer people will be employed in energy production from coal and other fossil fuel sources.[56] A "job demultiplier," which is likely at least as large as the multiplier assumed to be 2.5, and perhaps more, for reasons discussed below, would need to be applied to the lost jobs in those sectors. If a worker simply transfers from a job at a coal-fired electric plant to one at a wind-turbine electric plant, there is no job impact at all. This does not mean that wind energy production may not be a good idea, only that the job creation claims assume there is no alternative use for the resources devoted to this activity. It is likely that the net impact on employment is much lower and thus could even be an overall negative impact on the economy as we move away from the allocation of resources based on highest valued use in a competitive economy to allocation determined by political fiat.

Ignoring these net effects, green jobs estimates often claim credit for converting existing jobs into a "green" job. Retrofitting existing buildings, for example, is frequently cited as a major source of green jobs. The Mayors report predicts that:

> traditional contractors will develop their skill sets and expand their knowledge bases in ways that will allow them to transform large numbers of ordinary buildings into some of the most energy efficient in the world. The existing stock of energy inefficient buildings offers an opportunity to reduce total electricity demand and create jobs for these workers.[57]

This type of reasoning is endemic in the green jobs literature. Consider how it deals with the benefits of retrofitting existing buildings to higher energy efficiency standards. The CAP report argues that retrofitting would enable replacing "at least" the 800,000 construction jobs lost due to the housing downturn between July 2006 and July 2008[58] and so should be required by the government for "all public buildings" and induced in private buildings by "strong financial incentives including both loan guarantees and tax credits."[59]

The UNEP concedes that "exact figures are unknown" but nonetheless states that "it is easy to imagine that a worldwide transition to energy-efficient buildings could create millions or even tens of millions of jobs and would green existing employment for many of the estimated 111 million people already working in the sector."[60] Similarly, the UNEP report notes, "New green construction does allow for the possibility of some new jobs due to the increased investment in the construction phase. But most of the jobs created through green building practices are likely to occur from energy savings and reinvestment."[61] These jobs get counted as "new" because, as the UNEP report states, "[r]etrofitting buildings directly increases employment because without an attempt to make the building more efficient, the work would not have been done. Types of jobs that are likely to be created directly in the retrofitting process are auditors, engineers, estimators, project managers, and various jobs in the construction trades, including pipe fitters, sheet metal workers, HVAC technicians, engineers, electricians, and general construction workers."[62] This assumes that these workers have no alternative employment. Removing them from doing whatever it was they would have done otherwise—unless they were all unemployed—eliminates jobs and production in those other areas.

Conclusion

Politicians have long asserted, when shilling programs to voters, that programs will cost a fraction of what the true cost turns out to be. Something for nothing, or for very little, is always a good claim. In the private sector, that can be fraud, and making claims that are too good to be true can result in prison, as Bernard Madoff can aver. Politicians and policy advocates are under no such constraint. The result, over the years, has been the construction of one costly

8. Green Pork and the Green Economy

Many green jobs estimates focus only on job gains without considering job losses as employment shifts to favored industries, such as solar power, and away from disfavored ones, such as coal power plants. Even when green jobs estimates attempt to calculate job losses, they do so using inappropriate methodology. Subjecting any claims regarding a jobs program to a net jobs test is critical to informed decisionmaking, and a green jobs program should be no exception.

Before moving into the details about job estimates in the green economy, it is worth noting that at least one detailed study of the environmental industry found it to be unexceptional. Becker and Shadbegian used establishment-level data on manufacturers of environmental products to investigate whether the firms were different from comparable firms in other industries in their employment practices, productivity, or exports.[1] They found no evidence that firms in the environmental sector were systematically superior in performance. That is not a surprise. In a competitive economy, rates of return, costs, and other factors tend to be normalized. However, this casts doubt on those who assert that green industries provide superior employment impacts. Whether one is making green cars or nongreen cars, growing corn for ethanol or corn for pig feed, jobs are jobs.

A common thread among advocates of renewable energy and related programs is that they will create new jobs. The Center for American Progress report claimed that a $100 billion stimulus program in 2009 aimed at green jobs would "reduce the number of unemployed people to 6.8 million, down from 8.8 million" in one year.[2] In fact, stimulus spending was much larger than $100 billion in 2009 yet unemployment rose significantly. It was nearly $800 billion and was promised by Obama administration economists to generate 3.6 million jobs. It was not nearly as successful as promised, as even the 2010 Economic Report of the President claimed that employment was only about 1.8 million higher than it would have been in the absence of the stimulus.[3]

Perhaps the spending was not green enough. That promise was modest compared to the American Solar Energy Society report, which asserted that a scenario that "may be realistically feasible both economically and technologically" would create 40 million new green jobs by 2030.[4] More modestly, the U.S. Conference of Mayors report promised 2.5 million new green jobs over a decade.[5] As noted before, these jobs are pinpointed city by city. No doubt such promises have political appeal to help generate support from voters who hear that the programs will create clean energy and many new employment opportunities. Who can be opposed to jobs, especially green jobs? A significant problem is that the predictions are derived from an inappropriate technique. Using a forecasting methodology whose assumptions are not met by the conditions the green jobs literature assumes renders the results as unbelievable as they appear at first blush.

Multipliers were initially discussed in Chapter 5. As noted, a standard claim by those advocating green jobs is that the touted programs will have an even larger impact than it would appear at first blush because of the additional jobs and other benefits created. This claim rests on "economic multiplier" analysis. Economic multipliers are familiar in the applied policy literature, having been used to advocate for public subsidies for industries,[6] sports stadiums,[7] and other spending programs. Higher education has been shameless in claiming a multiplier impact from additional spending on that industry. The authors of one study reviewed 138 higher education economic-impact studies completed since 1992 and concluded that they are "public-relations documents masquerading as serious economic analysis."[8] A report on higher education in Michigan asserted that every dollar of state money spent on public universities generated $26 of economic impact. Only the most outlandish Ponzi schemes claim a 2,600 percent rate of return!

Multipliers are based on the idea that an increase in activity by one firm will lead to an increase in activity by other firms and employees that receive payment from the first. The contractor for a new football stadium buys concrete; the concrete subcontractor buys new tires for its trucks; all the firms' workers go out to dinner; and so forth. There are several standard models of how these interactions promulgate through the economy.[9] A literature review by staff of the International Monetary Fund provides both theoretical and empirical reasons to expect multipliers of various magnitudes. They conclude that multipliers will be larger and positive when increased government spending does not substitute for private spending, when it enhances the productivity of labor and capital, and when government debt is low. If these conditions do not obtain, the multiplier will be smaller and perhaps even negative.[10]

The fact that a job multiplier can be negative is illustrated by a study from Spain. That country has poured resources into renewable energy sources and is hailed as a leader in solar and wind power. Economists at King Juan Carlos University who studied the matter accepted the government claims of the number of jobs created by wind, mini hydroelectric, and photovoltaic (PV) energy projects. They found that the 50,000 green jobs created required an expenditure of 28.7 billion euros (U.S. $38 billion, meaning an astounding $760,000 cost per job).[11] The net employment effect was negative; the huge sums spent on green jobs drained resources out of the economy and raised energy prices. Each new job created is estimated to have destroyed 2.2 other jobs[12], and some companies moved production facilities to lower-cost energy countries.[13]

A fundamental question about these models is whether the multiplier is actually greater than zero. To see why this is a question, consider an economy at full employment. In such an economy, an increase in jobs in one industry must be offset by a decrease in jobs in another industry, so the multiplier equals zero. Of course, in the actual economy there are unused and underused resources. If investment that results in green jobs also induces some of these unused or underused resources to be put to good or higher-value use, then there could be an indirect effect that adds to the benefit. Harvard economist Robert Barro, summarizing his scholarly work on the matter, found that a multiplier of 0.8 is an upper bound for the impact of government spending.[14] That is, if the government spends $1, it generates, at most, $0.80 of economic activity. It is the case whether the spending was for military purposes or any other public purpose.[15] Since the degree of unused resources varies with economic conditions, analyses using multipliers should include forecasts under a range of economic conditions. None of the green jobs analyses do

141

so. Indeed, as U.S. economic conditions have changed dramatically over the past few years, what is most striking about the green jobs literature is that its predictions have remained constant.

Input-Output Analysis

In practice, multipliers are difficult to observe, and it is impossible to know them in advance. Therefore, they must be estimated by indirect means. The typical approach to constructing a multiplier is a technique known as "input-output analysis." This approach connects the ultimate destination of various products to their required components and allows estimates of the increased economic activity in multiple sectors induced by an increase in activity in a single area, such as green energy.[16] In input-output analysis

> the structure of each sector's production process is represented by an appropriately defined vector of structural coefficients that describes in quantitative terms the relationship between the inputs it absorbs and the output it produces. The interdependence among the sectors of the given economy is described by a set of linear equations expressing the balances between the total input and the aggregate output of each commodity and service produced and used in the course of one or several periods of time.[17]

The vectors are calculated using data on various industries that are combined into a single representation of the economy as a "matrix of technical input-output coefficients of all its sectors."[18] This structure of analysis makes some of the green jobs data problems we pointed to earlier fundamental for the accuracy of calculations.

Input-output analysis rests on two important assumptions. The first assumption is constant coefficients for production. In other words, the ratio of outputs to inputs is constant regardless of the scale of production or the time period. This assumption removes the possibility that inputs may be substituted for each other, either because of technical progress or because of changes in factor prices.[19] A typical assumption would be that if $1 of energy was required to produce $10 of steel at the time the input-output table was created, the same would be true in the future. Of course, if the price of energy increases, the relation is likely to change, as has been the case with steel. Higher energy prices would induce steel producers to change production techniques so as to reduce the amount of energy used per unit of steel. Even if that is not possible, it is not likely that the producer can fully pass along all of the increased energy costs to customers,[20] so that the ratio of energy cost to steel cost would change.

The assumption of constant coefficients production is particularly problematic in industries whose existence and growth are based on expectations of rapid technological progress that will enable changes in the needed inputs in various sectors of the economy and significant increases in energy costs. Since green jobs proponents commonly assert rapid technical progress will occur in alternative energy, input-output analysis is particularly inappropriate for use in estimating green jobs. In addition, increasing scale of output tends to increase capital intensity because of economies of scale in some capital investments. Thus, we would expect the amount of labor per unit of output to decrease relative to what input-output analysis would predict.

The second assumption on which input-output analysis rests is constant factor prices. This assumption was implicit in the lack of factor substitution already discussed, but it has an explicit role in the implementation of input-output analysis. In most cases, the relation between inputs and outputs is calculated using dollar values rather than physical quantities.[21] This approach is valid only if the physical quantities and the monetary values have a constant ratio. In other words, prices must be fixed. That is unlikely to be the case with respect to green jobs estimates. A common justification offered for supporting green technology is that oil and coal will become more expensive, either for technological reasons or because of a tax based on carbon dioxide emissions.[22] Because of the pervasive role that energy plays, such changes will alter factor prices throughout the economy, making the input-output analysis invalid. The role of oil as a nonenergy input into production of many materials, such as plastic, means that changes in oil price must have a direct impact on prices beyond the induced effect on the price of energy. Again, green jobs estimates are precisely the sort of analysis where input-output analysis is inappropriate.

We are not the only analysts to point out these difficulties in the green jobs literature. A recent study by the Congressional Research Service that looks at the employment impact of increased government infrastructure spending notes that "I-O models freeze technology and

143

productivity at a particular point in time."[23] The report goes on to point out that "[e]stimates of induced jobs or the multiplier are considered tenuous."[24] In addition, "[e]stimating the number of jobs dependent upon green infrastructure activities presents a greater challenge than estimates related to infrastructure projects as generally defined. . . . This recognized difficulty generally is either not mentioned, or how it is dealt with is not described, in the analyses of green job creation."[25]

In general, targeting subsidies to a particular area or industry, as the green jobs literature advocates, has not been supported by peer reviewed analysis. A survey of the evidence concluded "targeting is based on poor data, unsound social science methods, and faulty economic reasoning and is largely a political activity."[26] In a fundamental contribution to the literature, Courant outlined conditions under which subsidies can possibly increase economic welfare. He shows that unless a policy can increase productivity or bring in new resources to an area, then it will be a net burden on the region.[27] However, there is little guarantee that the political process will select a beneficial policy and little empirical evidence that such policies have been enacted where subsidies have been employed.

Subsidy policies are driven more by concerns about redistribution—a political issue—than by a concern about enhancing economic efficiency. The lack of emphasis on efficiency is unfortunate, as policies to improve efficiency are not only theoretically justified but empirically validated in some cases. After surveying the literature, one researcher concludes, "Although there is uncertainty in current research, I would argue that we do know some useful things: tax incentives for economic development are not self financing, but have significant costs per job created; some programs that promote productivity appear to be effective."[28]

Inappropriate Use of Multipliers and Input-Output Analysis

Suppose we overcome the difficulties in the kinds of data necessary to create a good multiplier. The next question is to what that multiplier should be applied. The green jobs literature's approach is to apply the multiplier to the gross amount of jobs in the green-energy sector.[29] This is likely to be an overestimate for two reasons: (1) the use of gross rather than net jobs and (2) the failure to account for deadweight losses.

144

Theoretically, the efficiency of employment "subsidy schemes is questioned because of the existence of non-additional employment and deadweight spending."[30] There is an additional technical flaw in much of the economic development literature, from which the green jobs literature also suffers. The discussion assumes that jobs are an unmitigated benefit, so that all of the wages should be considered as a net increase. In practice, there are unpleasant aspects to work, so that only the wages above some reservation amount should truly be considered an increment to welfare.[31] Because some of the gross job creation is not truly attributable to the subsidy, it is possible to develop inflated estimates of impact unless the true net impact is carefully analyzed. Noll and Zimbalist show how a gross economic impact of $760,000 conceals a true net impact of only $22,200 in an example from subsidizing a professional sports stadium, and even the studies done in support of subsidies find costs of as much as $1.8 million per job created.[32]

The deadweight loss problem is also serious, as it reveals that the green jobs literature also incorrectly treats the financing of the billions it advocates spending. Many of the green jobs reports start with the assumption that spending public money is the best method to induce additional economic activity. But that spending must be paid for, in some fashion, by higher taxes now or in the future. Because people engage in activities to avoid taxation, the cost of the tax exceeds the revenue yielded by the tax, a phenomenon known as deadweight loss. Because these effects are typically unobserved, they are generally not raised in public policy discussions. David Bradford illustrates the concept by hypothesizing a $1 million-per-pack tax on cigarettes. Such a tax would probably collect zero revenue. Thus, the tax would seem to have no impact. However, there is the lost pleasure of law-abiding smokers who no longer can obtain cigarettes. There might also be considerable activity by private citizens raising and curing tobacco for their own use, an activity stimulated as a result of this measure.[33] Another example is the result of the imposition of a door and window tax in France during the French Revolution and maintained until 1917.

> Its originator must have reasoned that the number of windows and doors in a dwelling was proportional to the dwelling's size. Thus a tax assessor need not enter the house or

measure it but merely count the doors and windows. As a
simple, workable formula, it was a brilliant stroke, but it
was not without consequences. Peasant dwellings were sub-
sequently designed or renovated with the formula in mind
so as to have as few openings as possible. While the fiscal
losses could be recouped by raising the tax per opening, the
long-term effects on the health of the rural population lasted
for more than a century.[34]

Subsidies, too, can have a deadweight loss as people alter their behavior to become eligible for the subsidy. James Sallee showed that
the imposition and expiration of tax incentives for purchase of hybrid vehicles led to the delay (waiting for imposition) or acceleration
(prior to expiration) of purchases of Toyota Prius automobiles.[35] A
more recent example of behavior modification was the rush of financial institutions to be classified as banks and thereby become eligible
for bailout funds.

Including deadweight loss in the analysis will reduce the net
benefit to which any multiplier should be applied. A counterargu-
ment might be that the public investment represents money allocated
from another source, so that the total tax revenue does not go up.
However, the reduced spending in the other area would have negative multiplier impacts that could mitigate the positive multiplier
effects of increased spending on green energy. Whether the source of
the subsidy is higher taxes or altered government spending, there is
a cost that reduces any net positive impact. The green jobs literature
does not incorporate estimates of deadweight losses into analyses
and so it does not provide net jobs calculations.

Who Pays for the Jobs?

The net jobs problem is a serious one. The issue is jobs that would
have been created had a subsidy not caused resources and jobs to be
shifted elsewhere. "For example, construction jobs are touted as new
jobs in targeting—say—an industrial park. But they are not; these
construction workers would have been working on other projects
if not reallocated to an industrial park by subsidies."[36] The proper
measure is not total jobs that exist in an area receiving a subsidy
but additional *net* new employment—jobs that would not otherwise
have existed.

This is a problem here because green jobs are substitutes for other jobs. An increase in electricity generation from wind, solar, or other sources will substitute for energy from, say, coal-fired generation, which in turn will reduce employment in coal mining and processing. The net impact on employment (before the multiplier) will depend on the relative labor intensity of energy production in the respective sectors at the margin of added or subtracted production.

Ignoring these issues renders the input-output analyses unconvincing. For example, studies that looked at jobs that were due to nonadditional employment or deadweight spending in other government projects, out of the total employment in a subsidized area, found that between 40 and 90 percent of the jobs should be classified as simply displacing existing jobs.[37] That is, only between 10 and 60 percent of the jobs that the reports claimed to have been created by a subsidy actually could be classified as jobs that might not otherwise have existed. A comprehensive study of European policies predicted that increased subsidies to renewable energy would increase employment by about 400,000 by 2020, while continuing current policies would increase employment by about 150,000, so that about 40 percent of the increased employment is not truly the result of the increased subsidies. Even this study, which unlike most of the literature presents both multiple scenarios and a reasonable benchmark, still suffers from the flaw that the subsidies to green jobs seem to come without any cost to the taxpayer.[38]

Even that measure does not consider the opportunity cost of the subsidy. Where else in the economy could the funds have been used more efficiently? The measure used here concerns only jobs that would have existed anyway but were falsely attributed to the subsidy and to "windfall gains" captured by firms that received subsidies. Studies of the job creation resulting from public projects have shown that the job creation that results often is of dubious value, because the cost per job created is high. For example, Oriole Park at Camden Yards, the Baltimore Orioles' stadium, was billed as a job-creating project.[39] However, the estimated cost per job created was $127,000.[40] In contrast, a review of 48 studies found that reducing state and local taxes resulted in greater business activity. On average, a 10 percent tax cut resulted in a 3 percent increase in business activity, which of course included new jobs that were voluntarily created.[41]

In another well-studied example, BMW, which has an assembly plant in upstate South Carolina, commissioned a study that reported it has a job multiplier of 4.3.[42] There were 5,400 direct BMW employees and 17,650 induced and indirect jobs for suppliers to BMW and local jobs created by economic activity of BMW employees. While the BMW plant is wonderful, the fact is that had it not been built there, it would have been built somewhere else in the country, so the net job issue is irrelevant for the nation as a whole. Even if it had been built in Canada rather than in the United States, it does not mean that those who earn their living in jobs related to BMW assembly in South Carolina would have had no alternatives. For all we know, employment opportunities may have been worse, the same, or better, making the job multiplier claims little more than happy talk. Job creation is a common argument for government subsidies of many projects around the world. Politicians find it to their advantage to cater to special interest groups while imposing the costs on taxpayers at large, all the while claiming to be increasing economic output and jobs.

Coates and Humphrey survey the evidence on the impact of sports teams on local economic activity. Most of the new construction of stadiums is accompanied by claims that their presence will boost the overall level of economic activity and especially employment. "Despite these claims, economists have found no evidence of positive economic impact of professional sports teams and facilities on urban economies." There are four main reasons for this finding. First, spending on sports is easily substitutable for spending on other leisure activities. Thus, the increase in spending on professional sports in Oklahoma City, say, as a result of the relocation of an NBA team, is almost entirely accounted for by a decrease in spending on movie tickets, greens fees, restaurant meals, and so on. Second, the attention paid to local sports teams could reduce worker efficiency as they spend time discussing the game rather than working. Third, the money spent on sports teams and facilities might reduce the amount spent on other public facilities and services. Because roads, fire protection, and other local government services can improve productivity, a reduction in spending on them could reduce productivity and thus overall economic activity. Fourth, the multiplier on spending for sports might be smaller than the multiplier for other activities. Because most of the money spent by sports teams reflects salaries to wealthy individuals who might not even reside in the region, it is unlikely to have the same impact that a similar amount of spending that directly affected local workers would have.[43]

These problems outlined here of input-output analysis point to a major flaw in the green jobs literature. In addition to the theoretical incoherence of the definition of "green" and the issues with the statistics used for its forecasts, its basic forecasting methodology is fundamentally flawed and largely discredited from its use in prior forms of economic planning.[44]

If the promised benefits are derived from input-output analysis and premised on technology that disrupts the relationship upon which the input-output analysis depends, the resulting data are unreliable. Perhaps most damning, these issues are not discussed in the green jobs literature even though they are widely known among economic analysts. What the input-output analyses do is clothe the proposals in the garb of scientific respectability. What they do not do is provide any confidence that the results are reliable.

Promoting Inefficient Use of Labor

The green jobs literature often defines a job as "green" based on the inefficient use of labor within a production process. While low labor productivity is a drag on the economy, it does not follow that it will lead to lower environmental impact. This focus on inefficiency stems in part from the efforts of those dissatisfied with free markets and their logical outgrowth, free trade, to use environmental issues to achieve political policy objectives for the economy.[45] Further, by focusing green jobs expenditures on economic activity with low labor productivity, resources can be forced to be shifted from capital to favored workers in line with these groups' economic priorities.

These proposals are often simply part of a "bootleggers and Baptists" coalition to achieve unrelated policy aims of the labor movement.[46] This idea, first published in the *Cato Journal*, builds on the old notion that politics makes for strange bedfellows. That is, those who wanted prohibition of alcohol (the Baptists) ended up on the same side of the issue as the bootleggers who profited from the existence of prohibition. Those parties have nothing in common but end up, inadvertently, in an alliance. That can be seen in certain environmental issues where environmental groups (the Baptists in this case) champion a policy, such as mass transit construction, that finds a natural alliance in labor unions that will profit from the union-wage construction jobs created and the companies that will provide the steel and rolling stock.[47]

Green jobs proponents have a curious attitude toward efficiency. On the one hand, they tend to see efficient use of nonlabor inputs such as energy and raw materials as crucial to creating a green economy. For example, the United Nations Environment Programme report states: "Greater efficiency in the use of energy, water, and materials is a core objective"[48] of a green economy. Discussing the cement industry, the report notes:

> Energy efficiency in the [cement] industry is gained as new cement plants are built. Inefficient, outdated processes are mainly found in small, regional plants. Manufacturers in countries or regions with stagnant levels of demand still rely on inefficient technologies, such as small-scale vertical kilns and the wet production process. Efficiency improvements are generally being made in countries with an increasing demand for cement. More-efficient rotary kilns utilize the dry production process and are replacing inefficient vertical shaft kilns. New plants built in developing countries are larger, cleaner, and more efficient than those built 10 to 30 years ago in developed countries.[49]

On the other hand, green jobs proponents see *increasing* the use of labor as a virtue, not a cost. For example, the UNEP report argues that a negative feature of today's economy is that it has increased labor productivity and so reduced the amount of labor necessary to deliver goods and services: "Any effort to create green jobs in food and agriculture must confront the fact that labor is being extruded from all points of the system, with the possible exception of retail."[50] Likewise, the same report criticizes the steel industry for increasing labor productivity. "Today steel is no longer a labor-intensive industry. It is marked by rising globalization, ongoing consolidation, substantial gains in labor productivity through automation and computerization, and strong competition, particularly from Asian producers."[51] A similar criticism is made of the oil industry, with the report observing "almost 40 percent of U.S. oil-refining jobs disappeared between 1980 and 1999; another 8 percent decline occurred between 2001 and 2006."[52]

Low labor productivity has critically important consequences. First, a society of low-labor-productivity jobs is an impoverished society in which output is restricted by the failure to make use of capital and in which wages are low by definition, for employees can receive only the value they generate absent transfer payments. Second, because green jobs proponents promise high-wage jobs, they will have to force compensation higher than the competitive wage, producing permanent high unemployment. This is not a matter of theory; a comparison of European and North American labor markets over the past 50 years reveals that promoting high-wage, low-labor-productivity jobs produces high structural unemployment.[53]

The ASES report asserts that "the net effect within a carbon-constrained energy economy is positive, creating roughly five jobs for each job lost,"[54] meaning that to produce the equal value in production of a given quantity of energy, five times as many bodies will be required. That implies a massive drop in productivity and, therefore, standard of living. At such low levels of efficiency, as much as a quarter of the entire workforce may have to be involved in this enterprise. ASES notes that, by 2030, 40 million workers in the United States—"about one in every four working Americans"—could be in the renewable energy and energy efficiency areas.[55] Similarly, the Renewable and Appropriate Energy Laboratory at the University of California at Berkeley found it a positive feature of alternative energy that "renewable energy creates more jobs per kilowatt hour than traditional energy sources."[56] Again, this is simply a fancy way of stating that renewable energy is more costly in labor terms than alternatives—hardly a virtue to anyone asked to pay for the energy produced.

Increasing labor productivity is what makes societies wealthier and better able to satisfy their wants and needs, ranging from better education to better access to health services and medicines, and allows them to have more leisure time.[57] Moreover, reducing the labor component of obtaining any energy service would, all else being equal, reduce overall costs to consumers, because for most services, the cost of labor generally exceeds the cost of materials, as anyone who has had the misfortune of getting a car, computer, or cell phone repaired can attest.

This glorification of inefficient labor practices captures a frequent mistake in the green jobs literature—mistaking the means for the end. For example, the UNEP study complains: "Economic systems that are able to churn out huge volumes of products but require less and less labor to do so pose the dual challenge of environmental impact and unemployment."[58] As a result, the study is critical of carbon capture and sequestration efforts because they are "capital intensive, and therefore the jobs created per million dollars of investment can be expected to be low,"[59] in contrast to the greater labor intensity of biofuels harvesting. "The labor intensity of biofuels harvesting compares favorably with conventional fuels. On average, biofuels require about 100 times more workers per joule of energy content produced than the capital intensive fossil fuel industry."[60]

Similarly, the operating efficiency of coal power plants compared to solar power plants is portrayed as a negative feature of the coal plants, because coal plants produce fewer jobs per delivered megawatt of power since a greater peak capacity is needed by a solar PV facility to produce the same amount of delivered power.[61] As a result, more construction jobs are created by a need for delivery of a megawatt of power from solar PV than from coal, because a greater solar peak capacity is required to deliver the same amount of energy.[62] The study criticizes extractive industries generally for not employing large numbers of people.[63] It also disapproves of the efficiency of farming in the United States and large retailers.[64] Even increased labor productivity in green industries such as rail transportation is characterized as a problem rather than as a benefit. Greater efficiency in rail services in China is, according to the UNEP report, a mistake.[65] This is so even though cutting labor costs would speed expansion of the green industry by lowering costs.

As a result, green jobs advocates often promote technologies that are inefficient users of labor precisely because the technologies are inefficient. For example, in discussing "bus rapid transit" (BRT) systems, the UNEP report notes:

> In BRT systems, the frequency of service is carefully calibrated, and therefore bus breakdowns and other operational failures need to be minimized. This in turn implies that buses must be kept in excellent condition. Hence BRT systems offer a substantial number of maintenance jobs. Maintaining high-quality service also means it is critical to ensure good working conditions for drivers, who need to be well trained and are expected to take responsibility for their performance. Thus, jobs for drivers and mechanics must be decent and well paying.[66]

Increasing the number and skill level of employees makes the BRT systems *more* expensive and *less* competitive relative to other means of transportation, such as personal automobiles or less labor-intensive bus systems, if the BRT must cover costs. It is a problem preventing the adoption of such systems, not a benefit, that they require more skilled labor than alternatives to deliver the same amount of transportation services.

Germany has long been active in promoting the use of renewable energy through the use of feed-in tariffs and other subsidies. Feed-in tariffs have only recently been introduced in the United States, although they have been used in Europe since the early 1990s. A feed-in tariff offers a higher price for electricity to producers if that electricity is generated in favored ways, such as through solar PV generation, than for other ways, such as natural gas–fired plants.[67] A study of the impact of these policies in Germany estimated that the subsidy per worker reached levels as high as $240,000, well above the wage. As a result, the jobs are unlikely to be sustainable when the subsidies are removed.[68] The study also found:

> Proponents of renewable energies often regard the requirement for more workers to produce a given amount of energy as a benefit, failing to recognize that this lowers the output potential of the economy and is hence counterproductive to net job creation. Significant research shows that initial employment benefits from renewable policies soon turn negative as additional costs are incurred.[69]

The selection of maximizing labor use as the measure of success presents several major problems. First, the goal of economic activity is not the employment of labor or of other resources but the production of goods and services that satisfy human needs and wants. Higher labor productivity makes societies wealthier and better able to satisfy wants and needs ranging from better education to better access to health services and medicines. It also allows people to have more leisure time and provides them the resources to enjoy that leisure.[70]

A new method of production that uses fewer inputs to produce the same outputs as an existing method frees up inputs for use in addressing additional human needs and wants. A prime example is agriculture. The labor intensity of agriculture in the United States has plummeted over the last 200 years, as farmers adopted mechanization, increased agricultural knowledge, and developed higher-yield seeds. Merely 1.4 percent of the U.S. workforce is engaged in agriculture today compared to over 21 percent in 1929,[71] yet production today is much higher.[72] The people who left agriculture are now employed in alternative occupations, creating goods and providing services that would be unavailable if those people had remained employed in agriculture. Under the definitions of green jobs used in these reports, however, this transition is a negative change in the "greenness" of American agriculture.

Second, even assuming that some substitution of capital and other inputs for labor has negative environmental consequences, it does not follow that such substitutions generally are either net negative contributions to the environment or inappropriate. Again, agriculture provides an example. Agriculture is a dangerous occupation, with farming "among the most hazardous of industries in terms of number of fatalities, fatality rates, number of non-fatal injuries, and non-fatal injury rates."[73] Much agricultural labor was previously devoted to backbreaking, low-productivity, unpleasant work that broke people down. New techniques that free people from dangerous, unpleasant work and increase production of food crops have benefits that offset the claimed negatives of more capital-intensive farming methods identified in these reports. As Martin Wolf notes, "Subsistence farming is among the riskiest of all human strategies, since starvation is one harvest away."[74]

Whether particular techniques are better or worse for the environment or for the individuals engaged in the labor is thus not an issue that can be settled by assuming that all labor-intensive methods are to be preferred to all capital-intensive ones. If, as some green jobs advocates insist, labor-intensive agriculture produces a desirable lifestyle, one would expect to find people volunteering to do that for a living. But you can't keep Johnny down on the farm. Prohibiting capital-intensive agriculture would indeed cause more labor to shift to agriculture as more people pick up hoes for a living, but the crash in standards of living from the loss of capital intensive technology would not mean quality, high-paying jobs. Yet this is precisely what the green jobs literature asserts will occur.

Third, even in the favored green industries, increasing labor efficiency has been an important component in making the technologies more commercially viable. For example, corn-based ethanol cost reductions in the United States over time have been driven in part by "upscaling farms" (i.e., introducing economies of scale) and the advanced technology necessary to convert corn into ethanol.[75]

Increasingly efficient use of labor was a significant factor in the remarkable economic growth of the U.S. economy during the 19th century. That growth was attributable to a significant degree to conditions of labor scarcity and a relentless drive to reduce the need for labor across industries. Labor scarcity led to high wages for American workers relative to workers elsewhere (an indicator of a good job, according to the UNEP report[76]). This then meant that, as an English investigative commission noted in 1854, "the whole energy of the people is devoted to improving and inventing labour-saving machinery."[77] As Nobel laureate Douglass North explained:

> The constant concern with labor saving machinery was considered by the [British] commissioners [investigating U.S. industry in the 1850s] to be a fundamental explanation of the indigenous development of such innovations, and the relatively high price of labor was considered the driving force. Important innovations developed in every industry, frequently in small shops and firms at the hands of mechanics with little or no formal scientific training.[78]

Labor was scarce in 19th-century America because the abundance of cheap, fertile land in the United States made agricultural output per person high and made it harder to lure people from agriculture into industry.[79] Labor scarcity meant that American manufacturers needed to organize their employees efficiently. For example, comparing English and American workers in the 19th-century textile industry, "The most conspicuous example of efficient use of labour is the training that the American manufacturers gave to their workers so that each was able to handle more looms."[80] Moreover, the increased training and skill levels of American workers then equipped those same workers to improve on the technology they used, "particularly when the worker had been self-employed earlier in life, and most of all when he had been a farmer, for he carried over into industry the inclination to seek his own methods of doing his job better."[81] Again, all these are indicia of good jobs according to the UNEP report, and all are the result of high labor productivity, not low labor productivity.

Busy Hands, Happy Heart?

The green jobs literature's focus on inefficient labor use thus embodies three highly peculiar assumptions about human well-being. First, it assumes that increasing labor productivity, which increases output, should be discouraged. This reduces human welfare by reducing the goods and services available to people. While many environmentalists have promoted reductions in consumption for decades,[82] adopting a policy of reducing the goods and services available to the general population should be done through open debate, not by smuggling it in through a green jobs policy. Such a policy will condemn those already poor to eternal poverty.

Second, low labor productivity does not produce high wages. Each factor of production receives its marginal productivity in a competitive economy. Since the green jobs literature insists that jobs must be high paying, creating a world of high-paying, low-productivity jobs requires an aggressively interventionist economic policy to shift rewards from high-productivity inputs (capital and resources) to low-productivity inputs (labor). Not only is such a policy inconsistent with an open market economy, but the payment of a wage above what productivity justifies will lead to unemployment.[83] It is simply not possible to mandate a world of high-paying, low-productivity jobs any more than it is possible to mandate that the second law of thermodynamics will no longer be taken into account in energy use. An aggressive set of policy measures would be required to force such a shift in an economy that would then be afflicted by declining standards of living.

Finally, subsidizing labor at the expense of capital could delay the development of technologies that increase the efficiency with which scarce resources are used. To the contrary, consider the example of petroleum refining. It is a highly capital-intensive process, but these increases in capital intensity have yielded dramatic increases in the amount of fuels and specialty chemicals obtained from a barrel of crude oil. Petroleum products are used in some chemical and pharmaceutical products. A 42-gallon barrel of crude oil yields over 44 gallons of petroleum products, including asphalt, petrochemical feedstock, and lubricants.[84] By increasing the yield from crude oil, these innovations have boosted the efficiency of use of natural resources. Biasing production away from capital intensity reduces the incentive to produce such innovations that raise standards of living.

Moreover, because environmental protection is itself often capital intensive (to the extent that it requires additional capital equipment to reduce emissions),[85] such a bias would likely increase the harm to the environment from the production that continued.

Conclusion

The problems with the methodologies of green jobs studies that we have identified are grounds for caution in accepting their policy proposals. Before trillions of dollars in public and private resources are directed into promoting a "green economy," we need to have a better understanding of the details of how such programs will transform our economy. We should worry about proposals that glorify low labor productivity, the modern version of the Luddites.[86]

Our survey of problems in the green jobs literature is not merely methodological nit-picking, although we do have many methodological issues with the literature. The issues we have identified have a common theme: the masking of critically important policy choices beneath a series of questionable assumptions and definitions. Before policies are adopted that are committed to an effort to remake human society on the basis of these assumptions, Americans deserve a full and open debate informed by the best data and analytical methods. Thus far, the push for green jobs has provided neither.

9. Green Cars, Trucks, and the Green Economy[1]

No area of the "green economy" has been subject to greater hype and had more predictions of amazing technological revolutions just around the corner than transportation. Politicians have been proclaiming the internal combustion engine and personal automobile to be the "most serious and dangerous source of air pollution in the Nation today" since at least 1974 (during a congressional debate over the Clean Air Act)[2], and regulators from Washington, D.C., to Sacramento, California, have long insisted that use of "zero-emission vehicles," replacing gasoline and diesel with new fuels, and replacing cars and trucks with buses and trains will both spark an employment boom and yield substantial environmental benefits.

Despite the constant predictions of transportation revolutions, we're still driving cars powered by internal combustion engines burning gasoline and still shipping goods in heavy duty diesel trucks. And in almost every year since World War II, we've done more of these activities than we did the year before. There has been considerable progress. Today's cars and trucks are individually much less environmentally damaging than their predecessors. The black-smoke-belching tailpipes of 1960s-era cars and trucks are no more; today's automobiles and heavy duty diesel trucks are cleaner than their counterparts from 1970, 1980, or 1990. Between 1970 and 1980 alone, new vehicles got 96 percent cleaner with respect to hydrocarbons, 76 percent cleaner with respect to NO_x, and 96 percent cleaner with respect to CO.[3] Cars and trucks have gotten cleaner in part because federal clean air regulations required it. Even if there had not been those regulations, however, there is good reason to believe there would have been major improvements in emissions.[4] From 1980 to 2007, new vehicles got another 37 percent cleaner with respect to NO_x and another 52 percent cleaner with respect to CO.[5] There is little pollution left to control. "Today's cars are 98 percent cleaner than those from the 1970s when considering conventional air pollution."[6]

One important consequence of the extent of these reductions in emissions from cars and trucks is that we have reached the point where further reductions in per-mile emissions from individual cars and truck of the main pollutants regulated under the Clean Air Act ("the criteria pollutants") will be both tiny and expensive. And these limits on future reductions of per-mile emissions of criteria pollutants are not ones that can be overcome by the discovery of a new catalyst for treating emissions or invention of a new end-of-the-tailpipe device. We have simply arrived at the point where there is little else we can do to make internal combustion and diesel engines or gasoline or diesel fuel cleaner that we have not already done.

There is one exception: to the extent that we can increase engine efficiency, we can reduce emissions per mile by reducing the amount of fuel that must be burned to move the vehicles a mile. If real gasoline prices increase in the next few years, we will undoubtedly see such improvements in engine efficiency. However, increasing efficiency results in the "Jevons Paradox" (named for 19th-century economist Stanley Jevons): greater efficiency in resource use leads to increased resource use because the reduced cost per unit increases the number of units purchased.[7] This offsets (at least in part) the impact of the higher cost of the resource. While higher gasoline prices will encourage the purchase of more fuel-efficient cars, that will in turn lower the cost per mile of driving and so increase the number of miles people drive.[8] Further, some of those increases in efficiency may come at the expense of increased emissions of pollutants, since many of the measures necessary to make vehicles more efficient necessitate trade-offs with controlling some pollutants.

The improvements in vehicle emissions are a remarkable success worthy of celebration. Air pollution in the developed world generally has been transformed from a visible problem with a real risk of acute injury and death into a debate over the impacts of quite small levels of pollutants. Killer smogs are no longer the concern in the United States, Japan, or Europe, having been relegated to the history books. Similarly, fuels have significantly improved. Lead in gasoline has ceased to be a major airborne pollutant; sulfur and other contaminant levels in both gasoline and diesel have declined dramatically;

and transportation fuels are cleaner and less polluting in virtually every dimension than they were in 1970. Unfortunately, the situation is quite different in developing countries, where indoor air pollution from burning wood, charcoal, dung, and other solid fuels continues to be a major problem, as we discuss in Chapter 12, and where transportation fuels are not always as clean.[9]

This success in reducing per-mile emissions of criteria pollutants and in raising overall air quality levels has not ended debate over mobile source emissions, however. First, despite (and in part because of) the decline in per-mile emissions, there are more Americans driving, and Americans are driving more than in the past—an upward trend that has continued virtually unchanged since the end of World War II. Economic conditions and fuel price spikes sometimes produce short-term declines, but the long run trend continues to be toward additional miles driven by passenger cars.

It's not just cars, however. More goods are being shipped by truck, and more things are available to be shipped; what some call the "Amazon effect" means online shopping is substituting delivery truck miles for passenger car trips to the mall. Between 1980 and 2004, the number of gallons of fuel burned by commercial trucks went from 19,960,000 gallons to 33,968,000 gallons because of "a substantial increase" in the number of trucks on the road and a doubling of the vehicle miles traveled per truck.[10] While the global recession that began in 2008 temporarily slowed commerce, and so reduced freight traffic, economic recovery will once again boost freight shipments because firms have discovered how to reduce their costs through logistics programs such as "just in time" delivery of inventory.

Total mobile source emissions in the United States and other developed countries are therefore likely to increase (or, at least, are highly unlikely to decrease significantly) as our ability to engineer reductions on a car-by-car, truck-by-truck basis reaches its technological limit and is overwhelmed by the rising numbers of miles driven by vehicles. And mobile source emissions worldwide are certain to climb regardless of what we do, as other countries' living standards improve and greater wealth in the developing world fuels the demand for mobility.[11] If we compare the number of vehicles per capita for various countries relative to that same number for the United States at different points in time, we can get a sense of where world motor vehicle use is headed.

For example, in 1994 China had the same number of cars per capita as the United States had in 1911; by 2005 the number had risen to the level equivalent to the United States in 1915.[12] Car sales in China continue to rise rapidly as the Chinese people grow more wealthy—year-on-year sales were up 48 percent for 2009 and 80 percent for the first three months of 2010.[13] Even if China adopts an aggressive program of urban design and builds mass transit comparable to that in Western Europe, bringing China to the level of vehicles of Western Europe in 2005 (the same level as the United States in 1970) will dramatically expand the number of cars and trucks in China. The automobile industry correspondents for *The Economist*, Iain Carson and Vijay Vaitheeswaran, concluded in their 2007 book on the future of automobiles that the Chinese government "does not dare tell the aspiring middle classes about to buy their first car that they must ride bicycles or crowd onto buses. And even if China's leaders tried, they would probably fail to kill the car."[14] By 1999, China had already shifted from an economy dominated by passenger rail to one dominated by road transportation, and motorization is "rapidly accelerating" in the higher-income regions on the coast.[15] Even if the gasoline prices in China double and economic growth is low, the Japan International Transportation Institute predicts a doubling of 2000 levels of energy consumption by vehicles in China by 2030.[16] That is probably a significant underestimate. Auto sales in 2009 rose about 35 percent over 2008 as China blew past the United States to become the largest auto market in the world.[17]

India is also rapidly increasing its truck and passenger car use, with a "significant shift" from rail to road for freight in the 1980s.[18] More recently, the development of the inexpensive "one lakh" car in India will dramatically expand automobile use not just in India but in developing countries around the world, a prospect that some environmental regulators say gives them "nightmares."[19] As Carson and Vaitheeswaran note, "The One Lakh car could do for rural Indians what Henry Ford's Model T did for early-twentieth-century Americans or André Citroën's 2CV did for French farmers impoverished after World War II."[20]

Growth in cars and trucks abroad is not the only challenge we face in making transportation "greener." In general, our choices are no longer—if they ever really were—simple ones between "clean" and "dirty" air. Because we now face a complex series of choices implicating a diverse set of trade-offs, there is no obvious "green" answer to many environmental regulation policy questions. Not only will we confront technological barriers qualitatively unlike those we have solved in the past, as we continue to tighten existing air quality standards (e.g., ozone) and regulate additional air pollutants (e.g., greenhouse gases), but having previously put into place the easy, relatively-low-marginal-cost pollution control measures, we now face difficult trade-offs in making future emissions control decisions. Do we increase the efficiency of combustion in engines, reducing particulates but increasing NO_X emissions, or the reverse? Do we emphasize controlling CO_2 by encouraging a switch from gasoline to diesel engines at the cost of increasing NO_X emissions?[21] Or do we focus on controlling particulates, at which gasoline-powered spark-ignition engines have an advantage over diesels?[22] If we choose to create incentives for diesel use, will the greater fuel efficiency of diesel engines relative to gasoline engines lower the cost of operation and encourage more mobile source use? Whatever answers to these questions regulators come up with, however, it is certain that the future of transportation will involve hard choices. We cannot avoid those choices by wishing for new technologies that will make the choices magically disappear.

In the next chapter, we examine mass transit issues; in this chapter, we will look at the use of cars and trucks and what green energy proponents have to say about them.

Mandating a Greener Transportation Future?

Green energy proponents often speak of transportation issues as if the cars and trucks we use could be significantly altered just by legislating new technologies. California has attempted for years to mandate "zero-emission vehicles" (ZEV) (regulator-speak for plug-in electric vehicles whose emissions would actually come out of power plant smoke stacks rather than tailpipes), although the regulation's requirements have been watered down repeatedly.[23] Green energy proponents similarly propose similarly unrealistic goals, ranging from implausible expansion of biofuels programs that have yet to prove to be either green or economically sustainable, to shifting potential future car owners in developing countries into bicycle rickshaws instead. Unfortunately, things are not as simple as politicians might wish—as the problems with implementing California's ZEV program have demonstrated.

Broadly speaking, we can imagine two sorts of vehicles: those powered by their own energy sources (e.g., internal combustion engines) and those powered by stored energy produced elsewhere (e.g., cars running on electric batteries). Green energy programs stress the environmental benefits of the latter without admitting that stored energy vehicles simply shift the pollution problem to the stationary sources that charge their batteries. And, of course, there are environmental consequences to the production of vehicles as well as to their operations—consequences that can reverse the sign on the net environmental impact of a vehicle. Thus some analysts have argued that the Toyota Prius hybrid has a larger negative environmental impact than the less-fuel-efficient Hummer because of the greater energy necessary to build the Prius and the pollution caused by the lead in its batteries.[24] Whether the Prius–Hummer comparison is correct or not, the important thing to keep in mind is that it is the *net* environmental impact of a technology that matters. Green energy proponents seem curiously unwilling to consider *net* impacts. Unfortunately, few green energy proposals about transportation perform such calculations.

Let's set aside the problem of whether a particular technology will be a net environmental benefit and assume that wise EPA engineers and scientists can figure that out for us. What sort of transportation do green jobs proponents imagine we have available in a green economy?

- "[B]icycles and modern bicycle rickshaws offer a sustainable alternative and create employment in manufacturing and transportation services."[25]
- "Denser cities and shorter distances," which will "reduce the overall need for motorized transportation," with walking and bicycling replacing cars for many.[26]
- Less freight, shipped shorter distances.[27]
- Less air travel.[28]
- Increasing labor costs in rail and bus systems.[29]
- Large scale displacement of gasoline and diesel by biofuels—more than 2.5 times as much as predicted by the EIA.[30]

This future is not one we think most people will be willing to accept, and certainly not one that could be considered something to actively attempt to create.

Clunkers

We do have one example of a green energy transportation measure: the 2009 Car Allowance Rebate System, or Cash for Clunkers, program. The Obama administration touted the program for its green impact: both boosting the economy by spurring new car purchases and improving the environment by "bringing forward the replacement of dirty (high-polluting) 'clunker' motor vehicles by cleaner, high-efficiency vehicles means there will be less pollution over some time period."[31] Green energy proponents at the Center for American Progress heavily promoted the idea while it was under consideration in Congress:

> Public spending on "cash for clunkers," however, as part of a larger green stimulus, would have ancillary benefits by reducing our dependence on oil, increasing innovation and investment in the auto industry, and avoiding the devastating social, economic, and environmental effects of global warming over the long term.
>
> Indeed, the transformation of our antiquated and carbon-intensive fuel and energy infrastructure around the platforms of efficiency and clean technology represents the great potential engine of American innovation, economic growth, and job creation in the immediate future and for coming decades. Cash for clunkers represents a step toward that low-carbon future.
>
> Moreover, by targeting those most affected by high oil prices yet most often absent from the larger energy and climate conversation, this program reaches new constituencies for a green economic renewal, and will focus national attention on the opportunity to invest in good jobs in a more energy-efficient economy.[32]

And in August 2009, CAP's *Climate Progress* blog called the program "wildly successful" and a "slam dunk," despite "inadequate" requirements for increased replacement vehicle mileage.[33] With sales of nearly 690,000 vehicles during the program's operation, it looked like a success. The White House Council of Economic Advisors calculated that the program produced 440,000 new car sales during the program's operation, which would not have occurred without the program's incentives.[34] *Climate Progress* dispensed with worries about distinguishing incremental sales from those that would have occurred anyway, arguing the program succeeded because of the volume of new car sales, with the increased mileage of the replacement cars "saving" the consumer $500 million per year (based on an assumed average gasoline cost of $3.50 per gallon).

These estimates of savings are flawed in many of the same ways that other green jobs estimates are. CAP simply made up numbers like its $3.50 per gallon gasoline price (far above prices current or forecast by neutral observers like the EIA for the same period).[35] CEA at least made an effort but based its calculations on newspaper reports of interviews with auto industry executives and investment reports, not even conducting its own interviews with industry experts.

Unfortunately, more careful analysis revealed the program to be a dud. Edmunds.com, an auto website devoted to accurately pricing new and used cars, looked at the results of the program.[36] Using historical data on car sales, Edmunds concluded that only 18 percent of the car sales during the program were sales that would not have otherwise occurred, making the cost to taxpayers per additional sale a whopping $24,000.[37] A National Bureau of Economic Research study issued in September 2010 found that most of the extra purchases made in 2009 were simply early purchases by people who would have bought in the following months, almost completely reversing its impact by May 2010."[38] Even *Saturday Night Live* parodied the clunkers program in a segment broadcast in November 2009 by having Chinese President Hu Jintao caution President Obama that the United States could not repay its debt to China in "clunkers." Finally, the overall impact of the program on jobs turned out to be much less than originally claimed, with the third-quarter GDP estimates revised downward to reflect a lowered 0.81 percent annualized growth impact rather than the 1.7 percent originally claimed for the program.[39] Thus our experience with the one green energy program that has already been fully implemented points to the problems we identified earlier with the green energy proponents' analyses: sloppy calculations, bad data, and assumptions biased to demonstrate success.

Structural Obstacles

Beyond the flaws in specific analyses like those discussed above, there are three even more serious problems with the green energy proponents' vision of our transportation future. First, it rests on un-realistic assumptions about the ease of changing our transportation infrastructure. The United States has an extensive infrastructure of pipelines, storage tanks, and refineries dedicated to providing gasoline and diesel to cars and trucks. This infrastructure produces large network effects that will be hard to duplicate for any new technology, making it likely that gasoline and diesel engines will continue to dominate transportation well into the future. Some vehicles, like centrally dispatched delivery fleets, can adopt a new fuel technology relatively easily because they return to a central refueling station regularly. For example, local delivery fleets have led the way in adopting compressed natural gas, but expanding such models to passenger cars is financially infeasible unless the relative prices of natural gas and petroleum change sufficiently dramatically to warrant the costs of building an entirely new network of fueling stations and pipelines.

Moreover, we have a network of highways that carries people and freight. Our homes, workplaces, and recreation are all intertwined with this network. Even if all Americans wanted to pay to embrace the radical changes in lifestyle that a mass-transit-oriented society would require—replacing our low density suburbs with high density, European-like cities—it would take decades and untold billions of dollars in construction and demolition costs to make such a shift. As former oil company energy economist Peter Tertzakian put it in his call for reduced oil use: "to really offset demand we need to see lifestyle changes today at the level that was accomplished in Japan and many European countries over the past three decades."[40] Moreover, there is no evidence that most Americans (or most of any country's people) want to embrace such a future. As *The Economist* correspondents Carson and Vaitheeswaran—generally harsh critics of both the automobile and oil industries—note: "a world without cars would be a dim, joyless place with much-diminished freedom, mobility, and prosperity."[41]

Second, virtually all our existing infrastructure is unsuited for fuels other than gasoline. Even a liquid fuel like ethanol will not work with existing infrastructure. It cannot be delivered by existing fuel pumps at blends above 15 percent ethanol or transported via gasoline pipelines because of its much greater attraction to water and corrosive properties. Blends of ethanol and gasoline above 15 percent ethanol pose serious problems for existing equipment, including engines. If we move away from liquid fuels entirely, we have no infrastructure for handling plug-in electric vehicles, which would require billions in investment in home charging stations, parking lot charging stations, and new electrical generation and transmission capacity. If a significant number of Americans began charging cars for the drive home while they are at work, it would dramatically alter existing patterns of electricity use, straining our capacity to provide power.

Replacing or duplicating our existing fuel infrastructure to handle plug-in vehicles or alternative liquid fuel vehicles would cost billions of dollars and could require taking property from tens of thousands of landowners for new pipeline or transmission line right of ways. Brazil, the darling of ethanol proponents, solved this problem in the late 1970s because its then-military dictator "simply ordered every gas station in the country to install an ethanol pump," paid for by the government because the stations were all run by a state-owned oil company.[42] Since there were hardly any cars in Brazil that could use ethanol, "these pumps had no customers."[43] Having solved the problem of creating a fuel network by fiat, the dictator then mandated production of cars capable of using ethanol. In 2006, then-Sen. Hilary Clinton proposed the United States follow the Brazilian example by having the federal government pay half the cost of installing hundreds of thousands of E85 pumps at existing gas stations, to jumpstart a market for higher concentrations of ethanol here, as part of a larger $50 billion-per-year alternative energy program.[44] She did not explain where the pipeline and other infrastructure would come from or who would pay the other 50 percent of the pumps' costs.

Third, our existing fleets of cars and trucks are long-lived, making changing the overall fleet a drawn-out process. A 2004 study by the Center for Sustainable Systems at the University of Michigan found that long replacement intervals of 15 years or more for passenger cars were optimal for most owners,[45] a result similar to an analysis by the Oak Ridge National Laboratory that found that 1990 model year cars had a useful life of almost 17 years.[46] Heavy duty trucks are similarly long-lived.[47] Changing the energy use pattern of half the U.S. automotive or truck fleet will thus take almost a decade *even if every new vehicle purchased starting tomorrow* were a plug-in electric vehicle or other new technology. Even critics of American reliance on petroleum, like ethanol proponent Robert Zubrin, agree that this is a serious barrier. As Zubrin notes, in arguing that fleet changes will take too long to spread new technology:

> About 17 million cars are sold each year in the United States, or roughly 10 percent of the total in active use. If *every* consumer were to buy a hybrid car offering a 30 percent fuel saving over their existing car, and *none* of these people choose to drive more because they now had a car offering better mileage, and there were *no* expansion in the US vehicle fleet, such an innovation would result in a reduction in gasoline use of 3 percent per year.[48]

Given the technical hurdles facing stored energy vehicles like plug-in electric cars[49] and the demand for individualized transportation, it seems fair to assume that people in the United States will continue to rely on large numbers of individual cars and trucks run by an engine that burns a liquid fuel well into the foreseeable future, even if they are persuaded that it would be a great thing to adopt a new technology instead.[50]

What about hybrids? Energy efficiency gains in operating vehicles are possible, albeit currently at high costs, from capturing waste energy during vehicle operation and converting it to a usable form. For example, hybrid vehicles make use of energy released by braking to charge batteries that can then power the vehicle. These technologies hint at the possibility of dramatically reducing energy costs for operation of vehicles, but it is important to remember that hybrids like the Prius are "not the car of the future" but are ways to "offer a huge boost to the internal combustion engine."[51] Of course, as the cost of operation falls, we would expect vehicle use to increase. (As *The Economist*'s auto writers noted mournfully, hybrids like the Prius "prolong oil addiction.")[52] Some of the reductions in pollution per mile from such technologies are thus likely to be offset by increases in total miles of vehicle operation due to lowered costs. And, once again, what matters is the net energy gain and net environmental impact. Since hybrids are, for now at least, more energy intensive to manufacture than nonhybrids, the benefits of adopting hybrid technologies have to be assessed over the life of the vehicle. Once again, proponents of pouring tax money into promoting this technology via tax credits and other incentives have not produced the evidence necessary to evaluate their proposals on the merits.

Policy Must Recognize Trade-offs

We noted earlier that car and truck engines have become so clean that engine designers must now balance further reductions in one pollutant against possible increases in another. For example, some air pollution from power generation in a truck or car is the result of incomplete combustion (e.g., particulate matter). Improving combustion efficiency thus reduces that pollutant. But other pollutants come from combustion; improving combustion efficiency increases those pollutants (e.g., CO_2). As a result, altering engine operation can result in increasing some pollutants while decreasing others. Consider just a few examples of the trade-offs involved in diesel engine operation and design (similar trade-offs occur in spark ignition engines):

- Soot from diesel engines can be reduced by higher injection pressure, but doing so will produce more NO_x.[53]
- The "natural trade-off between particulate emissions and NO_x" is "one of the critical challenges in the design of diesel combustion systems."[54]
- "While it is feasible to program new [diesel] engines with modified fuel injection timing that lowers NO_x emissions, doing so likely would have significant collateral consequences. These include increased engine overheating and decreased engine life due to sooting, excessive engine wear, decreased fuel economy, and the need for changes to the truck chassis to deal with these changes in engine operation."[55]

Unsurprisingly given the existence of these trade-offs, some quantities of pollutants in exhaust emissions vary inversely with one another as the air-fuel ratio is adjusted.[56]

Taking these trade-offs into account is particularly important for the future because "[m]ost trade-off curves are approximately hyperbolic in shape, so that the first increment of control produces only small degradation of performance while later increments cause accelerating degradation of performance."[57] Progressive tightening of emissions standards, as the EPA has done over the last 30 years with NO_x, will move trade-offs onto the less favorable portion of the curve, where large increases in emissions of other pollutants are the price of small increases in control of NO_x.

An additional trade-off is also important. Research on ozone formation has found that there are multiple mechanisms at work in the atmosphere leading to ozone formation. When there are high levels of hydrocarbons in the atmosphere, reducing NO_X cuts ozone formation. When there are high levels of NO_X, however, reducing hydrocarbon levels is the better strategy. As diesel trucks emit proportionately more NO_X than hydrocarbons, while automobiles do the reverse, the impact of the weekend drop in truck traffic is different depending on whether NO_X or hydrocarbons are the critical factor in determining ozone levels. As a result, in some areas ozone levels fall on the weekends and in others they rise.[58] The existence of this "weekend effect" tells us both that atmospheric chemistry is complex and that regulators' models of it are sometimes inadequate to even predict the direction of the changes that result from changes in regulations.

Fuels

Green energy proponents are enthusiastic about altering transportation fuels to include more biofuels (especially ethanol and biodiesel). Fuel formulation requirements have a long history that can help us assess the impact of such mandates. Since the late 1980s, federal and state regulators have introduced increasing levels of regulation of fuel formulation and distribution in an effort nominally aimed at reducing mobile source emissions. As one refinery executive noted, "Gasoline is not gasoline anymore. It is a specialty chemical."[59] Unfortunately, when combined with the legacy of decades of economic regulation of petroleum industries and special interest lobbying on biofuels issues, the results have been problematic.[60]

The problems with the regulation of fuel formulation can be seen from the first step taken in the area: the EPA's efforts to remove lead additives from gasoline in the 1970s. Lead had been added to gasoline beginning in the 1920s to boost octane ratings and reduce engine knocking.[61] Lead needed to be removed from gasoline partly because lead emissions from cars were a health hazard[62], but also because the presence of lead in exhaust gases prevented proper operation of the catalytic converters introduced after the 1970 Clean Air Act Amendments.[63] Anticipating the problem, the 1970 Amendments authorized the EPA to order refiners to alter gasoline formulations to protect the catalytic converters.[64] The EPA moved relatively quickly to ban lead additives.[65]

Not surprisingly, given the history of energy regulation, the politically astute and powerful small refiners[66] were the beneficiaries of special treatment, winning an exemption from the rule until January 1, 1977, "in recognition of [their] special lead-time problems,"[67] and then an additional partial extension from Congress through October 1, 1982.[68] The result was the appearance between 1979 and 1982 of "a small subindustry of 'blenders,'" firms created "to take advantage of the small refiner exemptions," which "would purchase inexpensive, low-octane gas from foreign markets and blend in just enough high-octane leaded gas to stay within the small-refiner exemption."[69] An important result of the lead-removal efforts was intensive and successful special interest lobbying. Future fuel formulation regulation proved no different, particularly as biofuel mandates appeared.[70]

What consumers think of as "gasoline" is not a specific formulation of a fuel but a wide range of products meeting a set of characteristics making it suitable for use in automobile engines. Refineries are specialized chemical plants that transform crude oil inputs into a wide range of outputs. Refinery operations are essentially the solutions of a complex constrained optimization problem, with operators facing constraints imposed by the characteristics of the input stream of crude oil, the equipment mix, and the desired characteristics of the output streams. As fuel formulation requirements grow in number, this problem becomes more complex to solve, and the solutions can lead to unforeseen consequences, particularly when mixed with the heady brew of politics that surrounds energy regulation.

This can be seen in microcosm by examining the response to the lead phase-out. Lead additives had played an important role in fuels, and their loss produced "a desperate search for ways to maintain the octane level of [refiners'] gasoline pool."[71] One method was to change how refineries operated. The prevailing solution was to change the output mix to increase higher octane product streams. Refiners were able to adjust, but the changes in production method this required reducing the volume of gasoline produced, making it a costly step.[72] Refiners sought lead substitutes that would boost octane.[73] Some turned to an alternative additive, methylcyclopentadienyl manganese tricarbonyl (MMT), previously approved by the EPA.[74] However, under the 1977 Clean Air Act Amendments, refiners were not allowed to market gasolines for catalytic converter–equipped vehicles that were not substantially similar to the gasolines used to certify the vehicle, hampering

MMT use.[75] And in late 1978, the EPA restricted refiners' use of MMT.[76] However, the agency approved the use of methyl tertiary-butyl ether (MTBE) as an octane-boosting additive a few months later.

Unfortunately, MTBE's introduction proved to be one of the best examples of the consequences of lack of knowledge among regulators. In 1990, Congress required adding oxygenates to gasoline to reduce emissions in carbon monoxide nonattainment areas[77] as "a relatively minor and late-arriving aspect" of the 1990 Clean Air Act Amendments.[78] The mandate was the result of a special interest coalition of environmental pressure groups and farm-state senators interested in boosting ethanol use, and it passed without any consideration of the environmental impacts of any of the additives, including MTBE.[79] The problem was that MTBE had major environmental problems, causing serious ground water pollution.[80] The end result was a series of new environmental problems, no obvious environmental gains, increased costs for refiners and consumers, and a further entanglement of regulators in the operation of refineries.

A second formulation requirement began in the late 1980s. The summer of 1988 delivered "some of the worst ozone excursions on record," and research fingered high volatility gasoline as a factor.[81] States initiated fuel formulation controls on volatility in an effort to address their ozone problems.[82] The EPA in 1989 set national upper volatility (RVP) limits for summer gasoline for the first time.[83] The Clean Air Act Amendments of 1990 "substantially expanded" the agency's authority over formulation, mandating a federal reformulated gasoline (RFG) program.[84]

The federal RFG requirement produced three fuels: a "northern" RFG, a "southern" RFG, and uncontrolled gasoline used outside the areas where states or the EPA mandated one of the RFG gasolines. These regulatory requirements produced several changes in gasoline refining. The first level of RFG controls was met primarily through reductions in the butane content of gasoline, which required compensating for the loss of octane from butane removal through additional processing steps that rearranged the hydrocarbon molecules, increasing both the cost of equipment and the cost of running refineries.[85] The next set of standards was met by adding still more processing of gasoline, once again requiring additional capital investment and operating costs.[86] Both of these steps required "large capital investments" by refiners.[87] An additional set of constraints on refiners came from the EPA's order under the 1990 Amendments that transportation fuels, including gasoline, have dramatically reduced sulfur content.[88] These restrictions reduced the permissible sulfur content in highway diesel.[89] Combined with the shift in world crude supplies to heavier, more sour (i.e., higher in sulfur) crudes, this required refiners producing fuel for the U.S. market to make substantial capital investments in equipment to remove the sulfur.

The EPA imposed additional requirements on fuel formulations, both requiring refiners to use a more complex model of fuels' emissions properties in 1998[90] and regulating deposit control additives in fuel after 1990.[91] Figure 9.1 shows a map of federal fuel formulation requirements created by ExxonMobil. (We were unable to locate an equivalent map from a federal source.) The key point is that as the regulations became more complex, the EPA's involvement in fuel design steadily increased.

Moreover, these "boutique" fuel requirements are not simply a matter of the government specifying a particular set of gasoline characteristics. The technique used to add one required ingredient could affect the completed fuel's characteristics in other dimensions. This complicated the process still further and required more regulatory interventions. For example, the EPA was concerned

> about potential abuse of the process of adding oxygenate to gasoline downstream of a refinery. This practice, called "splash blending," involves mechanical mixing of finished gasoline or gasoline blending stock having front-end volatility set at a typical warm season value (RVP of 7 to 8 psi) with a liquid oxygenate (such as ethanol). Splash blending, unlike refinery-performed match blending that renormalizes product output to the required properties of an RFG, can change the proportional constituents of a gasoline by diluting (replacing) their mass and volumetric share in each gallon. It also has the potential to increase the quantity of total fuel that evaporates from vehicles if the fuel's resulting RVP is significantly higher. EPA sought to obviate this possibility by requiring the type of oxygenate that can be added be stipulated at the refinery and thus maintain RVP integrity.[92]

States also began to impose formulation requirements through their Clean Air Act State Implementation Plans, as did local

Figure 9.1
U.S. GASOLINE REQUIREMENTS

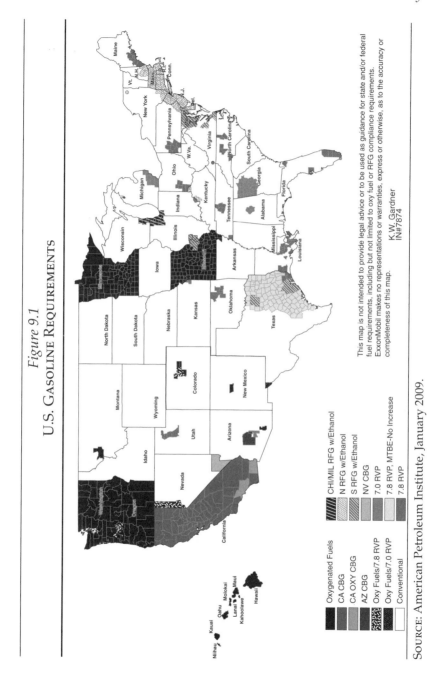

Oxygenated Fuels	CHI/MIL RFG w/Ethanol
CA CBG	N RFG w/Ethanol
CA OXY CBG	S RFG w/Ethanol
AZ CBG	NV CBG
Oxy Fuels/7.8 RVP	7.0 RVP
Oxy Fuels/7.0 RVP	7.8 RVP, MTBE-No Increase
Conventional	7.8 RVP

This map is not intended to provide legal advice or to be used as guidance for state and/or federal fuel requirements, including but not limited to oxy fuel or RFG compliance requirements. ExxonMobil makes no representations or warranties, express or otherwise, as to the accuracy or completeness of this map.

K.W. Gardner
IN#7874

SOURCE: American Petroleum Institute, January 2009.

governments.[93] While there is no comprehensive list of formulations mandated by all levels of government, there appear to be at least 17 different formulations (all made in multiple octane grades)— a major increase from the single standard (the lead standard) in place in the mid-1980s.[94] In addition, some state and local governments have imposed "biofuel" requirements.[95]

Formulation requirements have important effects on gasoline markets. First, they isolate some geographic markets from the overall gasoline market, making it harder to bring new supplies to a region or uneconomical to shift supplies out of a region. For example, if a boutique fuel is more costly to create than conventional gasoline, refiners may be unwilling to divert supplies of it to meet a shortage in an area that does not require the boutique fuel. There is evidence that boutique fuels are more costly to produce than standard gasolines.[96] Additional evidence indicates that the boutique fuel requirements, where they occur together with limited refinery capacity and pipeline connections to other regions, affect prices. After examining regional prices, the FTC found that differences in price variability across regions began appearing in 1992 and have increased since 1995.[97]

Second, additional capital investments are required to produce boutique fuels, limiting the number of current refineries able to produce a particular fuel, creating both incentives to exit a market and barriers to entry. Econometric investigations, comparing prices and price volatility between matched pairs of boutique fuel and non-boutique fuel cities, have found that not only is there evidence that boutique fuel requirements raise the cost of gasoline but also that the price impact varies with the geographic isolation and degree of competition in the relevant market.[98]

Finally, such mandates alter the path of technological change, diverting investment away from improving production processes to meet regulatory requirements. One summary of industry trends concluded that air pollution regulation "has driven the direction of our technological development."[99] Making cars and trucks cleaner is a good thing, of course, but having the technology developed to meet mandates rather than because it is the technologically superior alternative is a problem.

As discussed earlier, running a modern refinery is a complex optimization problem in which refiners must solve the problem of creating the highest value mix of end products by managing the streams of intermediate products manufactured at different stages.[100] The boutique fuel requirements thus increase the number of constraints in the optimization problem. If the constraints are binding (and they are meaningless if they are not), then the constraints have costs.[101]

This brief history of fuel formulation mandates provides four important lessons about how green jobs proposals for even more mandates will affect us. First, regulators' record with respect to fuel formulation mandates is not good. They have frequently made bad technological choices like the requirements to use MTBE and ethanol; let politics shape the regulatory framework and so rewarded special interest lobbying; and damaged markets' ability to improve product quality. Second, even when individual mandates make sense, the combination of an ever-increasing series of fuel formulation requirements is making refining transportation fuels an increasingly complex operation. Adding constraints to such complex systems is costly, both in dollar terms and in foregone outputs. Third, regulation breeds more regulation in a vicious circle. Increasing the complexity of the system requires additional layers of complexity to deal with unintended impacts of the previous round, creating a dynamic that ratchets the level of regulation ever upward. Finally, regulation opens the door to special interest rent-seeking, demonstrated here by the small refiner bias in virtually every energy program after World War II.

Vehicle Use Restrictions

Although green jobs proponents rarely mention it, one method of controlling pollution and reducing energy use has not been exploited: restricting how cars and trucks are operated and maintained. Differences in driving style can have significant impacts on emissions. For example, a 1998 study of 24 drivers operating a single vehicle on a standard route revealed statistically significant differences among drivers, which the study authors attributed primarily to differences in "intensity of operating with a mode rather than the frequency of different driving modes."[102]

Reducing emissions through altering owner/operator behavior is underexploited for a reason, however. Existing forms of use controls are extremely unpopular. The federal government's few efforts to alter individuals' vehicle use behavior have been serious failures. For example, efforts under the 1990 Clean Air Act Amendments to require employers to create "trip reduction programs" to shift commuters out of individual automobiles failed miserably.[103] Even programs requiring inspection and maintenance (I&M) of pollution control systems, which can play an important role in ensuring engines are properly maintained and so operate effectively, are often wildly unpopular and of questionable efficacy.[104]

While we doubt that many readers think that any American officeholder today would publicly endorse any proposal for use restrictions that went beyond the already unpopular I&M programs, note that the EPA is considering mandating a urea additive system to control diesel passenger car emissions, which would disable the car's engine if the urea tank was empty. Mercedes has already included this feature in its BlueTEC diesel vehicles.[105]

A Market Alternative

There is an alternative to the ever-tightening and changing cycle of mandates. At two key points in the 20th century, transportation fuel markets were relatively unregulated. During these periods, there were dramatic improvements in fuel quality, which demonstrate the power of market forces to improve fuels. Moreover, immediately before World War II and during the war, energy companies worked closely with aircraft engine manufacturers and the military to bring about a revolution in aviation fuel (which spilled over to gasoline production after the war), responding not to mandates but to price incentives and performance targets. The improvements in fuel and refining technology produced during this period, primarily by Royal Dutch Shell and Standard Oil of New Jersey, were critical to the Allied victory in the Battle of Britain.[106] We briefly describe both the competition that produced the first breakthroughs in refining technology in the first decades of the 20th century and the innovation during the late 1930s because these events show the power that market competition has to improve transportation fuels.

Demand for petroleum products, particularly gasoline, soared after World War I. The simple refining methods used prior to 1910 (essentially distillation) could not produce sufficient gasoline to keep up with demand. Seeking to improve yields, energy companies developed thermal conversion (or cracking) in the mid-1910s and boosted output by applying energy to the oil and breaking heavier molecules into the lighter ones in gasoline.[107] This was a period in which "the field of hydrocarbons chemistry took off in a series of revolutionary discoveries."[108] Hydrogenation, which allowed refiners to "produce any desired percentage of high-grade gasoline from a barrel of petroleum and to vary the percentage of various products according to desire," followed in the 1920s.[109] Seeking more control over output quantities and quality, energy companies continued to invest in research and development, yielding the catalytic cracking process—enhancing the ability to split large molecules into smaller ones by conducting the "cracking" in the presence of catalysts—in the mid-1930s.[110] Catalytic cracking was first put into commercial operation in 1936, and the capacity for it at U.S. refineries was at 122,000 barrels per day in 1940. By November 1944, catalytic cracking capacity by U.S. energy firms reached 1,011,650 barrels per day, a 729 percent increase in four years.[111]

Aviation fuel averaged 70 octane in the 1920s and was standardized at 87 octane in 1930 by the Army Air Corps.[112] The progress of technology was rapid: 100 octane aviation fuel began the decade as "a rare chemical costing $25 per gallon in the small quantities necessary for anti-knock testing purposes"; 1,000 gallons sold for $2 a gallon in May 1934; and the Air Corps bought 1 million gallons for $0.30 a gallon by September 1935.[113] This helped convince the Air Corps to raise its standard combat fuel to 100 octane in 1937.[114] By 1941, the Air Corps bought 100 octane aviation fuel for $0.25 per gallon in even larger quantities.[115] Standard Oil of New Jersey's capacity to produce 100 octane fuel in 1942 alone went from 15,940 barrels per day in the first half of the year to almost 43,000 barrels per day by December.[116] More generally, a 1941 review of the refining technology concluded that "[t]he constant practical application of chemical and engineering research to refining operations has resulted not only in improvement of products to meet changing conditions and requirements but also in the reduction of waste in processing and in the manufacture of an almost infinite variety of products."[117]

After the war, this technology was applied to motor fuel, leading to improvements in engines to take advantage of the higher octane.[118] The payoff from this investment has been significant. Gasoline production grew from 142,465 barrels per day in 1900 to 4.1 million barrels per day in 1960, reaching 8.3 million barrels per day in 2005.[119] The National Petroleum Council's assessment of technological change from 1945 to 1965 in refining concluded that

> The product specifications of all refinery products have been steadily changing since World War II to improve the performance of these products in end use. As the equipment and machinery using petroleum products have become more sophisticated, so have the treatment and finishing techniques. Technology advances have improved the operating and economic aspects, resulting in a beneficial influence on blending, as well as improvements in the uniformity of product quality.[120]

Gasoline before the war was "a simple mixture of largely unprocessed stocks with basic additives for octane improvement and storage stability."[121] By the 1960s, additives had become more sophisticated, and refineries produced a range of specific hydrocarbons to blend into the finished gasoline.[122]

The drivers for these improvements in fuels (and the resulting improvements in engines) were demand-driven. To meet growing consumer demand after 1910, energy companies invented the modern refinery, creating entirely new processes to increase both yields and quantities. To meet the Air Corps' and Royal Air Force's demand for 100 octane fuel during World War II, energy companies responded to bids based on performance standards and created technologies that radically reshaped transportation fuels by dramatically increasing quantity and quality, while cutting costs to a mere fraction of the level of just a few years earlier. This was the result of market competition at work, not political mandates.

Conclusion

Transportation is critical to our lives. We have an immense (and expensive) infrastructure in place that provides us with the ability to live and work where we wish; to buy foods ranging from fresh fruit from Chile to California wine to Maine lobsters, regardless of where we live; to travel the country and the world; and to buy products at prices lowered by efficient logistics that reduce inventory costs. Radically changing that infrastructure will be neither simple nor cheap, and any discussion of doing so must be based on clear analysis of sound data, not wishful thinking. Unfortunately, the type of political thinking, spurred by special interests, that produced the "Cash for Clunkers" program and fragmented our gasoline market is prevalent in the hype over greening transportation.

10. How Green Is Mass Transit?

We have already observed how the green jobs literature is constructed on a foundation of opposition to trade. In this chapter, we look in more detail at the one form of mechanical transportation endorsed in the green economy literature: mass transportation. More precisely, mass transportation by rail is promoted, as intercity air and bus and intracity bus are often ignored or criticized despite their often superior efficiency. Rail transportation is consistently touted as having the benefits of saving time, improving the environment, and saving costs over the life of projects. It seems a constant mystery why every city has not built a light rail transport system or why high speed trains do not carry us comfortably from one metro area to another.

Intermetropolitan Trade

Cities differ from each other in the goods and services they produce. As a result, not only do products need to travel from city to city, but so do people. There are four main modes of intercity travel: automobile, airplane, train, and bus. The green jobs literature attacks the first two, praises the third, and ignores the fourth. This set of priorities is not consistent with either environmental efficiency or human happiness. Let's briefly compare the private and social costs of each mode. For specificity, we'll focus on the trip from Cleveland to Cincinnati, as it is one of the proposed corridors for high speed rail.[1]

The driving distance from Cleveland's bus terminal to Cincinnati's is 248 miles, which takes four hours and eight minutes (according to MapQuest). The average fuel efficiency for a car is 22.4 miles per gallon, so the trip requires 11 gallons.[2] Assuming a gas price of $3 per gallon, the direct out-of-pocket cost for the trip is $33. The traveler would also need to park at the destination, but we will neglect that cost for the moment. Of course, this is not just the cost for one person but also the cost for any number of people up to the capacity of the car. In other words, there are economies of scale in automobile transportation up to the size of the typical household.[3]

There are three main social costs of driving: congestion, accidents, and pollution. The amount of congestion depends on the day and time of travel; the risk of accident also varies; and the amount of pollution varies with these factors, as well as with the way in which the vehicle is operated. Again using average figures, the congestion costs can be estimated at $0.05 per mile, accident costs at $0.03 per mile, and the pollution costs at about $0.029 per mile.[4] Total external costs are thus about 11 cents per mile, increasing the social cost of the Cleveland to Cincinnati trip by about $27. Total CO_2 emissions for the trip are about 250 pounds, and the costs of the emissions are included in the estimated social costs.

Airplanes have a higher out-of-pocket cost than cars, as a representative fare is $234.[5] The flight is scheduled for 70 minutes, which at first glance gives a huge time advantage. However, the traveler must get to the airport in both cities and be at the airport prior to the flight, which adds to the time cost, while parking costs and travel costs upon arrival also increase the monetary costs. Carbon emissions are estimated to equal 0.484 pounds of CO_2 per passenger-mile, or about 120 pounds (0.06 tons) for the trip.[6]

Now consider high speed rail. The Ohio Hub Plan proposal is for a train that will cover this distance in three and a half hours.[7] The plan reports[8] an expected one-way fare of $95, compared to an expected auto cost of $84 for business travel, $26 for other travel, and $186 one-way airfare. If a second person (or more) is making trip—a family going to celebrate Thanksgiving with relatives, for example—then the money costs are multiplied. As with planes, there are also some time and money costs involved in getting from home to station and from station to final destination.

The emissions from the train are 0.05 tons of CO_2 per passenger.[9] There are substantial monetary costs from constructing the train line. The current estimated cost for infrastructure is $4.9 billion. At a 10 percent amortization rate, this is $490 million per year, or about $190 per rider per year at the current projected ridership in 2025 of 2.6 million people per year.[10] These costs are borne by the general taxpaying public as they come from general funds. The report expects that 80 percent of the cost will come from the federal government. There is also the question of whether ridership will reach the predicted level. A study by Bent Flyvbjerg and colleagues found that ridership predictions for transit systems were systematically too high.[11] The Ohio Hub Plan[12] notes that all of its estimates are made using 2002 dollars, and increases in steel and concrete prices might imply that the costs will be higher.

There is bus service between Cleveland and Cincinnati at a current cost of $37.40 ($51 for a fully refundable fare).[13] The trip takes five hours, slower than the airplane or rail, but the cost is considerably lower those modes. In fact, the bus fare is comparable to the cost of driving, although this is not true if more than one person is traveling. This also neglects any costs in moving from the bus station to other destinations.

Because buses use the same highways as cars, the social costs are comparable. The CO_2 emissions are 0.18 pounds per passenger-mile, or about 45 pounds (0.0225 tons) for the trip. The congestion costs are higher because buses are less maneuverable than cars, but again this cost is distributed against all of the riders, so the net per capita congestion is not that different.[14]

Tables 10.1 and 10.2 summarize key information for the Cleveland to Cincinnati comparison. One sees that intercity bus is amazingly

Table 10.1
CLEVELAND TO CINCINNATI TRAVEL COMPARISON (1 RIDER)

Mode	Private Cost	CO_2 Emissions	Time (minutes)
Car	$33.00	250 pounds	248
Bus (per rider at capacity)	$37.40	45 pounds	300
Plane (per rider at capacity)	$234.00	120 pounds	70
Train (per rider at capacity)	$95.00	100 pounds	210

SOURCE: Authors' calculations. Sources include the surrounding materials that are cited in the notes.

Table 10.2
CLEVELAND TO CINCINNATI TRAVEL COMPARISON (4 RIDERS)

Mode	Private Cost	CO_2 Emissions	Time (minutes)
Car	$33.00	250 pounds	248
Bus	$149.60	180 pounds	300
Plane	$936.00	480 pounds	70
Train	$380.00	400 pounds	210

SOURCE: Authors' calculations. Sources include the surrounding materials that are cited in the notes.

efficient for mass transit, especially when compared to high speed rail. This is not unique to the Ohio corridor. An article in the *Washington Post* concluded that buses were better than trains even in the train-friendly Northeast corridor.[15] Harvard economist Edward Glaeser, analyzing a hypothetical Houston–Dallas rail line of about the same distance, found similar results.[16]

Although we have discussed high speed rail proposals as if they were concrete, there is some evidence that the proposals are being continually refined to garner maximum political support. For example, the Ohio Department of Transportation has introduced a proposal for 79 mph trains in order to participate in stimulus funding.[17] A civil engineering professor and transportation expert at the University of Minnesota, David Levinson, concluded a series of blog posts analyzing high speed rail in the following way: "There is sometimes a danger of a planner falling in love with his map. There is no danger here, even the same agencies have random maps. It seems as no one cares where the lines actually go, so long as they are high-speed rail."[18]

Intrametropolitan Trade

Metropolitan areas are complex systems that rely on modern communications and transportation. Some people have a mental model of the metropolitan area as monocentric, consisting of a single dominant commercial district surrounded by primarily residential areas.[19] This metropolitan structure was an accurate description of how cities were during a period from about 1880 to 1930. However, it has become increasingly inaccurate since then due to the development of the truck, car, and associated retail and manufacturing technologies. Electricity meant that each machine could have its own engine, allowing production to occur horizontally rather than vertically. This technology, combined with the truck, allowed manufacturing to leave downtown, to the relief both of the manufacturers and their neighbors.

Trade, whether international or local, is based on specialization. Within modern metropolitan areas, we see this specialization in the form of bedroom communities specializing in residential services, shopping malls specializing in retail services, large manufacturing plants, and so on. Before the invention of mass transit in the 1830s, all activities had to be located close enough so that people could walk to them.[20] The advent of transit, especially the electrified trolley in the 1880s, allowed people to move farther away from commercial activities.[21] Thus, mass transit's initial impact was to facilitate decentralization and specialization, the two key features of modern metropolitan structure. This "inconvenient truth" has been developed by researchers who hold no brief for the automobile, but it is ignored by modern transit advocates. Even more inconveniently, many transit systems were used as a loss leader to promote real estate development rather than as an investment in their own right. The inability of transit to cover its costs from the fare box is not a post–WWII phenomenon. In the historical record, mass transit is an anomaly, occupying a dominant role only for the brief period when its greater speed was enough to outweigh its inconvenience.[22]

Mass Transit

The love that green jobs advocates have for intercity trains is exceeded only by their love for intracity fixed rail transit. Unfortunately, the arguments in favor of streetcars, light rail, and subways are grounded on the same wishful thinking that afflicts so much of the green jobs literature.

The first problem with the analysis of mass transit is that much of the discussion focuses solely on commuting. The journey from home to work and back has accounted for an ever smaller fraction of total personal trips, now down to about 17 percent.[23] Because many people combine personal trips with commuting, even this figure is an overestimate of the percentage of traffic purely devoted to moving people from home to work. Moreover, a true analysis of fixed rail would include the time, money, and environmental costs of moving people from home to the train, subway, or trolley station. A book by Meyer, Kain, and Wohl is the classic reference.[24] They divide the commute into three parts: residential collection, line haul, and downtown distribution. The line haul is the part of the trip on the rail line, but the time costs of the other parts of the commute can be considerable. They find that even under the denser and less auto-dependent conditions of the 1960s, buses are more efficient than fixed rail except in a few extreme circumstances, such as Manhattan.

Wait, say the train advocates, the number of trips and their distance reflects the current reliance on automobiles. If we build more walkable communities centered on transit stations, then both these objections would be attenuated. A recent paper by the Political Economy Research Institute (the academics behind the Center for American Progress study) is an example. They point out that the relatively low elasticity of demand for auto travel with respect to gas prices would increase if lots of mass transit were constructed. They also expect that mass transit would be publicly funded out of general revenues.[25] Their argument is predicated on the considerable need for building in the next few decades. Arthur Nelson, in a widely cited study for the Brookings Institution, estimated that about half of the commercial and residential property that will be needed in 2030 did not exist in 2005.[26]

The dense, walkable, transit-centered neighborhood is a good location for many people. However, it is not possible to maintain the current range of retail options for consumers at current prices at a density that would attract most Americans. Randall Bartlett applies the so-called "popsicle test" to a range of commercial activities to identify the needed density to support walkable neighborhoods. The popsicle test is based on the idea that a child should be able to walk to a store and buy a popsicle without dealing with fast-moving cars. This test implies a radius of about a quarter-mile around a store, or an area of about 125 acres. Bartlett estimates (at 1479) that the median book and news store, for example, requires a minimum customer base of 7,576 using current technology and assuming that the residents do not shop at any other bookstore. This implies that the density surrounding the store would have to be at least 38,560 people per square mile, or more than 60 people per acre. Compare this figure to the median density in U.S. central cities of 3,207 people per square mile, and the scale of the discrepancy between the popsicle test and reality is apparent.[27]

Because it is not feasible for stores to survive on the basis of walking customers alone, it is inefficient to reduce accessibility of such stores to shoppers who drive (and to trucks bringing supplies). The planning and policy literature that equates "walkable" with "hostile to cars" is misguided. Given what we saw in Chapter 6 about the anti-trade bias of green jobs advocates, it is unsurprising to see an illogical belief in autarky at the local level as well. This hope for autarky is longstanding. Ebenezer Howard's book, *Garden Cities of To-Morrow* (1902), which is the ur-planning text, was based on garden cities that met all of their residents' physical and cultural needs. For reasons that are not apparent, these garden cities were connected by train lines, even though there would be no reason for travel or trade if Howard's vision were fully implemented.

It is not disputed that automobiles are the source of negative externalities. A standard response to negative externalities is to impose a price on the externality-generating activity to force individuals make more socially efficient decisions. In the case of cars, this price is assessed by taxes on gasoline. Because the major external cost of cars is congestion, a more targeted policy is to charge people to drive on roads at a given time. These tolls have been used in a variety of settings to improve traffic flow and generate revenue for either public-sector or private-sector road operators. The most interesting point about tolls, though, is that they can be valuable to consumers who are willing to pay in return for a more rapid trip. One study found that house prices in parts of Orange County were higher near toll roads. This was not because households like to pay tolls; rather, it reflects the willingness to pay for improved access to less congested roads.[28]

Tolling technology has improved rapidly in recent years because of the substitution of capital (in the form of transponders) for labor. Thus, the green jobs literature will discount the potential impact of tolls because unionized toll-takers are no longer needed. The transit advocates who are truly opposed to automobile traffic in general will also underestimate the potential benefits of tolls. The important role of road pricing is developed in a recent analysis by Duranton and Turner, who find that neither road construction nor public transit provision will relieve congestion unless congestion tolls are implemented.[29]

Another advantage of cars and buses relative to fixed rail transit is their promotion of infill development. If the transport options are largely restricted to walking and riding the streetcar, there will be development along transit corridors with nodes near stations. Cars and buses allow the areas between stations and between transit lines to be developed, promoting the density that is the defining characteristic of cities.

Environmental Impact of Mass Transit

Green jobs proponents often advocate investment in expanding public transportation as a way to create jobs with an environmentally friendly purpose. For example, CAP argues that building light rail and subway systems will produce "job growth in engineering, electrical work, welding, metal fabrication, and engine assembly sectors," and such investment in "both urban and rural communities . . . can be an engine for far broader economic activity."[30] More money for freight rail would "yield some immediate job gains in similar professions, creating substantial employment through both construction operations, alongside a down payment on more job creation over two years through improved maintenance and expansion of services."[31] In the short run, CAP advocates more bus and subway services, reducing public transportation fares, increasing federal support for mass transit "to deal with increased ridership," increased federal subsidies for employer-based mass transit incentives, and "[h]igher funding for critical mass transit programs currently bottlenecked for lack of federal dollars to encourage new ridership and more transportation choices."[32]

Similarly, the United Nations Environment Programme study contends that "a more sustainable system will have to be based on shorter distances. Reduced distances and greater density of human settlements enables a rebalancing of transportation modes—giving greater weight to public transit systems, as well as walking and biking. A modal shift away from private vehicles and toward rail and other public transport can generate considerable net employment gains, while reducing emissions and improving air quality."[33] Remember that "net employment gains" generally means higher costs due to lower productivity. Lower standards of living do not produce a greater level of sustainability for humans. It is simply an article of faith, not science, in the environmental community and government circles that mass transit (including different forms of rail travel) is more energy-efficient than automobiles. As the UNEP report explains, "Railways are more environment-friendly and labor intensive than the car industry."[34] This is so because "[p]ublic transit is less energy and carbon-intensive than automobiles."[35] A cursory examination of the amount of energy used to move one passenger one mile (a "passenger-mile") reinforces this belief.

Table 10.3, taken from O'Toole, shows the energy needed per passenger-mile for different modes of travel, arranged in the order of

Table 10.3
MODAL ENERGY CONSUMPTION AND CO_2 EMISSIONS
PER PASSENGER-MILE

Mode	Energy Expended (BTU)	Emissions (lbs. of CO_2)
Ferry Boats	10,744	1.73
Automated Guideways	10,661	1.36
Light Trucks	4,423	0.69
Motor Buses	4,365	0.71
Trolley Buses	3,923	0.28
All Automobiles[1]	3,885	0.61
Light Rail	3,465	0.36
Passenger Cars	3,445	0.54
All Transit	3,444	0.47
Heavy Rail	2,600	0.25
Commuter Rail	2,558	0.29
Toyota Prius†	*1,659*	*0.26*

[1] This figure includes passenger cars and light trucks.
SOURCE: Randal O'Toole, "Does Rail Transit Save Energy or Reduce Greenhouse Gas Emissions?" Cato Institute Policy Analysis no. 615, April 14, 2008.

increasing efficiency. Data for the Toyota Prius are shown at the very end to provide a sense of the possibilities of increasing efficiencies for automobiles. This table shows that bus transit is generally less efficient than automobiles in general, while rail transit is more efficient than automobiles. However, Table 10.3 is misleading in several important respects. First, the raw numbers do not account for the fact that for rail transit to function, it is necessary to have an extensive bus feeder system that moves people to the rail stops. Taking this into account reduces, and may even eliminate, the savings in energy or reductions in CO_2 emissions suggested by Table 10.3.

As O'Toole explains, transit agencies, to get people to the rail stations, typically increase bus service. Bus routes that used to serve the rail corridor are turned into feeder bus routes for the rail. However, since many people drive to rail stations, the average passenger load of the feeder buses tends to be smaller than it used to be for the corridor buses they replaced. Consequently, the advent of new rail transit lines could increase fuel usage because the average loads of the buses is reduced. For example, in 1991, before St. Louis built its light rail system, its buses averaged more than 10 riders and consumed 4,600 BTU per passenger-mile. After the light rail line opened, average bus loads in 1995 declined to seven riders and energy consumed per passenger mile increased to 5,300 BTU. CO_2 emissions increased from 0.75 pounds to 0.88 pounds per passenger-mile. Similarly, energy and CO_2 performance also deteriorated for Sacramento and Houston after rail transit was implemented.[36]

Second, ignoring costs, even if rail transit results in a net reduction in energy use and CO_2 emissions per passenger-mile, these improvements may be more than offset by the energy required to construct the rail system, and any resulting emissions. For example, Portland's North Interstate light rail line is estimated to save about 23 billion BTU per year, while its construction is estimated to have consumed 3.9 trillion BTU; it would take 172 years to offset the extra energy needed for construction.[37] Not only would this exceed the lifespan of the line, "long before 172 years, automobiles are likely to be so energy efficient that light rail will offer no savings at all."[38]

Similarly, Seattle's North Link light rail line is estimated to save about 346 billion BTU of energy in 2015 and 200 billion BTU in 2030.[39] The energy savings will not repay the construction energy cost of 17.4 trillion BTU until 2095.[40] Despite the claim that the light rail project should have about a 100-year lifespan, experience from the Washington and Bay Area metro systems indicate that the expected lifespan is probably closer to 40 years, before which additional capital and energy investments would need to be made to rebuild or replace the system.[41] Of course, any alternative to rail transit will also consume energy and emit CO_2. However, highways are likely more efficient than rail transit because, compared to the latter, each mile of urban highway typically carries far more passenger-miles. For instance, the average mile of light rail line moved only 15 percent as many passenger-miles as the average lane mile of urban freeway in rail regions.[42] Highways also carry millions of tons of freight that can share the cost of construction.[43]

Moreover, contrary to the claims of disproportionate spending on highways, mass transit already receives more than its share (as measured by passenger-miles) of government funds. Data for 2001–03 from the Bureau of Transportation Statistics indicate that although mass transit is responsible for less than 1 percent of the total passenger-miles moved in the United States, it receives about 23 percent of the federal transportation grants (in dollars).[44] This ratio is consistent with the 2009 stimulus bill; it allocates $27 billion for highway projects and $12 billion for rail and mass transit projects.[45] Highways, responsible for almost 90 percent of the passenger-miles, receive only about 70 percent of the grants.[46]

Such disproportionate spending on transit might be justifiable were mass transit to provide net social value. However, studies indicate that most transit systems may not be socially desirable.[47] As Winston and Maheshri observe in a broad study of all the major rail transit lines in the United States:

> Despite a decline in its mode share, investment to build new urban rail transit systems and extend old ones continues. . . . [Based on estimates of] the contribution of each U.S. urban rail operation to social welfare based on the demand for and cost of its service. . . . [w]e find that with the exception of BART in the San Francisco Bay area, every system actually reduces welfare and is unable to become socially desirable even with optimal pricing or physical restructuring of its network. We conclude rail's social cost is unlikely to abate because it enjoys powerful political support from planners, civic boosters, and policymakers."[48]

The main reason for rail's failure to attract sufficient patronage to cover costs is the ongoing evolution in urban structure. Ironically, the decentralization and specialization that characterizes the modern metropolitan area was initiated by and first developed along streetcar lines and other mass transit routes.[49]

Winston and Maheshri use empirical results to investigate whether a system provided along optimal routes using ideal pricing would reverse this finding. Even though they take into account the value of reduced congestion due to increased ridership, no system with the exception of San Francisco's BART provides benefits in excess of costs. Even BART provides an example of how mass transit ridership projections tend to be overestimated and their costs underestimated.[50] When BART service was extended to the airport, an additional 18,000 daily boardings were projected, but only 7,000 were realized.[51] The unexpected closure of the San Francisco Bay Bridge in October 2009 provided an opportunity to see the ridership response of BART when a major automobile corridor is restricted. There was record ridership, but the increase in trans-bay ridership of 75,000 was less than one-third of the 280,000 people that use the Bay Bridge on a daily basis. The reopening of the bridge brought BART ridership back to previous levels.[52] Winston and Maheshri conclude that:

> Unfortunately, transit systems have been able to evolve because their supporters have sold them as an antidote to the social costs associated with automobile travel, in spite of strong evidence to the contrary. As long as rail transit continues to be erroneously viewed in this way by the public, it will continue to be an increasing drain on social welfare.[53]

To summarize, mass transit provides few if any benefits over the automobile in reduced energy usage and lower greenhouse gas (GHG) emisions. In fact, it may even be counterproductive if one adds in the energy consumed during construction. Consequently, it makes little sense to continue to subsidize this form of transportation for the masses, and even less sense to add to these subsidies. In other words, it is the wrong sort of infrastructure on both economic and environmental grounds.

One logical fallacy in much of the discussion about private cars is the asymmetric treatment of innovation, which is a consistent problem in the green jobs literature. It is logically inconsistent to assume that technological progress will solve the current problems in generating and transmitting wind or solar power while simultaneously assuming no progress in solving problems of powering private automobiles. There is a bit of confusion in the green policy view. Cars should be eliminated in favor of mass transit and rickshaws because cars are dreadful polluters, but at the same time billions should be invested so cars can increase their miles per gallon of gasoline consumed. The green policy advocates are positive the car companies can do much better, if only they put their minds to it.

Even in the unlikely event that households suddenly reduced reliance on private automobiles, the switch to mass transit would have no dramatic effect on the metropolitan structure. A study of the various explanations of metropolitan decentralization in the United States found that a 10 percent reduction in households owning one or more cars would only reduce the size of a metropolitan area by about 0.5 percent.[54] For a typical metropolitan area of about 160 square miles, this implies a reduction in size of less than one square mile, hardly the source of a substantial new demand for mass transit, much less biking and walking.

Technical Neutrality and the Inefficiency of Subsidies

One recurring theme in the green jobs literature is the need for government subsidies to accomplish desired outcomes. Unfortunately, this theme is more of a reflection of political preferences than analytical rigor.

Suppose we wish to reduce carbon emissions. In general, there are two ways to do this. First, make it more costly to emit carbon. Second, subsidize activities or technologies that emit relatively less carbon than currently popular activities or technologies.

When expressed in this fundamental way, the problem with subsidies as a way of accomplishing environmental objectives is apparent. By subsidizing activities that emit carbon, even if less intensively than other activities, the policy works against itself. Consider the case of subsidies for hybrid vehicles. Reducing the relative price of hybrids should encourage people to purchase them instead of other cars. If we suppose that these vehicles emit less carbon than standard automobiles, then the subsidy should reduce carbon emissions.

While hybrids use less gasoline, the total carbon emissions of hybrids depends not only on the gasoline that they use but also on the fuel used to power electric generations (for plug-in hybrids) and the carbon emissions during production. However, a reduced price per mile driven (in both financial and environmental terms) might encourage people to drive more with a hybrid than they otherwise would have. Thus, the subsidy could induce some additional carbon emissions, offsetting at least in part the reduced emissions from the hybrid technology.

Another problem with subsidies as currently implemented is that they are not neutral across technologies. A policy is neutral across technologies if it costs the same per unit to reduce emissions (such as a ton of carbon dioxide) regardless of the technology used. The approaches used in the United States are nonneutral even in situations that are seemingly neutral. For example, geothermal energy and wind energy both qualify for a 2.1 cent per kilowatt hour production tax credit. However, geothermal energy can replace base load production, which is typically coal, while wind can only replace peaking capacity, which tends to be natural gas. As a result, geothermal energy reduces carbon emissions by more per unit of energy generated, so that the subsidy per ton of CO_2 is $7.74 as compared to a subsidy of $12.28 per ton for wind.[55]

Subsidies for automobiles are designed to be nonneutral. For example, there is no subsidy for cars powered by internal combustion engines, even though there are opportunities to improve their efficiency. In addition, the subsidy for hybrids is phased out once sales reach a particular level. As a result, cars with very similar fuel efficiency offer a different marginal cost per gallon saved. Gilbert Metcalf calculates the tax credit per gallon of gasoline saved for several models of car. In order to do so, he assumes that the new car replaces one that has a fuel mileage of 20 miles per gallon and is driven 12,000 miles per year. Some cars qualify for tax credits, while others do not. In addition, the credit per gallon saved will vary depending on the fuel efficiency of the new car. Metcalf estimates that the tax credit per gallon of gasoline saved ranges from $0 to $11.68 for a selection of 2009 model year cars. The $0 credits are for the Toyota Corolla and Prius, which have no subsidy because of their pure internal combustion engine (Corolla) or because their sales exceed the subsidized level (Prius). The $11.68 subsidy is for a Chrysler Aspen

Hybrid, which has a rated 21-miles-per-gallon fuel efficiency, not much better than the base case of 20 miles per gallon.

A generic carbon tax does not suffer from these problems. However, a carbon tax does not allow the government to choose individual firms or groups of firms as winners, reducing the incentive of lobbyists to court government officials. In addition, the reduction in emissions from a carbon tax is straightforward to calculate, at least when compared to the analogous calculation for a subsidy program. This transparency allows voters to weigh the benefits and costs of the policy. Transparency and neutrality are costs to the government and to well-connected companies. These political economic imperatives often outweigh the efficiency calculations.

Conclusion

The green economy approach to transportation relies on a faulty idea of modern metropolitan structure and a misleading characterization of the efficiency of alternative transportation modes. There is no question that automobiles generate negative externalities. However, that observation does not automatically imply that automobiles should be banned or even restricted. Rather, it implies that policies that lead people to account for the externalities should be followed. Then the creative power of entrepreneurs can be unleashed to find ways to meet demand for transportation. While this does not meet the political economy test of green jobs advocates—steering jobs to favored clienteles—it does meet the efficiency test of the market.

Taxing vehicles for their emissions and for the congestion that they cause is a more flexible and effective way to address externalities than spending billions of dollars on intercity and intracity passenger rail. The anti-automobile agenda of the green energy literature would require major reductions in living standards. It should not be imposed on people by stealth.

11. The Politics of Green Energy

Green energy proposals are extremely popular. It seems as if almost everyone, except for some nit-picking university faculty, is excited about them. To take just a few examples:

- The AFL-CIO, which put $1 million into a Center for Green Jobs in February 2009, to help "make progressive energy and climate change a first order priority."[1]
- 2008 Republican presidential candidate John McCain, who during the campaign said, "We can move forward, and clean up our climate, and develop green technologies, and alternative energies for battery-powered cars, so that we can clean up our environment and at the same time get our economy going by creating millions of jobs."[2]
- Secretary of Labor Hilda Solis, who touted $55 million in green grants as "part of the administration's long-term commitment to fostering both immediate economic growth and a clean energy future. It's an investment that will help American workers do well while doing good. . . . These grants provide an immediate return, and they are part of a larger green initiative that will help lead to increased job placements and promote economic growth."[3]
- Independent Vermont Senator Bernie Sanders, who argues that "[i]f we get our act together as a nation and start addressing the major environmental problems of our time—global warming and our dependence on fossil fuels—we can create millions of good paying jobs. . . . In other words . . . good environmental policy is good economic policy."[4]
- General Electric CEO Jeff Immelt, who told a business group in Copenhagen at an environmental "summit" that "[i]n business you always say when is the right time, and we think the right time is now. . . . If you have high unemployment, this is one of the ways to create jobs. Everyone wants to lead in green technology."[5]

If Republicans, Democrats, and the U.S. Senate's lone indepen-dent-socialist-progressive, the AFL-CIO, and GE's CEO all endorse green energy programs, their support is impressively broad. The problems with the green energy proposals we describe in this book are not particularly hard to understand. We can summarize them as bad data used in poor quality models designed with flawed assump-tions about economics producing unreliable analysis upon which unsupported recommendations are based. So why are so many peo-ple so enthusiastic about the idea of spending billions or trillions of dollars on green energy programs?

There are three key interest groups promoting green energy pro-grams, each of which stands to benefit from increasing green energy spending. First, there are economic interests that will benefit by creat-ing markets for products they sell, getting subsidies for their sales or research, and making life difficult for potential competitors. Energy magnate T. Boone Pickens, for example, proposed to build a massive wind farm in the Texas panhandle, but he needs the government to spend billions to build power lines to connect it to the electrical grid.[6] Agribusiness giant Archer Daniels Midland promotes corn-based eth-anol, turning a substantial profit because of billions in taxpayer subsi-dies.[7] GE executives believe the company could "bring in as much as $192 billion from projects funded by governments around the globe, such as electric-grid modernization [and] renewable-energy genera-tion." As GE's CEO notes, "The government has moved in next door, and it ain't leaving."[8] Unions benefit from the strings attached to many green energy programs that require paying union-level wages, hampering lower cost, nonunion firms from competing for the jobs produced by the grants.[9] And unions use environmental laws like the Endangered Species Act to create roadblocks for environmental proj-ects that use nonunion labor.[10] Importantly, none of these interests depend on the programs actually being successful at creating a net social gain, an improvement in environmental quality, or a net in-crease in jobs—what matters to each of them is that money be spent in ways that benefit them.[11]

The second major interest group is politicians, at all levels of gov-ernment. Local politicians love programs that bring funding for projects. Governors and mayors like to cut ribbons at plant openings and announce federal grants for projects such as insulating school buildings. Members of Congress need to bring home the bacon so they can demonstrate how their clout in Washington makes them such a valuable asset for their constituents that they should be reelected. It is bipartisan politics.[12] Presidential candidates need signature issues, particularly ones popular with motivated groups of influential voters. For example, Iowa's corn farmers, a key constituency in the Iowa presidential caucuses, are the main reason why most presidential candidates from both parties have been strong ethanol supporters.[13] The benefits of green energy spending flow to the politicians whether or not the programs actually accomplish anything useful: there will be media coverage of the ribbon cutting at the new wind turbine assembly plant; there will not be any at the coal plant closing down the road.

The big Washington, D.C.–focused environmental groups like the Sierra Club and the Environmental Defense Fund are the third major interest group with a stake in green economy programs. These groups excel at lobbying Congress and the executive branch, allowing them to take to massive government programs like ducks to water. They need apparent policy successes to report to their memberships to show that membership dues help make it possible to further what the members presume to be part of a worthy agenda. They need opportunities to build alliances with other interest groups, such as labor unions, to create a coalition in Congress for measures they could not obtain on their own. As with the other groups, these organizations benefit from the programs regardless of whether the programs actually improve environmental quality or create net jobs.

The problems we identified with green energy proposals come about because these interests' rewards are not connected to the success of the programs they are touting but instead are aligned with producing the maximum sizzle rather than the biggest steak. This lack of a link between rewards and performance makes it critical that the rest of us ask the hard questions necessary to separate proposals that create a net gain from those that do not. Next, we untangle the politics of green energy to help identify where pressure needs to be applied to ensure those questions do get asked.

Bootleggers and Baptists

Green energy proposals are a version of Yandle's "bootleggers and Baptists" coalition, discussed earlier.[14] Yandle named his theory after the coalition behind laws banning the Sunday sale of alcoholic beverages. (Note: these laws do not restrict Sunday *consumption* of alcoholic beverages, only their legal sale.) If an area were dominated by opponents of alcohol consumption, Sunday closing laws would not be a mystery—the majority would support such laws and politicians seeking voters' favor would vote for bans on Sunday sales (or even sales generally). But we observe Sunday closing laws even where alcohol opponents lack a majority. The explanation for Sunday closing laws even where there is no majority for restricting alcohol consumption is a tacit alliance between well-organized and respected opponents of the consumption of alcoholic beverages. They feel strongly about the matter and so pay attention to how representatives vote on the issue, and those who can gain a competitive advantage from restricting *legal* sales.

Unsurprisingly, Sunday closing laws are supported by groups opposed to the sale of alcohol generally, including religious opponents such as Baptists. In addition, they are supported by bootleggers, who obviously have no objection to either the sale or consumption of alcohol. Why do bootleggers tacitly ally with Baptists to support restrictions on alcohol sales? Bootleggers have a financial interest in the higher prices and enhanced profits that result from reduced competition on Sundays, as they continue to sell on Sunday and can charge higher prices if there are no legal sellers on that day. Regulations shutting down legitimate sellers on Sunday thus align the bootleggers' economic interest with the moral interest of the Baptists.

The bootleggers need the Baptists because the Baptists play an important role in monitoring enforcement of laws restricting Sunday sales and because the Baptists provide the politicians voting for the Sunday closing laws with a legitimate moral reason that they can use to explain their votes. The Baptists need the bootleggers because they lack the political strength to pass the Sunday closing laws on their own. Both groups—bootleggers and Baptists—lobby for the same outcome, but for vastly different reasons. This coalition has its limits, however. Baptists' overall opposition to alcohol prevents any explicit alliance with the bootleggers, and bootleggers' economic interests lead them to disagree with many broader extensions of Baptists' anti-alcohol policy (e.g., rules affecting the consumption of alcoholic beverages).

Yandle generalizes the Sunday closing law story to the following proposition: durable regulatory bargains are possible even among groups with quite different goals, where interest group benefits can be cloaked with a more politically acceptable purpose. One group, the "Baptists," brings a public, altruistic interest to the political debate, trumpeting this with enough fanfare to give the politicians a publicly acceptable reason to support the regulatory bargain. "Bootleggers" bring an economic interest that generates the campaign contributions and other support that closes the deal with the politicians. The public interest rationale provides cover to the quiet self-interest; the invisible coalition of nonallies greases government machinery for action.

Green Pork

Given the vast amount of money flowing to projects proclaimed to produce "green energy," it should be no surprise that profit-making enterprises have zeroed in on the chance to share in the rewards. GE has been particularly successful at finding green products to sell, doubling its "green" sales from 2005 to 2007 to $12 billion.[15] A year later, sales were up another 21 percent to $17 billion.[16] As we noted earlier, ADM has profited enormously from biofuels subsidies seemingly custom-designed to funnel money to the firm. It's not just American companies profiting from U.S. green spending: European giant Siemens AG, whose profits from its wind energy business have been increasing, forecast higher profits from the U.S. stimulus package green energy program.[17]

Companies making money off of environmental improvement is a great thing—when it happens in the marketplace because their products meet a demand from consumers.[18] But when companies create a demand for products that they would not otherwise sell, by using the government, it is not such a good thing. This is nothing new, of course. Remember Enron? An internal company memo boasted that if the Kyoto Agreement (to limit carbon emissions) were implemented, it would "do more to promote Enron's business than almost any other regulatory business." Enron perfected the technique of mining environmental regulations for money. Former Enron analyst Robert Bradley termed Enron's wind energy venture, Enron Wind, "Enron's first fraud" and concluded that Enron's "green" strategy was at the core of its business problems *and* legal problems.[19] And we are not singling out GE and Siemens for abuse here. In May 2009,

Bjorn Lomborg listed among the sponsors of the World Business Summit on Climate Change in Copenhagen:

- Generation Investment Management (Al Gore's investment firm), which promotes green energy;
- Vestas, the world's largest wind turbine manufacturer, which sponsors CNN's *Climate in Peril* program and lobbies for wind energy;
- Rhodia SA, a French chemical manufacturer, which could earn more than $1 billion over seven years by destroying its nitrous-oxide emissions at its South Korean and Brazilian plants, earning pollution credits it can sell under a UN program aimed at helping developing countries, not European multinationals. The equipment necessary cost the company only $15 million, and the emissions credit business earns Rhodia more than the underlying production at the plants, which is barely profitable;[20]
- Duke Energy, a large U.S. utility that promotes a U.S. cap and trade regime, but only one that gives utilities free credits; and
- European energy companies, which were given free carbon credits under Europe's cap and trade system.[21]

Green pork draws corporate rent-seekers like flies because a successful green rent-seeker needs three things, all of which these companies have. First, green pork requires a staff of lobbyists able to ensure that a rent-seeker's operations fit the legal description of projects eligible for the subsidies. For example, Aptera Motors, Inc. was dismayed to learn that its proposed three-wheeled vehicle was ineligible for a $75 million subsidized loan from the Department of Energy to promote the development of more fuel-efficient cars because the agency ruled that the legislation establishing the program required it to define "automobile" as "any four-wheeled vehicle."[22] But since the company's investors "include some big-money donors to the Democratic Party" and it is based in California, whose congressional delegation could be enlisted "to help a home-state enterprise," the company launched a lobbying effort to get the definition changed by Congress.[23] This paid off later in 2009, and Aptera could receive the loan.[24]

Second, a successful raid on the public purse requires an ability to find clever ways to hide the pork in federal legislation. Outright grants are easy for budget hawks to spot;[25] a tweak to a tax provision can be no less lucrative but easier to slip into a bill without as much public notice.[26] For example, the Bush administration's fall 2008 bank bailout bill included "a line so that utilities that install smart meters, which allow consumers real-time access to their energy usage and two-way communication with utilities, can depreciate the cost of the meters in 10 years instead of 20." Why was this important? "By halving the time over which the companies can write off their investments, they double the amount of money they can save on their taxes."[27] How much? An estimated $915 million.[28]

Third, getting a full plate of green pork requires having the staff to spot exactly how to tweak the legislation to maximize your take while minimizing the political fallout. Consider the plug-in hybrid electric vehicle tax credit tacked onto the 2008 bank bailout. Getting a credit for plug-in hybrids into a bank bailout took some astute lobbying to begin with—it's not obvious that's an appropriate place to set tax policy, particularly with respect to technologies. But since the banking system was uncomfortably close to a meltdown, lobbyists knew that something had to pass quickly. All they needed was to attach their clients' green pork to the bill and it would become law with little scrutiny. But the cleverness of the green pork lobby didn't stop with finding the perfect host for the bill. Lots of lobbyists got in on the action—the original draft of H.R. 1424 (the financial bailout bill) was three pages long; the final bill was 451 pages long and included the infamous "wooden arrow" provision, a tax exemption for wooden arrows no more than 5/16 inch in diameter and which are neither finished nor laminated.[29]

The plug-in credit was set at $2,500 plus $417 for each kWh of battery-pack capacity in excess of 4 kWh, up to a maximum of $7,500 for light duty vehicles.[30] These are somewhat peculiar numbers—why $417? The draft bill used $400 per kWh, and $417 is not a number that seems like a clear focal point, like multiples of 5 or 10. The answer is that the Chevy Volt has a 16 kWh battery, and 417 is the number necessary to provide it with the full $7,500 credit.[31] Even better, the credit can be applied against the Alternative Minimum Tax, making the entire $7,500 available to the wealthy individuals most likely to be shelling out $45,000 for a Volt. And a whopping $1 billion was set aside for this tax credit, allowing many of those wealthy taxpayers subject to the AMT to buy Volts. And, as a final gift to General Motors, the 4 kWh minimum capacity *excludes* Toyota's (and likely some others') first-generation plug-in hybrid.[32] Such artistry in drafting is impressive—and out of the price range of most.

Because large firms like Enron, GM, and GE, and politically well-connected firms like Aptera, have the resources to acquire all three of these prerequisites, they can win big at the green pork game. When they spot an opportunity to have some "Baptists" drum up support for green pork, they're ready to assist—just as long as their lobbyists have the chance to steer some porkbarrel spending in their direction.

Selling Green Pork

The group whose role is easiest to understand is politicians. The vendors of green pork are members of Congress who can influence the outcome of bills. Committee chairs, appropriations committee members, conference committee members, and a host of others all have opportunities to fiddle with the text of legislation. Agency staff write regulations to implement legislation, another arena for tweaking definitions to make green pork available. In return, politicians need three things. First, they need votes and the campaign contributions necessary to get votes.[33] Money and office operations for their campaign committees are crucial, as is money for their political action committees to donate to others, creating obligations that will help them on the campaign trail themselves, in the quest for higher office, in gathering support for their efforts, or mounting a defense against everything from ethics charges to political smears. Green pork consumers are efficient providers of campaign funds. GE employees, for example, have made over $17 million in campaign contributions since 1990, split roughly evenly between Democrats and Republicans, with contributions to congressmen on the House Select Energy Independence and Global Warming Committee getting the largest average contributions.[34] Even more impressively, Enron employees remained on the top 100 campaign contributors list into 2008 despite not having given any money since 2002.[35]

Second, politicians need "green labels" for themselves. The League of Conservation Voters provides an annual scorecard of "environmental votes" that certifies an incumbent as "green."[36] Many of these are votes on procedural and technical matters that are hard for voters to understand but which accurately gauge fidelity to environmental pressure groups' agendas.[37] Other organizations provide endorsements, giving politicians the chance to tell voters about their "green" credentials.[38]

Finally, they need the mobilization efforts of organized groups to get voters to the polls, efforts that some analysts have found to be important in congressional races, and environmental groups have been playing a role in this since 1994.[39] In-kind assistance from organizations in mobilizing voters is increasingly important in elections where turnout is critical.[40]

Green energy programs provide politicians with something new to sell—no longer just a jobs or infrastructure program, they can now tout a *green* program, which is appropriate regardless of overall economic conditions. Moreover, by allowing the label "green" to be applied to special interest provisions like the plug-in hybrid giveaway to General Motors, favors can be doled out to preferred recipients (GM) and denied to others (Toyota) without attracting negative attention. And the threat of denial of a "green" label will be enough to motivate unorganized interests to form organized groups to seek certification. As Northwestern University law professor Fred McChesney puts it, politicians who merely threaten action can obtain "money for nothing."[41] Thus, green pork programs extend the product line that elected officials have "for sale," offering them new opportunities to gather resources.

Making the Green Mission Acceptable

The green pork coalition has an additional twist on Yandle's example. The "Baptists" in the green pork coalition are the environmental groups. Their broad mission of improving the quality of air, water, and land is so widely accepted in American politics today that, as Richard Darman, President George H.W. Bush's director of the Office of Management and Budget, put it in 1990:

> We are all environmentalists. . . . The President is an environmentalist, Republicans and Democrats are environmentalists. Jane Fonda and the National Association of Manufacturers, Magic Johnson and Danny DeVito, Candice Bergen and The Golden Girls, Bugs Bunny and the cast of Cheers are all environmentalists.[42]

Darman captured a crucial truth about American politics, one that reflects a widespread change from the 1960s: no one today seriously argues that environmental protection is not an important public policy goal, although there are disagreements over the merits of particular measures or priorities.

If environmentalism means only a preference for clean air or clean water when no costs are being considered, the concept is so vague that the "environment" disappears from the political radar screen.

> It is hard . . . to make a campaign issue out of a matter when voters tend to be in agreement. No candidate is going to say that he favors dirty air and polluted water, wants to see more dolphins killed, or hopes to build a Wal-Mart in the middle of Yosemite.[43]

Thus environmental groups have to find issues on which they can distinguish themselves from the general agreement that clean air and clean water are good things if they are going to motivate potential members to join and contribute money. A green energy program offers one possible product.

Green energy programs are important for environmental pressure groups for a second reason. Modern environmental pressure groups have a much broader agenda than simply advocating cleaning up rivers or the air. Environmental historian Hal Rothman distinguished "environmentalism" from beliefs he labels "conservationism," which he argues dominated environmental thinking before the 1960s. Modern environmentalism is "saving the planet from the excesses of the human race. . . . Human beings [are] entitled to clean air, clean water, open spaces, and a pristine and inspiring environment as well as the life, liberty, and pursuit of happiness enshrined in the United States Constitution." [sic][44] Conservationism, on the other hand, was "the idea of using resources in a manner to further the goal of the 'greatest good for the greatest number in the long run'. . . ."[45]

Other analysts have similarly noted that environmental pressure groups and their leaders make broad moral claims about what constitutes a good society. University of Maryland economist Robert Nelson argues that "[t]he distinctive feature of the contemporary environmental movement . . . is not a goal to improve public health but its rethinking of the basic relationship between human beings and nature—a central topic of religion for thousands of years."[46] Philip Shabecoff, the long-time chief environmental correspondent for the *New York Times,* distinguished environmentalism from conservationism by its focus on "social change and political activism" to address issues related to "pollution and toxic substances" rather than "on the land and wildlife preservation."[47]

Modern environmentalism is also marked by a belief that technology and modern society has divided humanity from nature. To take just a few examples, historian Mark Dowie lists a "return to nature" for humanity and recognition that humanity is not "the crowning achievement of evolution" among his predictions of a future environmental consensus.[48] Former Vice President Al Gore analogizes humanity's relationship to nature as similar to that of children in a dysfunctional family: "we internalize the pain of our lost sense of connection to the natural world, we consume the earth and its resources as a way to distract ourselves from the pain, and we search insatiably for artificial substitutes to replace the experience of communion with the world that has been taken from us."[49] "Deep ecologists" Bill Devall and George Sessions argue that "[t]echnological society not only alienates humans from the rest of Nature but also alienates humans from themselves and from each other."[50] Rothman argued that the Wilderness Act came about because "Americans recognized that wilderness—for many just the *idea* of wilderness—helped make them whole, helped obviate the sense of loss that stemmed from urbanization and suburbanization."[51] Professor Linda Graber contends that such views are valuable to the ardent believer in a cause because "the purist is encouraged to see himself as part of the advance guard for a higher level of civilization, which is a much more pleasant self-image than 'nature nut.'"[52] Alienation surfaces as an important factor in Kempton et al.'s analysis of environmental thinking. They found that alienation is one of the explanations raised primarily by environmentalists rather than by the full range of their interviewees.[53]

Moreover, many environmental pressure group leaders subscribe to an apocalyptic narrative about the current state of the environment. For example, Rachel Carson dedicated *Silent Spring* to Albert Schweitzer, who she quoted as saying: "Man has lost the capacity to foresee and to forestall. He will end by destroying the earth."[54] John Bellamy Foster's influential *The Vulnerable Planet* set out the apocalyptic narrative in typical fashion:

> The litany of ecological complaints plaguing the world today . . . include: overpopulation, destruction of the ozone layer, global warming, extinction of species, loss

> of genetic diversity, acid rain, nuclear contamination, tropical deforestation, the elimination of climax forests, wetland destruction, soil erosion, desertification, floods, famine, the despoliation of lakes, streams and rivers, the drawing down and contamination of ground water, the pollution of coastal waters and estuaries, the destruction of coral reefs, oil spills, overfishing, expanding landfills, toxic wastes, the poisonous effects of pesticides and herbicides, exposure to hazards on the job, urban congestion, and the depletion of nonrenewable resources.[55]

Deep ecologists argue that environmentalism provides "a single motivating force for all the activities and movements aimed at saving the planet from human exploitation and domination."[56] Or, as Shabecoff put it, "The mission of environmentalism is to mobilize society at all levels to confront the danger and disorder into which human activity has propelled us and to guide us to a safer, saner way of living on this planet, now and in the time of our posterity."[57]

Having a great purpose can be inspirational. For example, in *Encounters with the Archdruid,* John McPhee praised David Brower, a founder of many environmental organizations, as effective because he was "a visionary . . . an emotionalist in an age of dangerous reason."[58] Former Vice President Al Gore's labeling of "the climate crisis" as "an opportunity to experience something that few generations ever have the privilege of knowing: a common moral purpose compelling enough to lift us above our limitations and motivate us to set aside some of the bickering to which we as human beings are naturally vulnerable"[59] appears to be popular. Environmental historian Thomas Dunlap argues that

> Environmentalism campaigns for new laws, but it also gives moral weight to the apparently trivial decisions of daily life. It tells you what kind of grass to put in the front yard, how to get to work, even what kind of diapers to put on the baby. It makes a brick in the toilet tank an expression of virtue. It asks not just that we change policies or even our habits, but that we change our hearts, not just that we recycle papers, cans, and bottles, but that we form a new relationship with nature. Finally, it invokes the sacred, holding some areas and species in awe and finding in wilderness the opening to ultimate reality.[60]

Robert Nelson calls environmentalism a "secular Puritanism,"[61] and argues that it is the quasi-religious nature of environmentalism that explains why

> the Arctic National Wildlife Refuge (ANWR) has become so religiously important to the environmental movement. It is not just the on-the-ground environmental features of the area—in both Alaska and Canada there are in truth many other similarly desolate and isolated places bordering the Arctic. The one truly distinctive feature of ANWR is that so much valuable oil and gas there—amounts that have an estimated gross worth of as much as one trillion dollars. . . . If this area is instead left "untouched," the ANWR "church" conceivably would be the most expensive cathedral to the glory of an environmental god and the American environmental movement.[62]

The point of the statement made by foreswearing development of ANWR is that it is the preservation of a place without direct utility for humans, a powerful sacrifice indeed and one that is without immediate utility.

These calls to a higher purpose are undoubtedly exhilarating to those who respond to them with near religious fervor. But there are limits to the proportion of the population which can be motivated by jeremiads.[63] In particular, the efforts in the 1960s and 1970s by environmental groups to focus on "the population problem" using similarly charged language proved "so controversial that they were dropped."[64] Where the high moral purpose of environmentalism collides with people's other priorities, environmental pressure groups run into a problem: not only does everyone not want to be an environmental Calvinist, but environmental pressure groups are unable to persuade even a majority to don the hair shirts they proffer on many issues. As Philip Shabecoff summarizes the problem, "A number of environmentalists, political experts, and scholars interviewed . . . said that the poor political record of the environmental community can be explained by the poor job it does in demonstrating how its agenda links up with the real problems and needs of the American people. . . . Although the polls may show that people are concerned about the environment, the environment as an abstraction fails to motivate electoral decisions."[65]

THE FALSE PROMISE OF GREEN ENERGY

As a result, even some of the most fervent environmental thinkers argue that advocacy of the movement's goals cannot succeed politically. For example, deep ecologist theoretician Arne Naess has argued that "[t]he shallow ecological argument carries today much heavier weight in political life than the deep. It is therefore often necessary for tactical reasons to hide our deeper attitudes and argue strictly homocentrically."[66] But even committed environmentalists find that this strategy carries risks of its own, leaving supporters "in an existential hell, trapped between two flatly incompatible visions of reality," one of which is an impending "collapse of the very systems that sustain life on the planet, with a terribly small chance of avoiding cataclysm if we manage to fundamentally reshape global society in four years," and the other with climate change "a most serious problem and getting worse, but we have made major progress and there's considerable room for hope; indeed, climate change provides us an opportunity to rebuild our society along more sustainable and equitable lines."[67]

Moreover, since the mid-1980s, the national environmental organizations have faced a challenge from grassroots environmental groups focused on local issues, who do not automatically accept the national organizations' agenda or values. In particular, these local groups often emphasize the need to preserve jobs in their communities while addressing environmental issues and argue that the national organizations have neglected the issue of jobs. For example, Richard Moore of the grassroots Southwest Network for Environmental and Economic Justice, criticized the Sierra Club in 1993, saying it "has been a co-conspirator in attempting to take resources away from our communities . . . supporting policies that emphasize the clean up and preservation of the environment on the backs of working people, and people of color in particular."[68]

These grassroots organizations have two significant advantages over the national pressure groups. First, they address issues of day-to-day concern to the lives of their members. Rather than a global apocalypse based on confusing technical models and contested science, grassroots groups stir up their members about the emissions from the chemical plant next door or the development of property that the members know well. These more relevant messages have helped them in the competition for members by allowing them to criticize the national pressure groups as "tame, corporate and compromising."[69]

Second, they operate on much smaller budgets, avoiding the high priced salaries, consultants, and Washington headquarters.[70]

Green energy programs offer the national pressure groups something unique—a positive program in which environmental improvements are linked to improvements in human needs. Green energy programs offer an image of how doing the right thing environmentally can also be the right thing for individuals in place of the drudgery of sorting one's trash for recycling[71] or a future defined by resource constraints and reduced consumption.[72]

Green economy programs also offer a chance to build an alliance with organized labor and politicians looking for resources to distribute, enabling environmentalists to build a majority that will enact at least some of their policy preferences as part of the overall package. For example, most green energy projects involve switching to sources of energy that are more expensive, raising the cost of energy use. Mass transit projects included as green transportation projects subsidize environmentalists' preferred transportation modes. Straightforward efforts to raise energy prices or put additional resources into costly mass transit projects, however, would be a nonstarter politically since the costs they would impose would be obvious to voters.

Green energy programs thus solve three political problems for environmental pressure groups. First, they create a pool of resources whose distribution can buy support for the pressure groups' goals from organized labor and politicians. Second, they offer a positive program that is more politically appealing to voters than a repetition of the apocalyptic themes used by environmental groups so far and which offers voters a way out of their "existential hell." Third, they enable the national pressure groups a chance to bid away support from their grassroots competitors, by shifting the focus of action back to the halls of Congress and the Washington bureaucracy, where the national organizations' lobbyists and lawyers have a competitive advantage over the grassroots organizations.

Conclusion

The politics of green energy means that the incentives are all wrong with respect to getting a careful assessment of green energy proposals. No decisionmaker in Washington has an incentive to scrutinize a proposal for a $4 billion appropriation here or a $1 billion tax credit there. Everyone involved in the process has an incentive to jump on the bandwagon and get their share of the green pork. Members of Congress all want the coveted green label for the next campaign, the contributions and mobilization aid from environmental pressure groups, and the campaign contributions from the industrial beneficiaries of their largesse. Businesses line up at the trough to gorge themselves on green pork, finding the payoff from their lobbying efforts in a definition here and tweak to a bill there. Environmental pressure groups gain allies for measures they could not win on the merits, buying support by looking the other way while billions are shunted to a firm in a congressperson's district or a program whose eligibility requirements fit only a selected few.

If we are to have a fair assessment of these multibillion dollar programs before they are embedded in spending bills, tax codes, and environmental regulations, people outside the environmentally sustainable iron triangle of the green industrial complex will need to press hard to have questions like those we raise in this book answered: How much does it cost? How will borrowed money be repaid? When will the benefits appear? Who benefits?

The promise of a green economy—of millions of high paying, environmentally sensitive jobs—is beguiling. It would be wonderful if wind and solar installations used "free" energy to produce electricity, if useful fuels could be squeezed from common plants without significant energy inputs, or if wrapping public buildings in insulation could cut government energy costs deeply and quickly enough to repay the investment in just a few years. All these are laudable goals, and ones we think the market has already provided incentives to entrepreneurs to attempt to meet. But we must not forget that once these wonderful visions are reduced to legislation in the corridors and committee rooms of Congress, and the details written into regulations by administrative agencies, those actions are simply politics as usual. The devil is in the details—the details that decide whether GM or its competitors will reap the rewards of a tax credit, whether three-wheeled vehicles are automobiles or not, and whether utilities can write off their investments in smart meters in 10 years or 20. Billions of our (and our grandchildren's) dollars turn on those decisions. It is criminally naive for Americans to think that good intentions will suffice to ensure that those billions will be allocated from taxpayers' pockets to special interests in an open, transparent, and fair way.

12. Forward to the Past?

The world suffers from profound environmental problems. It always has. The World Health Organization estimates that 1.6 million deaths per year can be attributed to air pollution.[1] That makes it the eighth largest source of death. The impact is primarily on children and women. The immediate cause of death is pneumonia or some other disease triggered by exposure to high levels of pollutants from the burning of biomass such as wood or agricultural residue.

This is, of course, not the low levels of air pollution people in the United States and the EU are exposed to but the high levels of pollutants suffered by billions of people as they burn wood, dung, or other material in their homes to meet basic energy needs—cooking and heating. These people do not have the luxury of using electricity or natural gas to produce energy for such purposes. The power sources that help provide for our high standards of living and health, and energy sources that the poor would love to have, are under assault. Coal, natural gas, and other carbon-based energy sources are being declared to be major environmental problems. The question is, compared to what?

Americans suffered from much higher levels of indoor air pollution in the not-to-distant past. Using 1940 as the baseline, scholar Indur Goklany shows that major indoor pollutants in the United States dropped rapidly over the next several decades—down to a small fraction of what had been experienced before.[2] No regulations forced that to happen—indoor air quality is essentially unregulated. Why did indoor air get cleaner? Market-generated technology and wealth. Smelly coal- and oil-burning furnaces were replaced with electric heat or natural gas furnaces, and combustion technology improved, so fuel burned more efficiently. As people enjoyed higher incomes, they bought cleaner sources of heat, just as wood-burning stoves were abandoned in favor of cleaner, more efficient sources of heat for cooking. The air in homes, and the outdoor air, improved.

The makers of furnaces and stoves competed to make ever-better appliances for us to enjoy.

Peasants in India, Africa, and other places cannot adopt the wonderful benefits we enjoy, but fortunately their options are improving. Clever inventors have come up with little stoves that burn less fuel more efficiently and produce lower emissions. Health improves as people in little homes breathe fewer emissions. The cost of securing material to burn also drops as fewer inputs are needed to produce heat. One foundation (there are others) working on this is Envirofit International. Based in Fort Collins, Colorado, and funded in part by the Shell (Oil) Foundation, it worked with scientists at Colorado State University to produce low-cost, efficient stoves that burn traditional biomass materials. "The design was developed using advanced Computational Fluid Dynamics, heat transfer modeling, and robust emissions and durability testing to optimize the geometry and materials of the stove."[3] As lawyers and economists, we are not sure what that means, but we understand that it has new technology that could improve the lives of millions.

Stove users enjoy a better life from breathing cleaner air and spending less time and money gathering material to burn. The rest of us benefit too. Envirofit reported on its website in July 2009 that 60,000 stoves had been sold in India: "Over the next five years these 60K cookstoves could keep over 400,000 tons of CO_2 and over 85,000 kg of black carbon from entering the atmosphere, while garnering savings of over 900 million rupees ($18M USD) for some of India's lowest-income consumers."[4]

While charitable people will be glad to know that lives are improved for a pittance, the extra benefit is that greenhouse gas (GHG) emissions may be reduced too. We are not experts on atmospheric science so will not make assertions about the impact of GHGs on the environment and climate, but there are people who work on that subject. "There is new but intriguing evidence that a large cloud of particulate pollution originating mainly in India is a major source of greenhouse warming."[5] Black carbon (soot) is estimated to be account for 18 percent of GHGs, so the stoves have environmental and economic benefits.

> There's a large experience and some analytical literature on the kinds of efforts that could be needed which probably involve deployment of advanced cookstoves for heating and cooking.

Measurements from drones flown into the brown cloud suggest that just a few states in India are the main source of the pollution and thus the effort could initially concentrate in those locates .... Getting a handle on the exact global warming benefit of a large-scale deployment of advanced cookstoves is difficult but it could be on the order of the equivalent of one third of India's anthropogenic greenhouse gas emissions.[6]

No authority in Congress, in Washington, D.C., or in New Delhi told Envirofit to invent the stoves. Environmental entrepreneurs, who are now called enviropreneurs, saw a problem and came up with something nifty that helps individuals have a better life and may well help the global environment.[7]

Imagine distributing a thousand times as many stoves: 60 million. That would serve a small fraction of the 3 billion people who might benefit from such technology. The CO_2 savings would be immense, perhaps 400 million tons. That is equal to about a quarter of the CO_2 emissions from coal burning in the United States.[8] If we want cost-effective ways to reduce emissions, it may be a lot cheaper to buy a bunch of stoves for poor people in India than to blanket the U.S. countryside with corn, wind turbines, and solar panels in a dubious effort to reduce emissions from coal.

Small Can Be Beautiful

There are many lessons to draw from the clean-burning stoves. Cost effective solutions are more likely to come from the bottom up—including from a little outfit in Fort Collins—than from the Senate Commerce or House Energy committees doling out huge sums in the federal budget to the pork recipients lucky enough to get a cut of the action. But as discussed in the previous chapter, luck has nothing to do with getting on the federal gravy train; it takes serious lobbying to get funding for a bridge to nowhere or for a federal clean-burning stove program. GE and other big organizations with Washington offices can belly up to the table for such goodies.[9] Little organizations are less likely to be able to rely on green pork for a living. Most smaller firms focus on being clever and cost-effective so as to have a chance to outperform the competition that may play by different sets of rules, including access to our grandchildren's purse, thanks to Congress.

As we have seen, when green energy and jobs advocacy groups talk about "innovative" projects, they are not focusing on clever stoves that previously unknown inventors come up with. They want cash or special tax goodies given to specific (generally unionized) projects that use existing technology. The regulatory process tends to lock in that technology; it does not encourage thinking outside the federal box. The continual improvements in energy efficiency that evolved over the past two centuries did not come at the behest of central planners. They came from good firms, including GE, working hard to do a little better job than their competitors for current and future customers. There is nothing cute about the competitive process; it leaves many bankrupt firms in its wake. But it is an important part of why progress occurs.

The little stoves will help people in India thanks to the mechanism we call international trade. American know-how designed the stoves. Envirofit is selling them in India (with a five-year warranty!). The green jobs trade-naysayers give the impression that every community can invent and produce everything it needs. Without trade, Indians may not have gotten such benefits to improve their lives; the environment would not have benefitted; and American inventors would have had less reason to design this useful product. Trade creates new wealth.

We enjoy the highest standard of living and highest health standards ever enjoyed by humans. We hope more people can share in this bounty. Peasants in India suffering lung disease from open cooking fires can have a better life by obtaining a little stove. Many of the green energy and jobs proposals would halt economic progress and, as we have discussed, may reverse it, eliminating hope for many. If CO_2 emissions are a major problem, then we should address it in the most cost-effective manner possible, while retaining as much personal and market freedom as possible. Little stoves and many other innovations are likely to provide more cost-effective solutions to emissions than bloated political mandates for wind turbines, Synfuel, corn ethanol, or federal window-caulking programs. It is profoundly puzzling why, if the green jobs advocates are actually interested in the environment, they do not search for the many cost effective solutions that may emerge, rather than focus on a litany of federal mandates that would push the country further into debt, reduce personal and market freedom, and hinder technical progress.

Pay More to Live Worse

The costs of the green programs proposed by the interest groups that authored the reports we examined, and others with less fully developed proposals, are staggering. The federal government committed $62 billion in direct spending and $20 billion in tax incentives to green jobs programs as part of the 2009 stimulus bill.[10] And keep in mind that this money is all borrowed and must be repaid with interest. Worse, the price tag is open ended. Even the proponents are reluctant to give firm cost estimates since one can, of course, add or subtract pieces of a program that can encompass many things. For example, the United Nations Environment Programme report concludes:

> No one knows how much a full-fledged green transition will cost, but needed investment will likely be in the hundreds of billions, and possibly trillions, of dollars. It is still not clear at this point where such high volumes of investment capital will come from, or how it can be generated in a relatively short period of time.[11]

The scale of social and economic change that could be imposed is immense. To take just one example, the worldwide production of cement in 2008 was 2.84 billion metric tons.[12] Cement is ubiquitous in modern society. As you read this, you can likely see cement. Yet we are told that "[t]he cement industry will only become sustainable if the building industry finds completely new ways to create and use cement or eventually figures out how to replace it altogether."[13] And, as we have described in this book, green jobs advocates propose equally dramatic shifts in energy production technologies, building practices, and transportation. These calls for dramatic changes in every aspect of modern life are wrapped in a bright, shiny package in the green jobs literature, promising not only a revolution in our relationship with the environment but the creation of millions of high-paying, satisfying jobs.[14] Despite the new green packaging, these calls for creating a new society through central planning are as old as human history. The failure of the 20th century's utopian experiments suggests caution in undertaking such widespread transformations of society.

Other countries that have experience with renewable energy provide concrete evidence of what it means in practice. Germany is considered a leader in renewable energy technology. The price paid for PV electricity "is more than eight times higher than the wholesale electricity price at the power exchange and more than four times the feed-in tariff paid for electricity produced by on-shore wind turbines."[15] Solar PV, which produced only 0.6 percent of electricity in the country, cost more than $12 billion in 2008, which is almost all from subsidies. Over the decade ending in 2010, German electricity users will have paid out about $73 billion for that miniscule addition to the electrical system.[16] Wind energy, "widely regarded as a mature technology," requires a price as much as 300 percent that paid for conventional electricity.[17] The subsidies for all "green electricity," which is a small fraction of all electricity, adds 7.5 percent to household electricity prices.[18] The cost of the subsidy per worker in the PV industry is about $240,000.[19] One may counter that the benefit is reduced carbon emission. But the cost is about $1,050 per ton of CO_2 emission averted, which is 53 times the cost of buying carbon credits in the open market for PV-generated electricity and four times the cost for wind power.[20] The touted emission reductions from costly fuel programs may be mythical and governments may suppress that bad news: "Biofuels such as biodiesel from soy beans can create up to four times more climate-warming emissions than standard diesel or petrol, according to an EU document released under freedom of information laws."[21]

The green energy advocates suffer from a lack of faith in technology and innovation. Windmills have been around for centuries; modern wind turbines are nifty but do not, at least as yet, offer a serious solution to the need for stable power sources. The same issue of lack of consistent production affects solar power, as we have discussed. We have no doubt these technologies will improve over time, but those are not the only likely sources of development. Since many environmentalists have their heads stuck in Luddite sand, they ignore exciting possibilities that are on the horizon. Little stoves and many other innovations are constantly evolving to improve technology and thereby reduce emissions. Tomorrow will not look like today unless regulations lock us into current technology. Americans would be wise to turn their attention to critically examining pending federal legislation, such as the Clean Energy Jobs and American Power Act, to see if it is in their, and their children's, best interests.[22]

Claims versus Facts

The analysis provided in the green energy and jobs literature is deeply flawed, resting on a series of myths about the economy, the environment, and technology. We have explored the problems in the green jobs analysis in-depth; we conclude by summarizing the major claims about green jobs, give brief rebuttals based on empirical evidence and standard economic logic to the greenspeak, and then provide questions that should be addressed to current or wannabe politicians touting green jobs proposals:

Claim: There are "green jobs."

Fact: There is no coherent definition of a green job. Green jobs are asserted to be ones that pay well, are interesting to do, produce products that environmental groups prefer, and usually do so in a unionized workplace. Yet such criteria have little to do with the environmental impacts of the jobs. To build a coalition for a far reaching transformation of modern society, "green jobs" have become a mechanism to deliver something for every member of a real or imagined coalition to buy their support for a radical transformation of society.

Claim: Creating green jobs will boost productive employment.

Fact: Green jobs estimates include huge numbers of clerical, bureaucratic, and administrative positions that do not produce goods and services for consumption. Simply hiring people to write and enforce regulations, fill out forms, and process paperwork is not a recipe for creating wealth. Much of the promised boost in green employment turns out to be in nonproductive (but costly) positions that raise costs for consumers.

Claim: Green jobs forecasts are reliable.

Fact: The forecasts for green employment optimistically predict an employment boom, which is welcome news. Unfortunately, the forecasts, which are sometimes amazingly detailed, are unreliable because they are based on questionable estimates by interest groups of tiny base numbers in employment, extrapolation of growth rates from those small base numbers, and a pervasive, biased, and highly selective optimism about which technologies will improve. Moreover, the estimates use techniques (input-output analysis and multipliers) that are inappropriate to the conditions of technological change presumed by the green jobs literature itself. This yields seemingly precise estimates that give the illusion of scientific reliability to numbers that are simply the result of the assumptions made to begin the analysis.

Claim: Green energy and green jobs promote employment growth.

Fact: Green energy/jobs estimates promise greatly expanded (and pleasant and well-paid) employment. This promise is false. The green energy/jobs models are built on promoting inefficient use of labor and capital, favoring technologies because they employ large numbers rather than because they make use of labor efficiently. Similarly, green energy projects divert scarce capital away from other, non-politically driven uses, with greater expected economic return. The green energy/jobs literature dooms everyone to live in a shrinking economy. Economic growth cannot be ordered by Congress or the United Nations. Interference in the economy by restricting successful technologies in favor of speculative technologies favored by special interests will generate stagnation.

Claim: The world economy can be remade based on local production and reduced consumption without dramatically decreasing human welfare.

Fact: The green jobs literature rejects the benefits of trade, ignores opportunity costs, and fails to include consumer surplus in welfare calculations to promote its vision. This is a recipe for an economic disaster, not an ecotopia. The 20th century saw many experiments in creating societies that did not engage in trade and did not value personal welfare. The economic and human disasters that resulted should have conclusively settled the question of whether nations can withdraw into autarky. The global integration of wind turbine production, for example, illustrates that even green technology is not immune from economic reality.

Claim: Mandates are a good substitute for markets.

Fact: Green energy and jobs proponents assume that they can reorder society by mandating preferred technologies. But the responses to mandates are not the same as the responses to market incentives. We have reviewed powerful evidence that market incentives induce the resource conservation that green jobs advocates purport to desire. The cost of energy is a major incentive to redesign production processes and products to use less energy. People do not want energy; they want the benefits of energy. Those who can deliver more desired goods and services by reducing the energy cost of production will be rewarded. There is little evidence that command-and-control regimes succeed in accomplishing conservation.

Claim: Technological progress ordered by politicians will happen, and be cost-effective, because promoters want it to be so.

Fact: The preferred technologies in the green energy and jobs literature face significant problems in scaling up to the levels proposed. These problems are documented in readily available technical literature but resolutely ignored in the green jobs reports. At the same time, existing technologies that fail to meet the green energy and jobs proponents' political criteria are simply rejected out of hand. This selective technological optimism/pessimism is not a sufficient basis for remaking society to fit the dream of planners, politicians, patricians, or plutocrats who want others to live lives they think other people should be forced to lead.

Green energy and green jobs proposals sound great. "Invest"[23] in them and see jobs created that pay above-average wages and help enrich the country, including future generations, while improving the environment. The claims are similar to those promised by Bernard Madoff in his multibillion dollar Ponzi scheme, except he left off the part about improving the environment.

We want future generations to enjoy more wealth and have a better environment, but we believe that when somebody—especially somebody seeking political office, looking for funding for an advocacy group, or trying to peddle something that isn't selling well—says he can "beat the market," it is time to step back. It is one thing when an investor gets suckered into a bad deal. It is another when government force is used to extract billions of dollars from unwilling "investors," and their grandchildren, who are politely told that their money is being used for their own good, whether they know it or not. If we thought the scheme could work, then the merits of using political force to make it happen might be debatable. But we believe this is the worst of all worlds—a very costly spending program, falsely called an investment, that will leave most of us poorer, will impinge on personal freedom, will damage markets, and will not improve the environment. There is no upside to this, except for assorted special interests that will suck in revenues and benighted environmentalists who do not wish to be confused by facts.

Questions for Green Energy/Green Jobs Advocates

What can you do to have an impact? We believe that if enough people ask enough questions about these programs before they are enacted, we can break the hold of the "green-industrial complex" and force some common sense into the policy process. Based on our analysis of the evidence and basic economic logic reviewed in this book, we've prepared 30 questions that can be posed to those proposing to spend taxpayers' money on green energy and jobs. Take these with you to public meetings; include them in letters to the editor or opinion pieces in your local paper, your blog, or in discussions with your friends; and write to your representatives and ask them how well they have investigated these issues. If we can shift the process even 10 degrees toward an effective due diligence, we will save billions and prevent many of the worst of these projects from being funded.

1. Who will receive the money if this project is funded?
2. What ties do decisionmakers have to the companies that will receive the money?
3. What kind of analysis was done to calculate the benefits of this program? Who did the analysis?
4. If an input-output analysis was performed, how do proponents justify violating the method's basic assumptions of constant technology and constant relative prices?
5. Some green energy advocates want to eliminate power from coal, oil, natural gas, and nuclear plants. Do you believe wind turbines, solar power generators, and other costly technologies, such as large biomass-burning facilities, can replace most of the sources of our current reliable electricity at reasonable prices?
6. In absolute number terms, rather than percentages, how many new facilities would have to be built to achieve the goals of a

program such as that called for by the Conference of Mayors advocating going from 3 percent to 40 percent electricity from so-called renewable sources by 2038 (e.g., how many wind farms, solar farms, ethanol plants)?

7. If the project involves wind farms or solar PV fields, what provisions have been made for backup generation that can come on-line instantly when the wind dies or the sun sets? Who will pay for this system that duplicates power generation capability?

8. How much will electricity prices be likely to increase for households and businesses?

9. Costly solar power in Spain has driven businesses out of that country to those with more competitive prices. Do you think businesses in the United States will leave for Canada, Mexico, China, or other countries with lower-priced energy if we build costly "renewable" sources?

10. Since nuclear power plants emit almost no greenhouse gases, why are they not included in green energy and green jobs plans?

11. Do you know what a "green job" is? The government does not.

12. Green jobs advocates consistently claim that green jobs will pay above average. Since many green jobs are no different from ordinary jobs, such as secretaries, project managers, and such, why are these individuals paid a premium wage for doing such jobs that simply have something to do with environmental matters?

13. If every new car or truck bought in the next five years had the new technology proposed for them, what percentage of the U.S. fleet would have the new technology? What impact would that have on the environment?

14. How much per-unit gain (reduced carbon emissions, etc.) does this program cost? How does it compare to alternative uses of the money?

15. What interest rate is being paid on the borrowed funds used for this project? How was that rate chosen?

16. How will borrowed funds for green energy/green jobs projects be repaid if they have negative rates of return?

17. If a project claims a payback period of less than 10 years, why has it not already been done? What prevented people from choosing to accomplish this on their own?

18. Most green jobs projects require union scale to be paid. That eliminates many companies from competing for green energy

and jobs grants. Why not allow open competition for such projects?

19. Do you believe that trade with foreign nations should be limited as part of green jobs programs, as is often advocated? That is, why should they have "buy American" provisions?

20. If you think we should "buy American," should wind farms built in the United States be allowed to purchase wind turbine technology from foreign producers?

21. Prime locations for wind turbines are in places such as the coast of California. Since those who oppose looking at turbines can tie up proposed projects in court for years, do you support ending procedures that allow opponents to block construction of new wind projects and new power lines?

22. Senator Diane Feinstein of California proposes making huge areas of California desert off-limits from solar panel sites for electricity. Do you agree that construction of renewable power sources should be prohibited wherever some people oppose construction? Do you know of locations where people are lobbying in favor of construction?

23. Some green energy/green jobs advocates, focusing on reducing carbon emissions, recommend forcing people to live in high density cities to reduce reliance on cars. Do you favor such forced reorganization of where people live?

24. Why is the "smart grid" project called smart when it is agreed that it will result in higher electricity bills?

25. Do you have any estimates of the average cost of a so-called "green job" that is paid for by taxpayers? In Europe, the costs have been in the hundreds of thousands of dollars per job created to create overpriced electricity. How does that benefit taxpayers?

26. Since so-called renewable electricity—such as from solar or wind—costs much more than regular electricity, how can U.S. manufacturers stay competitive with companies that produce in other countries not burdened by such costly projects?

27. Green jobs proponents assert that government must pay for insulation and other energy-saving improvements on property because private property owners do not recognize the value of such improvements. Do you think property owners are too

dumb to realize the value of energy-saving improvements and, if they are, should taxpayers pay for such things?

28. Is it sensible for Americans to be forced to pay for expensive vehicles that use costly fuel sources to reduce emissions a miniscule amount if the rest of the world is rapidly adding to their vehicle fleets?

29. Since there is no evidence that the net environmental cost of mass transit systems, such as the light rail system in Portland, is lower than if the riders drove cars, what is the justification for forcing taxpayers to cover such expensive projects that cannot be commercially successful?

30. While new intercity train routes are much in vogue, they are incredibly costly and cannot be supported by passengers, and they produce more carbon emissions than do bus systems. Why should we not rely on more cost-effective and environment-friendly bus systems to move people from city to city?

Conclusion

To attempt to transform modern society on the scale proposed by even the most modest bits of the green jobs and green energy literature, such as the Conference of Mayors report, is an effort of staggering complexity and scale. To do so with borrowed money, based on the combination of wishful thinking and bad economics embodied in the green energy and green jobs literature, would be the height of irresponsibility. We have no doubt that there will be significant opportunities to develop new energy sources, new industries, and new jobs in the future. Just as has been true for all of human history thus far, as we have shown in this book, we are equally confident that a market-based discovery process will do a far better job of developing those energy sources, industries, and jobs than could a series of mandates based on imperfect information and faulty assumptions about the environment and economy.

Notes

Chapter 1

1. Roger Meiners et al., "Green Jobs Myths," *Missouri Environmental Law and Policy Review* 16 (2009): 326; Roger Meiners et al., "Seven Myths about Green Jobs," *PERC Policy Series* 44 (2009). Both available at http://papers.ssrn.com/sol3/papers .cfm?abstract_id=1357440.

2. Chapter 6 incorporates, updates, and expands upon our earlier article: Roger Meiners et al., "Advocating Autarky: A Flaw in Green Jobs Policy Proposals as They Pertain to Renewable Energy," *Texas Journal of Oil, Gas, & Energy Law* 5 (2010): 155.

3. Robert Bradley and Richard Fulmer, *Energy: The Master Resource* (Dubuque, IA: Kendall/Hunt, 2004).

4. Kenneth Green and Aparna Mathur, "Measuring and Reducing Americans' Indirect Energy Use," *AEI Energy and Environment Outlook* 2 (December 2008); Kenneth Green and Aparna Mathur, "Indirect Energy and Your Wallet," *AEI Energy and Environment Outlook* 2 (March 2009).

5. Ibid., p. 1.

6. See, e.g., Mathis Wackemagel and William E. Rees, *Our Ecological Footprint: Reducing the Human Impact on the Earth* (Gabriela Island, BC: New Society Publishers, 1996).

7. U.S. Energy Information Administration, "U.S. Energy Consumption by Energy Source, 2004–2008," http://www.eia.doe.gov/cneaf/alternate/page/renew_energy_ consump/table1.html.

8. Ibid.

9. For a list of Not In My Back Yard (NIMBY) energy projects, state by state, including dozens of wind farms, see *Project No Project*, sponsored by the U.S. Chamber of Commerce, http://pnp.uschamber.com/.

10. While the EIA figures we cite do not break out oil and natural gas separately for capacity, the overwhelming majority of electricity generated from those sources comes from natural gas. EIA does break these out in its energy consumption analysis, and there it shows use of over 5 quadrillion BTU of natural gas and just 1.18 quadrillion BTU of all liquid fuels for 2009, including LPG, kerosene, and distillate fuel oil. U.S. Energy Information Administration, "Annual Energy Outlook 2010," Table 2, http://www.eia.doe.gov/oiaf/aeo/aeoref_tab.html.

11. U.S. Energy Information Administration, *Annual Energy Review 2008* (Washington: Energy Information Administration, 2009), pp. 68–71, http://www.eia.doe.gov/ aer/pdf/aer.pdf.

12. Eric Onstad, "BP Drops Plans for UK Wind Farms – Paper," *Reuters*, November 6, 2008, http://www.reuters.com/article/rbssEnergyNews/idUSL731612820081107.

13. Ed Wallace, "The Great Ethanol Scam," *Business Week*, May 14, 2009, http:// www.businessweek.com/lifestyle/content/may2009/bw20090514_058678.htm.

14. Ibid.

15. Problems with biodiesel include increased NO_x emissions, slight decreases in fuel economy and power, and limited availability of biodiesel. Scott Hess, "How Biodiesel Works: The Cons," Howstuffworks.com, June 18, 2003, http://auto.how-stuffworks.com/fuel-efficiency/alternative-fuels/biodiesel4.htm.

16. See, e.g., Samuel Jackson, "Biodiesel: A Primer," Office of Bioenergy Programs, University of Tennessee Extension, http://www.utextension.utk.edu/publications/spfiles/SP700-C.pdf.

17. Data from U.S. Energy Information Administration, "Residential Energy Consumption Survey," http://www.eia.doe.gov/emeu/recs/recs97/contents.html.

18. "Group Faults Al Gore on Environmental Claims," NPR, *All Things Considered*, February 28, 2007, http://www.npr.org/templates/story/story.php?storyId=7648708.

19. "Despite Home Upgrades, Gore Still 'Hypocrite' on Energy Usage, Group Says," *Nashville City Paper*, June 18, 2008, http://www.nashvillecitypaper.com/content/city-news/despite-home-upgrades-gore-still-%E2%80%98hypocrite%E2%80%99-energy-usage-group-says.

20. National Resources Defense Council, "How to Reduce Your Energy Consumption," http://www.nrdc.org/air/energy/genergy/easy.asp.

21. John Funk, "FirstEnergy Corp. Unsure of Next Step after Light Bulb Uproar," *Plain Dealer (Cleveland)*, October 10, 2009.

22. Ohio Department of Development, "Ohio Energy Efficient Appliance Rebate Program," http://www.ohioappliancerebate.com.

23. The costs are high and the environmental benefits are not as much as expected. See Anselm Waldermann, "Wind Turbines in Europe Do Nothing for Emissions-Reduction Goal," *Spiegel Online*, February 10, 2009, http://www.spiegel.de/international/business/0,1518,606763,00.html.

24. See Linda R. Cohen and Roger G. Noll, *The Technology Porkbarrel* (Washington: Brookings Institution Press, 1991), pp. 259–320 (describing the synfuels program and concluding it had an "almost farcical economic basis").

25. Elizabeth Williamson and Paul Glader, "GE Pursues Pot of Government Stimulus Gold," *Wall Street Journal*, November 17, 2009, http://online.wsj.com/article/SB125832961253649563.html.

26. Progressive Automobile X Prize, http://www.progressiveautoxprize.org. For the use of prizes as incentives, see Jonathan H. Adler, "Eyes on a Climate Prize: Rewarding Energy Innovation to Achieve Climate Stabilization" (presented at Rethinking the Foundations of Climate Change Law and Policy, University of Pennsylvania School of Law, October 23, 2009).

27. Edward H. Crane and Carl Pope, "Fueled by Pork" *Washington Post*, July 30, 2002, http://www.cato.org/pub_display.php?pub_id=4090.

28. The White House proposed developing energy performance labels for homes and standardized home energy performance measures in October 2009. See Executive Office of the President of the United States, Middle Class Task Force Council on Environmental Quality, "Recovery through Retrofit," pp. 5–6, http://www.whitehouse.gov/assets/documents/Recovery_Through_Retrofit_Final_Report.pdf.

29. The Department of Energy announced the L Prize to create a better 60 watt light bulb. James Brodrick, "The Race is On for DOE's L Prize," *NEMA Electroindustry*, February 2009, http://apps1.eere.energy.gov/buildings/publications/pdfs/ssl/nema-ei-lprize_02-09.pdf.

30. One honest green technology advocate is Ted Trainer, who argues that "renewable energy cannot sustain a consumer society" in his book *Renewable Energy Cannot Sustain a Consumer Society* (Dordrecht, Netherlands: Springer, 2007).

31. http://www.merriam-webster.com/dictionary/green-collar; Maura Judkis, "Merriam-Webster Adds Green Words to Dictionary," *US News and World Report*, July 1, 2009, http://www.usnews.com/money/blogs/fresh-greens/2009/07/13/merriam-webster-adds-green-words-to-dictionary.html.

32. Edith C. Stein, *The Environmental Sourcebook* (New York: Lyons and Burford, 1992), gives an overview of materials related to "green" nonprofits, companies, and investment funds resulting from the "frenzy" of Earth Day.

33. Nicholas Basta, *Environmental Jobs for Scientists and Engineers* (New York: Wiley, 1992), p. v; see also Nicholas Basta, *The Environmental Career Guide* (New York: Wiley, 1991).

34. Basta, *Environmental Jobs*, p. v. He estimated 3.5 million green-collar jobs in 1992 and at least 7 million by 2000.

35. Ibid., p. 28.

36. Ibid., pp. 155–56.

37. Alan Thein Durning, "7 Sustainable Wonders," *USA Today Magazine*, July 1995.

38. Alan Thein Durning, *Green Collar Jobs: Working in the New Northwest* (Seattle: Northwest Environment Watch, 1999).

39. Ibid., p. 91.

40. Alan Thein Durning, *Cascadia Scorecard 2005: Focus on Energy* (Seattle: Northwest Environment Watch, 2005).

41. "Wired in the Woods," *The Economist*, July 31, 1999. "These new 'green-collar' jobs (Mr. Durning's phrase) should be every economic planner's dream."

42. Gerry Gray, "Green Collar Jobs: An Opportunity for Environmentalists and Economists Alike," *American Forests* 45 (2009): 43–44; jobs listed on p. 6 of Executive Summary. At http://bss.sfsu.edu/raquelrp/.

43. "California Green Corps: Putting Federal Economic Stimulus Dollars to Work Training California's Youth to Excel in Emerging Green Jobs," Office of the Governor Fact Sheet, March 16, 2009, http://gov.ca.gov/index.php?/fact-sheet/11753/.

44. California Energy Commission, "California's Appliance Efficiency Program," http://www.energy.ca.gov/appliances/.

45. United States Conference of Mayors, *U.S. Metro Economies: Current and Potential Green Jobs in the U.S. Economy* (Lexington, MA: Global Insight, 2008), http://www.usmayors.org/pressreleases/uploads/greenjobsreport.pdf.

46. Van Jones, *The Green-Collar Economy: How One Solution Can Fix our Two Biggest Problems* (New York: Harper Collins, 2008), pp. 165–70. But see: http://www.chicagoreader.com/TheBlog/archives/2009/09/03/the-green-mayors-green-policy-maker-is-leaving-for-vancouver. This blog claims Mayor Daley's environmental accomplishments are "mixed" and in jeopardy because Seattle has hired his environmental adviser.

47. Davis Gonzalez, "Greening the Bronx, One Castoff at a Time," *New York Times*, April 21, 2008, http://www.nytimes.com/2008/04/21/nyregion/21citywide.html.

48. Cynthia Gordy, Brentin Mock, and Regina R. Robertson, "The Green Awards," *Essence*, May 2009, p. 131. Other green economy advocates are also featured.

49. Van Jones, see note 46, pp. 165–70.

50. Gordy, Mock, and Robertson, see note 48, p. 130.

51. Van Jones, see note 46, p. v.

52. Scott Wilson and Garance Franke-Ruta, "White House Advisor Van Jones Resigns amid Controversy over Past Activism," *Washington Post*, September 6, 2009, http://voices.washingtonpost.com/44/2009/09/06/van_jones_resigns.html.

53. Van Jones, see note 46, pp. 84–88.

54. Ibid., p. 145.

55. Ibid., pp. 146–49.

56. Ibid., pp. 160–61.

57. Office of Hilda Solis, "House Committee Passes Solis' Green Jobs Act," Press Release, http://solis.house.gov/list/press/ca32_solis/wida6/greenjobscomm.shtml.

58. Ibid.

59. George W. Bush, "Remarks on Signing the Energy Independence and Security Act of 2007," Weekly Compilation of Presidential Documents, 2007, p. 1612. In his previous State of the Union address, President Bush had joined the chorus of recent presidents (starting with President Nixon) saying that America is addicted to oil.

60. Advocacy groups were disappointed that only $22.5 million was appropriated for green jobs training for fiscal year 2009. Goodwill Industries International Correspondence, "Green Jobs Act," June 2008, http://www.goodwill.org/c/document_library/get_file?folderId=1142299&name=DLFE-11505.pdf. The Recovery Act added $500 million to the original $50 million budgeted for green jobs training in FY 2010. http://www.dol.gov/opa/media/press/oasam/OASAM20090489.htm.

61. Margaret Kriz, "Shades of Green," *National Journal*, June 21, 2008, http://www.nationaljournal.com/njmagazine/nj_20080621_6762.php.

62. Barack Obama Campaign, "Barack Obama and Joe Biden: New Energy for America," www.barackobama.com/pdf/factsheet_energy_speech_080308.pdf. For a scientific analysis of various clean energy technologies as of 2008, see Trevor M. Letcher, ed., *Future Energy: Improved, Sustainable, and Clean Options for our Planet* (Oxford: Elsevier, 2008).

63. Bureau of Labor Statistics, "Occupational Employment Statistics (OES) Highlights: Jobs for the Environment," http://www.bls.gov/oes/highlight_environment.htm.

64. Linda Levine, "Job Loss and Infrastructure Job Creation Spending During the Recession," Congressional Research Service Report for Congress R40080 (2009), p. 4. "Although numerous studies on the emerging green economy have been released in the last several years, no consistent definition of green jobs exists at present."

65. Ibid., p. 10.

66. CAP's web page states it was founded in 2003 "to provide long-term leadership and support to the progressive movement" and to "develop new policy ideas, critique the policy that stems from conservative values, challenge the media to cover the issues that truly matter and shape the national debate." Center for American Progress, "About the Center for American Progress," http://www.americanprogress.org/aboutus. On energy, CAP says it is "pioneering progressive, 21st century policy proposals to transform our nation and our economy in ways that protect the global environment, boost global prosperity, and create sustainable sources of clean energy to reduce the world's reliance on dirty, carbon-based energy. Our low-carbon policy priorities encourage comprehensive upgrades in the efficiency of energy production and consumption as well as environmentally safe and sustainable energy diversification. And our commitment to sound scientific energy and environmental technology innovation exemplifies progressive ideals and pragmatism at work." Center for American Progress, "Where We Stand on Energy and the Environment," http://

www.americanprogress.org/issues/energy. Major CAP individual funders include such stalwarts of the left as George Soros, Peter Lewis, and Herbert Sandler (who was memorably lampooned for profiting from selling $122 billion of adjustable rate mortgages to Wachovia in 2006 during the financial crisis by a *Saturday Night Live* sketch, which NBC later edited to remove the Sandler reference after Sandler complained to NBC. "Former Golden West CEO Herb Sandler Speaks Out," *KTVU.com*, October 5, 2008, http://www.ktvu.com/news/17630347/detail.html; SourceWatch, "Center for American Progress," http://www.sourcewatch.org/index.php?title=Center_for_American_Progress. It is also heavily funded by Wal-Mart.

67. Levine, see note 64, pp. 11–12. For example, even the most well-run and well-intentioned state program that retrains unemployed workers to weatherize houses may be overwhelmed if its budget were instantly increased from $100,000 per year to $1,000,000 per year.

Chapter 2

1. United Nations Environment Programme, *Green Jobs: Towards Decent Work in a Sustainable, Low-Carbon World* (Nairobi: U.N. Publishing Services Section, 2008), http://www.unep.org/labour_environment/PDFs/Greenjobs/UNEP-Green-Jobs-Report.pdf.

2. Alister Doyle, "Science Academies Urge 50 Percent CO_2 Cut by 2050," *Reuters,* June 9, 2008, http://www.reuters.com/article/environmentNews/idUSL0911742120080610.

3. "State Laws Set Bold Pace for Large Carbon Cuts," *U.S. PIRG Citizen Agenda*, Summer 2007, http://www.uspirg.org/html/newsletters/summer07/topstory.html. Noting that the 80 percent goal has been signed into law in New Jersey and endorsed by other politicians, including the Republican governor of Florida.

4. UNFP, p. 3.

5. Ibid., p. 5.

6. Ibid.

7. Ibid., p. 83.

8. Ibid., p. 77.

9. Ibid., p. 78.

10. Ibid., p. 6.

11. Ibid., p. 131.

12. Ibid.

13. Ibid., p. 12.

14. Ibid., pp. 12–14.

15. Ibid., p. 149.

16. Ibid., p. 151.

17. Ibid., p. 152.

18. Ibid.

19. Ibid., pp. 14, 167.

20. Ibid., p. 13.

21. Ibid., pp. 14–18.

22. Ibid., p. 219.

23. Ibid., p. 242.

24. Ibid., pp. 216–17 (describing Egyptian "Zabaleen" or informal garbage collectors and South Asian ship dismantlers).

25. Ibid., p. 40.

26. Ibid., p. 19.

27. Ibid.

28. Ibid.

29. Ibid., pp. 19–20.

30. Ibid., p. 19.

31. Ibid., pp. 19–20.

32. Ibid., p. 19.

33. Ibid., pp.19–21.

34. Ibid., p. 20.

35. Ibid., p. 22.

36. Ibid.

37. Ibid., p. 23.

38. Ibid., p. 24.

39. Most measured technological progress has occurred in about the last 200 years, and much of it has to do, one way or another, with increases in efficiency.

40. Paul L. Joskow, "Energy Policies and Their Consequences after 25 Years," *Energy Journal* (October 2003): 17, 37.

41. Ibid.

42. This is referred to as the Jevons Paradox—as efficiency in energy use increases, production costs drop, the economy grows, thereby allowing consumers to purchase more goods, which increases the demand for energy. See John Polimeni et al., *The Jevons Paradox and the Myth of Resource Efficiency Improvements* (London: Earthscan, 2008).

43. See, for example, Paul R. Ehrlich, *The Population Bomb* (New York: Ballantine Books, 1968); William Paddock, *Famine, 1975!: America's Decision: Who Will Survive?* (Boston: Little, Brown, 1967).

44. Joskow, see note 40. For a scholarly history of oil, see Morris R. Adelman, *The Genie Is out of the Bottle* (Cambridge, MA: The MIT Press, 1995).

45. Short-run price fluctuations are often confused with the prospect of long-term energy shortages. Worry that we will "run out" of coal, oil, or other major energy sources has been a constant theme in scholarly and popular literature for more than a century. For a balanced discussion of this issue, and why we are not about to grind to an economic halt due to a collapse of supplies, see the many works by the distinguished Canadian researcher Vaclav Smil, such as *Energy in Nature and Society* (Cambridge, MA: The MIT Press, 2008).

46. Fred Sissine, "Energy Efficiency: Budget, Oil Conservation, and Electricity Conservation Issues," CRS Issue Brief for Congress, Congressional Research Service Report No. IB10020, 2006, https://www.policyarchive.org/bitstream/handle/10207/744/IB10020_20060120.pdf?sequence=23.

47. Paul L. Joskow and Donald B. Marron, "What Does a Negawatt Really Cost? Evidence from Utility Conservation Programs," *Energy Journal* 13(4) (1992): 41. A more recent study on this is David Loughran and Jonathan Kulick, "Demand-Side Management and Energy Efficiency in the United States," *Energy Journal* 25(1) (2004): 19. A rebuttal to this may be found in Maximilian Auffhammer et al., "Demand-Side Management and Energy Efficiency Revisited," *Energy Journal* 29(2) (2008): 91.

48. Scott Carson, "How Boeing Fights Climate Change," *Wall Street Journal*, May 23, 2009, http://online.wsj.com/article/SB124303177241948493.html.

49. Federal Reserve Bank of Dallas, *The New Paradigm: 1999 Annual Report* (Dallas: Federal Reserve Bank of Dallas, 2009), http://www.dallasfed.org/fed/annual/1999p/ar99.pdf.

50. Ibid., p. 14.

51. Ibid., p. 12.

52. Peter Lund Simmonds, *Waste Products and Undeveloped Substances; or, Hints for Enterprise in Neglected Fields* (London: Robert Hardwicke, 1862).

53. Karl Marx, *Capital: A Critique of Political Economy: Vol. III – Pt. I*, ed. Friedrich Engels (New York: Cosimo Classics, 2007), pp. 120–21.

54. Pierre Desrochers, "Did the Invisible Hand Need a Regulatory Glove to Develop a Green Thumb?" *Environmental and Resource Economics* 41 (2008): 519, 526.

55. Pierre Desrochers, "By-product Development before the Modern Environmental Era," *Enterprise and Society* 8 (2007): 353–54.

56. See Tables 2.1 and 2.2; see also Jesse H. Ausubel, "Technical Progress and Climate Change," *Energy Policy* 23 (1995): 411–16.

57. Roger Fouquet and Peter J.G. Pearson, "Long Run Trends in Energy Services, 1300–2000" (Fiji: Center for Environmental Policy, University of the South Pacific, Fiji, Working Paper, 2005): 11, http://www.webmeets.com/files/papers/ERE/WC3/154/HisEnS10.pdf.

58. Ibid., p. 1

59. UNEP, see note 4, p. 49 (higher energy and materials productivity is "particularly critical" in industries like steel that consume a great deal of energy and natural resources).

60. Ibid., p. 15. If the steel market was uncompetitive, major steel makers around the world would not have collapsed over the years, and, more recently, prices would not have plunged during the recession in 2008. Monopolists keep control of markets and prices.

61. American Iron and Steel Institute, "US Steel Industry: World Leaders in Energy Efficiency," http://www.steel.org/AM/Template.cfm?Section=Environment1&CONTENTID=21986&TEMPLATE=/CM/ContentDisplay.cfm.

62. U.S. Environmental Protection Agency, *Energy Trends in Selected Manufacturing Sectors: Opportunities and Challenges for Environmentally Preferable Energy Outcomes* (Washington: Environmental Protection Agency, 2007), pp. 3–53 to 3–54, http://www.epa.gov/sustainableindustry/pdf/energy/report.pdf.

63. William T. Choate and John A.S. Green, *U.S. Energy Requirements for Aluminum Production: Historical Perspective, Theoretical Limits and New Opportunities* (Columbia, MD: BCS Corporation for U.S. Department of Energy, 2003), Appendix B, p. B-1, http://www.secat.net/docs/resources/US_Energy_Requirements_for_Aluminum_Production.pdf.

64. Ibid., p. 59.

65. Ibid., Appendix L.

66. Ibid.

67. This isn't just your mother's household cleanser; in 2006, 146.5 million tons were produced, as it is a common ingredient in a wide range of products. "Ammonia – Wikipedia: The Free Encyclopedia," http://en.wikipedia.org/wiki/Ammonia.

68. International Fertilizer Industry Association, *Energy Efficiency and CO_2 Emissions in Ammonia Production* (Paris: International Fertilizer Association, 2009), p. 2, http://www.fertilizer.org/ifa/Home-Page/LIBRARY/Publication-database.html/Energy-Efficiency-and-CO2-Emissions-in-Ammonia-Production.html.

69. Ibid.

70. International Energy Agency, *Worldwide Trends in Energy Use and Efficiency: Key Insights from IEA Indicator Analysis* (Paris: International Energy Agency, 2008), p. 35, http://www.iea.org/Textbase/Papers/2008/Indicators_2008.pdf.

71. Ibid.

72. Ibid., p. 37.

73. Jonathan Remy Nash and Richard L. Revesz, "Grandfathering and Environmental Regulation: The Law and Economics of New Source Review," *Northwestern University Law Review* 101 (2007): 1691, 1692, 1694, 1708–1712; Bruce Yandle, "Public Choice and the Environment," in *Political Environmentalism,* ed. Terry L. Anderson (Stanford: Hoover Institution Press, 2000).

74. International Energy Agency, *Energy Labels and Standards* (Paris: International Energy Agency, 2000), p. 107, http://www.iea.org/textbase/nppdf/free/2000/label2000. pdf; California Energy Resources Conservation and Development Commission, *Regulations for Appliance Efficiency Standards Relating to Refrigerators, Refrigerator-Freezers and Freezers* (Sacramento, CA: California Energy Commission, 1977), http://www.energy .ca.gov/appliances/appl_regs_1976-1992/1977_12_22_Appl_Regs.pdf.

75. Lawrence Berkeley National Laboratory, U.S. Department of Energy, "Energy Efficiency Standards: The Standard Setting Process," http://ees.ead.lbl.gov/ node/2; *National Appliance Energy Conservation Act of 1987.* Public Law 100-12, 101 Stat. 103 (1987).

76. Ibid.; see also IEA, see note 74, pp. 173–75; Senate Report no. 100-6, reprinted in U.S.C.C.A.N., 100th Cong., 1st Sess., vol. 2, pp. 52–54.

77. Building Technology Program, U.S. Department of Energy, "Appliances and Commercial Equipment Standards: History of Federal Appliance Standards," http:// www1.eere.energy.gov/buildings/appliance_standards/history.html; Weatherization Assistance Program Technical Assistance Center, "Weatherization Program Notice 00-5," http://www.waptac.org/sp.asp?id=6897; Lawrence Berkeley National Laboratory, "Energy Efficiency Standards"; see also Energy Conservation Standards, Public Law no. 100-12, section 3 (amending section 322(a) of the Energy Policy and Conservation Act, 42 U.S.C. 6292(a)(1)-(13)).

78. Building Technology Program, Weatherization Assistance Program Technical Assistance Center, 42 U.S.C. 6292(a)(4) (water heaters).

79. Building Technology Program, Weatherization Assistance Program Technical Assistance Center, Energy Conservation Standards, Public Law 100-12, Section 5.

80. Building Technology Program, Energy Policy Act of 1992, Public Law 102-486, 106 Stat. 2776 (1992).

81. Ibid.

82. Building Technology Program; Preemption of State Regulations (Energy Conservation Program for Consumer Products), 10 C.F.R. 430.33 (2009).

83. U.S. Energy Information Administration, Appendix A, Table A4, "Annual Energy Outlook 2010," http://www.eia.doe.gov/oiaf/aeo/aeoref_tab.html.

84. Mark Ellis et al., "Do Energy Efficient Appliances Cost More?" (Conference proceeding of European Council for an Energy Efficient Economy 2007 Summer Study: Saving Energy—Just Do It! 2007): 1129, http://www.leonardo-energy.org/drupal/node/4038; IEA *Energy Labels and Standards,* pp. 107–08.

85. IEA, see note 74, p. 108.

86. U.S. Energy Information Administration, *Annual Energy Review 2008* (Washington: Energy Information Administration, 2009), p. xxiv, Figure 20, http://www.eia. doe.gov/aer/pdf/aer.pdf.

87. W.J. Spencer and T.E. Seidel, "International Technology Roadmaps: The U.S. Semiconductor Experience," in *Productivity and Cyclicality in Semiconductors: Trends, Implications, and Questions—Report of a Symposium,* eds. Dale W. Jorgenson and Charles

W. Wessner (National Academies Press, 2004); Nadejda M. Victor and Jesse H. Ausubel, "DRAMs as Model Organisms for Study of Technological Evolution," *Technology Forecasting and Social Change* 69 (2002): 243–62.

88. See, e.g., Association of Home Appliance Manufacturers, "Appliance Milestones," http://www.aham.org/consumer/ht/a/GetDocumentAction/id/1408; Electrolux International Company, "History of Frigidaire," http://www.frigidaire-intl.com/history.asp; see also Frigidaire Company, "Frigidaire: 85th Anniversary," http://www.frigidaire.com.hk/download/~Frigidaire%20history%20-%2085th%20anniversary%202004.pdf.

89. IEA, see note 74, p. 109.

90. IEA, see note 70, p. 15.

91. Almost 150 years ago, the noted economist William Stanley Jevons predicted the demise of the British economy within a generation due to an impending coal shortage: W. Stanley Jevons, *The Coal Question* 3rd ed. (London: Macmillan, 1906). Jevons has been followed by many doomsayers since his day. See, among many others, Harold Hotelling, "The Economics of Exhaustible Resources," *Journal of Political Economy* 39 (1931); Amory Lovins, "Energy Strategy: The Road Not Taken?" *Foreign Affairs* 55 (1976); and John Holdren, "Energy in Transition," *Scientific American* (September 1990). The belief that Cassandra knows the energy future and that it can, therefore, best be managed by strict government management of resources under the guidance of skilled professionals at the behest of political leaders seems to be a perpetual academic and policy folly that we consider in more depth in the following chapters.

Chapter 3

1. Kristin Choo, "The War of Winds," *ABA Journal*, February 2010, http://www.abajournal.com/magazine/article/the_war_of_winds/.

2. The Cape Wind project was approved by Secretary of the Interior Ken Salazar in April 2010, but more legal challenges remain. Katherine Q. Seelye, "Big Wind Farm off Cape Cod Gets Approval," *New York Times* (April 28, 2010), http://www.nytimes.com/2010/04/29/science/earth/29wind.html?hp.

3. Choo, see note 1.

4. Malcolm Keay, "CO_2 Emissions Reduction: Time for a Reality Check?" *Oxford Institute. for Energy Studies* (2005), http://www.oxfordenergy.org/comment.php?0502.

5. See Friends of the Earth, American Rivers, and Trout Unlimited, *Dam Removal Success Stories* (Friends of the Earth, American Rivers, and Trout Unlimited, 1999), http://sunsite2.berkeley.edu/wrca/damremoval/documents/DRSuccessStories1999.pdf; Greg Pahl, *The Citizen Powered Energy Handbook: Community Solutions to a Global Crisis* (White River, VT: Chelsea Green, 2007).

6. U.S. Energy Information Administration, *Annual Energy Review 2008* (Washington: Energy Information Administration, 2009), Table 6.4h, http://www.eia.doe.gov/aer/pdf/aer.pdf.

7. U.S. Department of Energy, *20% Wind Energy by 2030: Increasing Wind Energy's Contribution to U.S. Electricity Supply* (Oak Ridge, TN: Department of Energy, 2008), p. 13, http://www.nrel.gov/docs/fy08osti/41869.pdf.

8. Dan Charles, "Renewables Test IQ of Grid," *Science* 324 (April 2009): 172–75.

9. Center for Politiske Studier, *Wind Energy: The Case of Denmark* (Copenhagen: Center for Politiske Studier, 2009), p. 2, http://www.cepos.dk/fileadmin/user_upload/Arkiv/PDF/Wind_energy_-_the_case_of_Denmark.pdf.

10. Renewable Energy Foundation, *Response to Department of Energy and Climate Change* (London: Renewable Energy Foundation, 2009), pp. 6–7.

11. EIA, "Annual Energy Outlook 2010," Table 117. This report, issued each year, provides the Departmernt of Energy's best estimate of future supply and demand for the energy sector, based on its judgments about economic growth, labor supply, technological change, and so forth. It "generally assumes that current laws and regulations affecting the energy sector remain unchanged" throughout the projection period (2030 for this document). In this respect, it differs from the Department of Energy study cited previously (DOE, *20% Wind Energy by 2030*), which is an analysis of the consequences of meeting a target for wind energy to increase to 20 percent its contribution to total electricity generation. On the importance of subsidies, see Jeffrey Ball, "Clean Energy Sources: Sun, Wind, and Subsidies," *Wall Street Journal,* January 15, 2010, http://online.wsj.com/article/SB126290539750320495.html (quoting the CEO of Dong Energy, a Danish company building wind power plants: "Without [subsidies, wind plants] won't work").

12. EIA forecasts 15.8 percent of U.S. electricity will come from all renewables in 2030; 20 percent of 15.8 percent is 3.16 percent. See U.S. Energy Information Administration, "Energy in Brief," April 22, 2009, http://tonto.eia.doe.gov/energy_in_brief/renewable_energy.cfm.

13. U.S. Energy Information Administration, *Monthly Energy Review: December 2008* (Washington: Energy Information Administration, 2008), http://tonto.eia.doe.gov/FTPROOT/multifuel/mer/00350812.pdf.

14. EIA, see note 6, Tables 1 and 17.

15. Electric Reliability Council of Texas, "Report on the Capacity, Demand, and Reserves in the ERCOT Region, May 2008." See also Drew Thornley, *Texas Wind Energy: Past, Present, and Future* (Austin: Texas Public Policy Foundation, 2008), p. 3, http://www.texaspolicy.com/pdf/2008-09-RR10-WindEnergy-dt-new.pdf.

16. Massachusetts Technology Collaborative, "Small Wind Progress Briefing Summary," June 12, 2008, http://www.masstech.org/RenewableEnergy/sm_renew/Progress%20Briefing%20Summary%2061208.pdf.

17. This is more than a problem of people shivering in the cold or sweltering in the summer when the power goes off. Hospitals must have constant, reliable power. People who use electric-powered oxygen machines or ventilators require reliable power. "Britain's wind farms have stopped working during the cold snap due to lack of wind, it has emerged, as scientists claimed half the world's energy could soon be from renewables. The Met Office said there has been an unusually long period of high pressure across the UK for the last couple of weeks, causing the cold snap and very little wind." Louise Gray, "Wind Energy Supply Dips during Cold Snap," *Daily Telegraph,* January 10, 2009, http://www.telegraph.co.uk/earth/energy/windpower/4208940/Wind-energy-supply-dips-during-cold-snap.html.

18. Matthew Wald, "The Energy Challenge: Wind Energy Bumps Into Power Grid's Limits," *New York Times,* August 29, 2008, http://www.nytimes.com/2008/08/27/business/27grid.html?_r=1&pagewanted=print.

19. DOE, see note 7, pp. 95, 98.

20. Jonathan H. Adler, "Foul Winds for Renewable Energy," *National Review Online,* September 28, 2007, http://article.nationalreview.com/?q=Mjg1YWVjNDZjZTBkNDhlODUzZjVkZThmM2U0YjAwNjE=#more. The Cape Wind farm has some regulatory approvals after years of planning—are all such permit requirements to be swept aside? It was proposed in 2001; by early 2009, it only had some permits but was

not done yet. *Cape Wind: America's First Wind Farm on Nantucket Sound*, http://www. capewind.org/. These rapid growth rates are assumed to be capable of transforming the economy at large as well. "[T]he creation of green employment in key parts of the economy has the potential to 'radiate' across large swaths of the economy, thus greening commensurately large sections of the total workforce. For example, providing clean energy supplies means that any economic activity has far less environmental impact than today, when fuels and electricity are still produced largely from dirty sources." United Nations Environment Programme, *Green Jobs: Towards Decent Work in a Sustainable, Low-Carbon World* (Nairobi: U.N. Publishing Services Section, 2008), p. 300, http://www.unep.org/labour_environment/PDFs/Greenjobs/UNEP-Green-Jobs-Report.pdf.

21. See United States Conference of Mayors, *U.S. Metro Economies: Current and Potential Green Jobs in the U.S. Economy* (Lexington, MA: Global Insight, 2008), pp. 6–7, http://www.usmayors.org/pressreleases/uploads/greenjobsreport.pdf, regarding high costs; Tom Wright, "India Windmill Empire Begins to Show Cracks," *Wall Street Journal*, April 18, 2008, http://online.wsj.com/article/SB120846287761023921. html; Michael Connellan, "Spinning to Destruction," *Guardian*, September 4, 2008, http://www.guardian.co.uk/technology/2008/sep/04/energy.engineering (Danish government requires mandatory service checks on all windmills in country after cracking problems develop); U.S. Energy Information Administration, "Renewable Energy Consumption and Electricity Preliminary 2007 Statistics," May 2008, http://www.eia.doe.gov/cneaf/alternate/page/renew_energy_consump/reec_080514. pdf; see Table 3 of the report for details of electricity generation from renewable sources.

22. State Energy Conservation Office, "Texas Renewable Energy Resource Assessment 2008," Chapter 4: "Wind Energy," http://www.seco.cpa.state.tx.us/publications/renewenergy/windenergy.php.

23. Ibid.

24. *See supra* tbl.1.

25. EIA, *Annual Review 2006*, Tables 2 and 17.

26. Ibid., Table 17.

27. Ibid., Tables 1 and 17.

28. Severin Borenstein, "The Market Value and Cost of Solar Photovoltaic Electricity Production" (Center for the Study of Energy Markets, Working Paper no. 176, 2008), http://www.ucei.berkeley.edu/PDF/csemwp176.pdf; Borenstein, "Response to Critiques of 'The Market Value and Cost of Solar Photovoltaic Electricity Production,'" http://faculty.haas.berkeley.edu/borenste/SolarResponse.pdf.

29. Ibid.

30. Ibid.

31. Ibid., p. 26.

32. Richard S.J. Tol, "The Social Cost of Carbon: Trends, Outliers and Catastrophes," *Economics: The Open-Access Open-Assessment E-Journal* (August 12, 2008): 9–10, http://www.economics-ejournal.org/economics/journalarticles/2008-25/view.

33. Borenstein, Response, see note 28, p. 1.

34. Borenstein, "Market Value," see note 28, p. 24.

35. See U.S. Energy Information Administration, "Total Electric Power Industry Summary Statistics," http://www.eia.doe.gov/cneaf/electricity/epm/tablees1a.html.

36. Jesse H. Ausubel, "Renewable and Nuclear Heresies," *International Journal of Nuclear Governance, Economics and Ecology* 1 (2007): 229–43.

37. France leads among larger nations at nearly 80 percent of power from nuclear sources. World Nuclear Association, "Nuclear Power in the World Today," March 2009, http://www.world-nuclear.org/info/inf01.html.

38. John Deutch et al., *The Future of Nuclear Power: An Interdisciplinary MIT Study* (Cambridge, MA: MIT, 2003), http://web.mit.edu/nuclearpower/pdf/nuclearpower-full.pdf; Anna Momigliano, "Russian Gas Cut-off Energizes Nuclear Comeback," *Christian Science Monitor*, January 16, 2009; "Gas Row Shakes Europe's Trust in Russian Energy," *Kyiv Post*, January 21, 2009, http://www.kyivpost.com/business/33934.

39. U.S. Nuclear Regulatory Commission, "Fact Sheet on the Three Mile Island Accident," August 2009, http://www.nrc.gov/reading-rm/doc-collections/fact-sheets/3mile-isle.pdf. The disaster at the Chernobyl reactor in the USSR in 1986 was another matter. An improperly run Soviet reactor caused a large radiation leak and loss of life. See World Nuclear Association, "Chernobyl Accident," November 2009, http://www.world-nuclear.org/info/chernobyl/inf07.html.

40. See, e.g., EIA, note 25, p. 312.

41. In each case, the main website was used. The term "nuclear power" was entered in the site search box and the quotes come from the first page that appeared.

42. Sierra Club Conservation Policies—Nuclear Power, http://www.sierraclub.org/policy/conservation/nuc-power.asp. This is a 1974 resolution from the board of directors—subject to many qualifications, but no significant change in position since 1974.

43. Greenpeace USA, "Nuclear," http://www.greenpeace.org/usa/campaigns/nuclear.

44. National Audubon Society and National Wildlife Federation, "Global Warming: Impacts, Solutions, Actions," January 2008, p. 10, http://www.audubon.org/local/pdf/Global_Warming_Users_Guide_short.pdf. No other comment is made about nuclear power in the report.

45. WWF, "Climate Solutions: WWF's Vision for 2050," p. 28, http://www.worldwildlife.org/climate/Publications/WWFBinaryitem4911.pdf. The report calls for a "phase-out of nuclear power" (p. 1) "due to its costs, radiotoxic emissions, safety, and proliferation impacts" (p. 8).

46. Environmental Defense Fund, "Questions and Answers on Nuclear Power," http://www.edf.org/article.cfm?contentid=4470.

47. UNEP, see note 20, p. 89.

48. Noelle Straub and Peter Behr, "Energy Regulatory Chief Says New Coal, Nuclear Plants May Be Unnecessary," *New York Times*, April 22, 2009, http://www.nytimes.com/gwire/2009/04/22/22greenwire-no-need-to-build-new-us-coal-or-nuclear-plants-10630.html.

49. Nuclear Energy Institute, "New Nuclear Plant Licensing," http://www.nei.org/keyissues/newnuclearplants/newnuclearplantlicensing/.

50. National Research Council, *Review of DOE's Nuclear Energy Research and Development Program* (Washington: National Academies Press, 2008), http://www.ne.doe.gov/pdfFiles/rpt_NationalAcademiesReviewDOEsNE_RDProgram_2008.pdf. The report notes that the federal nuclear energy research budget "had collapsed to $2.2 million" in fiscal year 1998, p. 9. It rose during the Bush administration but has been reduced by the Obama administration.

51. Deutch et al., see note 38.

52. John M. Deutch et al., *Update of the MIT 2003 Future of Nuclear Power* (Cambridge, MA: Massachusetts Institute of Technology, 2009), http://web.mit.edu/nuclearpower/pdf/nuclearpower-update2009.pdf.

53. Ibid., p. 1 (emphasis in original).

54. Lawrence Livermore National Laboratory, "National Ignition Facility and Photon Science," https://lasers.llnl.gov/.

55. Robert Pollin et al., "Green Recovery: A Program to Create Good Jobs and Start Building a Low Carbon Economy," Center for American Progress, Political Economy Research Institute, September 2008, pp. 2, 5, 8, and 25 ("next-generation"); pp. 6, 8, and 9 ("advanced"); p. 29 ("low-carbon" and "cellulosic"), http://www.american progress.org/issues/2008/09/pdf/green_recovery.pdf.

56. UNEP, see note 20, p. 118. This report dedicates 10 pages to the issue at this point, noting that increased use of biofuels threatens the affordability of food for the poor and may cause increased cultivation of land. So there are a host of economic and environmental trade-offs. Of greatest concern is that biofuels will come from mechanized agriculture; the report advocates using labor-intensive methods of cultivation of the plants devoted to such use.

57. U.S. Energy Information Administration, "Federal Financial Interventions and Subsidies in Energy Markets 2007," Report #:SR/CNEAF/2008-01, 2008, p. xviii, http://www.eia.doe.gov/oiaf/servicerpt/subsidy2/index.html.

58. Tom Capehart, "Renewable Energy Policy in the 2008 Farm Bill," Congressional Research Service Report, no. RL34738, 2008, p. CRS-4, http://assets.opencrs.com/rpts/RL34738_20081107.pdf; I.R.C. Section 40(h)(2) (2008).

59. Ibid., I.R.C. Section 40(b)(6)(B) (2008) (Cellulosic biofuels credit); 7 U.S.C. 8111(d)(2)(B) ($45 per ton maximum biomass assistance).

60. Capehart, p. CRS-5; Food, Conservation, and Energy Act of 2008, Public Law no. 110-234. Ethanol Tariff Extension (through 1/1/2011), 122 Stat. 923, p. 1516. For actual tariff imposed, see http://www.eia.doe.gov/oiaf/aeo/otheranalysis/aeo_2008analysispapers/ffttc.html.

61. Capehart, pp. CRS-1, CRS-2; Public Law 110-140, 121 Stat. 1492, (Dec. 19, 2007).

62. Brent D. Yacobucci, "Waiver Authority under the Renewable Fuel Standard (RFS)," Congressional Research Service, Report no. RS22870, 2008, p. CRS-2, http://www.nationalaglawcenter.org/assets/crs/RS22870.pdf; 42 U.S.C. 7545(o)(2)(B)(i) (2007); 42 U.S.C. 7545(o)(2)(B)(i)(I) (2009).

63. Agricultural Sector Creates Global Opportunities for LSGI Investors, LSGI Advisors Report, Nov. 4, 2010. http://www.lsgifund.com/LSGIRMK/agriculture.pdf. This is, of course, a reason why food prices have been rising world wide.

64. Yacobucci, see note 62, p. CRS-3.

65. "EPA Rejects Landmark Attempt to Cut Ethanol Mandate," *Climate Wire*, August 8, 2008, http://www.eenews.net/climatewire/2008/08/08/archive/3?terms=rfs+perry+waiver.

66. E.g., Want to Know It? Answers to Life's Questions, "Advantages of Biofuels," http://wanttoknowit.com/advantages-of-biofuels/; the administrator may use the traditional administrative rulemaking process to modify congressionally mandated greenhouse gas reduction percentages, but not below 40 percent for advanced biofuel and biomass diesel, 10 percent for renewable fuel, and 50 percent for cellulosic biofuel; 42 U.S.C. 7545(o)(4) (2009).

67. Indur M. Goklany, "Unintended Consequences," *International Herald Tribune*, April 24, 2007, http://www.iht.com/articles/2007/04/23/opinion/edgolany.php.

68. Dale Buss, "Bush Comments Lend Another Boost to Cellulosic Ethanol," *Edmunds Auto Observer*, February 29, 2008, http://www.autoobserver.com/2008/02/bush-comments-lend-another-boost-to-cellulosic-ethanol.html.

69. E.g., David Pimentel and Tad W. Patzek, "Ethanol Production Using Corn, Switchgrass, and Wood; Biodiesel Production Using Soybean and Sunflower," *Natural Resources Research* 14 (2005): 65–76; Tad W. Patzek, "Thermodynamics of the Corn-Ethanol Biofuel Cycle" (2006), http://petroleum.berkeley.edu/papers/patzek/CRPS416-Patzek-Web.pdf (updated version of Tad W. Patzek, "Thermodynamics of the Corn-Ethanol Biofuel Cycle," *Critical Reviews in Plant Sciences* 23 (2004): 519–67; Justus Wesseler, "Opportunities (Costs) Matter: A Comment on Pimentel and Patzek, 'Ethanol Production Using Corn, Switchgrass, and Wood'"; "Biodiesel Production Using Soybean and Sunflower," *Energy Policy* 35 (2007): 1414–16; Michael Wang, "Key Differences between Pimentel/Patzek Study and Other Studies," Argonne National Laboratory, 2005, http://eerc.ra.utk.edu/etcfc/docs/pr/MichaelWangResponse~7-19-05.doc.

70. See, e.g., Timothy Searchinger et al., "Use of U.S. Croplands for Biofuels Increases Greenhouse Gases through Emissions from Land-Use Change," *Science* 319 (2008): 1240.

71. Robert Edwards et al., "Biofuels in the European Context: Facts and Uncertainties," European Commission Report, 2008, p. 22, http://ec.europa.eu/dgs/jrc/downloads/jrc_biofuels_report.pdf. EU research on biofuels has been controversial, with the news agency Reuters having to sue under freedom of information laws to force disclosure of some. See Pete Harrison, "Once-Hidden EU Report Reveals Damage from Biodiesel," *Reuters*, April 21, 2010, http://www.alertnet.org/thenews/newsdesk/LDE63J1FP.htm.

72. Intergovernmental Panel on Climate Change, 2007, *Climate Change 2007: The Physical Science Basis* (Cambridge, UK: Cambridge University Press, 2007).

73. See, e.g., Jörn P.W. Scharlemann and William F. Laurance, "How Green Are Biofuels," *Science* 319 (2008): 43–44; Searchinger et al., see note 70, p. 1238.

74. Joseph Fargione et al., "Land Clearing and the Biofuel Carbon Debt," *Science* 319 (2008): 1235–38; Searchinger et al., see note 70.

75. Ibid.

76. Ibid., p. 1236, Figure 1D.

77. Searchinger et al., see note 70.

78. Ibid., p. 1238.

79. Bruce Dale, "Biofuels, Indirect Land Use Change and Life Cycle Analysis: Do We Now Know Enough to Know that We Don't Know?" (presentation to Low Carbon Fuels Webinar, July 25, 2008), http://www.ncbioconsortium.org/vertical/Sites/%7B2CDC9F83-EF8C-48DE-BCA4-C099640B955B%7D/uploads/%7BA292DD0E-EF23-4121-B96C-973EDC3CDC2B%7D.PDF.

80. Ibid.

81. Pollin et al., see note 55, pp. 2, 5, 8, 25.

82. See, e.g., Searchinger et al., note 70; Carey W. King and Michael E. Webber, "Water Intensity of Transportation," *Environmental Science and Technology* 42 (2008): 7866–72.

83. Millennium Ecosystem Assessment, "Ecosystems and Human Well-Being," 2005, p. 117, http://www.millenniumassessment.org/documents/document.356.aspx.pdf; Indur M. Goklany, "Saving Habitat and Conserving Biodiversity on a Crowded Planet," *BioScience* 48 (1998): 941.

84. Rainer Zah, "LCA of Biofuels in Switzerland: Environmental Impacts and Improvement Potential?" (presentation to LCM 07 Zürich, August 28, 2007), http://www.lcm2007.org/presentation/Tu_2.07-Zah.pdf.

85. Scharlemann and Laurance, see note 73, pp. 43–44; Jörn P.W. Scharlemann and William F. Laurance, "How Green Are Biofuels?" *Science Supporting Online Material* (2008), http://www.sciencemag.org/cgi/data/319/5859/43/DC1/1.

86. Scharlemann and Laurance, see notes 73, 85.

87. Dan Morgan, "Subsidies Spur Crops on Fragile Habitat," *Washington Post*, December 7, 2008; David Streitfield, "As Prices Rise, Farmers Spurn Conservation Program," *New York Times*, April 9, 2008.

88. Ibid.

89. UNEP, see note 20, pp. 117–26.

90. Fargione et al., see note 74.

91. Searchinger et al., see note 70.

92. E.g., Siobhan Hughes, Ian Talley, and Anjali Cordeiro, "Corn Ethanol Loses More Support," *Wall Street Journal*, May 3, 2008.

93. UN Food and Agricultural Organization, "High-Level Conference on World Food Security: The Challenges of Climate Change and Bioenergy," report of the High-Level Conference on World Food Security, Rome, June 2008, http://www.fao.org/fileadmin/user_upload/foodclimate/HLCdocs/HLC08-Rep-E.pdf.

94. UN Food and Agricultural Organization, *State of Food Insecurity in the World 2008: High Food Prices and Food Security – Threats and Opportunities* (Rome: Food and Agriculture Organization of the United Nations, 2008), p.11, ftp://ftp.fao.org/docrep/fao/011/i0291e/i0291e00.pdf. (The FAO estimates that in 2007–2008, 4.7 percent of global cereal production will be used for biofuel production.)

95. Ibid., p. 2; FAO, see note 93.

96. In 2008, the FAO modified its recommendations for the minimum daily energy requirement (MDER) for an individual in order for the individual to survive and fulfill basic functions. The MDER varies with the country, age group, and levels of daily activities a person may indulge in. This change, along with new population estimates and other methodological changes, resulted in a net reduction in earlier estimates for the total number of chronically undernourished in developing countries of less than 8 percent for 1990–1992. FAO, see note 94, p. 45–47. Estimates for 1969–1971, previously estimated at 37 percent, were, however, not revisited. Indur M. Goklany, *The Improving State of the World: Why We're Living Longer, Healthier, More Comfortable Lives on a Cleaner Planet* (Washington: Cato Institute, 2007), pp. 44–48, 82–85. Based on the changes in numbers using the latest methodologies and assumptions, 30–35 percent would, therefore, seem to be a reasonable approximation for 1969–1971.

97. FAO, see note 94.

98. Ibid.

99. Former President George W. Bush stated that, "The solution to the issue of corn-fed ethanol is cellulosic ethanol." Amanda Paulson, "U.S. Eyes Shift Away from Corn Ethanol," *Christian Science Monitor*, May 1, 2008, http://www.csmonitor.com/2008/0501/p03s03-usec.html. That is, there are "good" biofuels and "bad" biofuels. This argument was most cogently summarized by a *New York Times* editorial:

> It is time to end an outdated tax break for corn ethanol and to call a timeout in the fivefold increase in ethanol production mandated in the 2007 energy bill. . . .

This does not mean that Congress should give up on biofuels as an important part of the effort to reduce the country's dependency on imported oil and reduce greenhouse gas emissions. What it does mean is that some biofuels are (or are likely to be) better than others, and that Congress should realign its tax and subsidy programs to encourage the good ones. Unlike corn ethanol, those biofuels will not compete for the world's food supply and will deliver significant reductions in greenhouse gases. . . .

Congress's guiding principle should be to tie federal help to environmental performance. The goal is not just to stop the headlong rush to corn ethanol but to use the system to bring to commercial scale promising second-generation biofuels—cellulosic ethanol derived from crop wastes, wood wastes, perennial grasses. These could provide environmental benefits and reduce dependence on oil without displacing food production.

Editorial, "Rethinking Ethanol," *New York Times,* May 11, 2008.

100. Indur Goklany, "Wishful Thinking on Cellulosic Ethanol," Cato-at-Liberty Blog, May 1, 2008, http://www.cato-at-liberty.org/2008/05/01/wishful-thinking-on-cellulosic-ethanol/.

101. Searchinger et al., see note 70.

102. Ibid., pp. 1238, 1240.

103. See, e.g., Jonathan H. Adler, "Rent Seeking behind the Green Curtain," *Regulation* 19 (4) (1996): 26 (describing rent-seeking in 1990s ethanol programs); Jonathan H. Adler, "Clean Politics, Dirty Profits: Rent-Seeking behind the Green Curtain," in *Political Environmentalism: Going Behind the Green Curtain,* ed. Terry L. Anderson (Stanford, CA: Hoover Institution Press, 2000), pp. 1–2; Jonathan H. Adler, "Clean Fuels, Dirty Air" in *Environmental Politics: Public Costs, Private Rewards,* eds. Michael S. Greve and Fred L. Smith, Jr. (New York: Praeger, 1992), p. 19 (clean fuels program as ethanol subsidy).

104. UNEP, see note 20, p. 33.

Chapter 4

1. "Measuring Green Jobs," http://www.bls.gov/green/.

2. Phillip Bastian, "On the Grid: Careers in Energy," *Occupational Outlook Quarterly* (Washington: Government Printing Office, Fall 2008), p. 32; Alice Ramey, "Going 'Green': Environmental Jobs for Scientists and Engineers," *Occupational Outlook Quarterly* (Washington: Government Printing Office, Summer 2009), p. 2.

3. United Nations Environment Programme, *Green Jobs: Towards Decent Work in a Sustainable, Low-Carbon World* (Nairobi: U.N. Publishing Services Section, 2008), p. 299, http://www.unep.org/labour_environment/PDFs/Greenjobs/UNEP-Green-Jobs-Report.pdf.

4. Ibid., p. 4, http://www.merriam-webster.com/dictionary/greenwashing. Entities (often corporations) that overly exploit environmental concerns to sell products or policies are sometimes accused of "greenwashing."

5. See, e.g., Kenneth Clarkson and Roger Meiners, "Institutional Changes, Reported Unemployment, and Induced Institutional Changes," Carnegie-Rochester Conference Series on Public Policy, Elsevier, Vol. 10 (1979), pp. 205–35. Discouraged workers reentering the workforce (and again being included in the official count) may actually increase the rate of unemployment, even as the overall number of new jobs created increases, as occurred in the United States in 2010.

6. Emergency Economic Stabilization Act of 2008, Public Law no. 110-343, § 503, 122 Stat. 3765, 3877 ("Exemption from Excise Tax for Certain Wooden Arrows Designed for Use by Children"); Section 308, Increase in Limit on Cover Over of Rum Excise Tax to Puerto Rico and the Virgin Islands. 122 Stat. 3765, 3869.

7. Gordon Tullock, "Rent Seeking," in *The New Palgrave: A Dictionary of Economics,* eds. John Eatwell, Murray Milgate, and Peter Newman (Houndmills UK: Palgrave Macmillan, 1987), pp. 147–49.

8. United States Conference of Mayors, *U.S. Metro Economies: Current and Potential Green Jobs in the U.S. Economy* (Lexington, MA: Global Insight, 2008), p. 5, http://www.usmayors.org/pressreleases/uploads/greenjobsreport.pdf. The report included jobs involved in the production of corn and soy to the extent the corn and soy are used for biofuels.

9. Ibid., p. 12 (nuclear power jobs "are not included in our projection scenario").

10. UNEP, see note 3, p. 3.

11. Ibid.

12. Ibid., p. 4.

13. Ibid., p. 15 ("Making steel mills greener and more competitive is a must for job retention").

14. Ibid., p. 89.

15. Gary Gardner and Michael Renner, "Opinion: Building a Green Economy," Worldwatch Institute, Eye on Earth, November 12, 2008, http://www.worldwatch.org/node/5935 ("Wind and solar technologies are not just more environmentally benign than oil, coal, and nuclear power, but also more jobs-intensive").

16. See, e.g., Mayors, see note 8, p. 21 ("one of the promising aspects of Green Jobs is that the vast majority of them are not restricted to any specific location, so cities and their metro areas across the country can and are expected to compete to attract this job growth").

17. World Nuclear Association, "Nuclear Power in the World Today," http://www.world-nuclear.org/info/inf01.html.

18. "Sweden Wants to Lift Reactor Ban," *New York Times,* February 6, 2009, http://www.nytimes.com/2009/02/06/world/europe/06sweden.html?ref=world.

19. Jeremy Plester, "Environmentalists May Go Nuclear," *Times (UK),* January 3, 2005; Ira Flatow, "Some Environmentalists Warming Up to Nuclear," *Talk of the Nation/Science Friday,* NPR, June 2, 2006.

20. William Tucker, *Terrestrial Energy: How Nuclear Power Will Lead the Green Revolution and End America's Energy Odyssey* (Savage, MD: Bartleby Press, 2008). See also Max Shulz, "Nuclear Recovery," *American Spectator,* December 2008 (reviewing Tucker and contrasting Tucker's views to those of Amory Lovins and Thomas Friedman).

21. See, e.g., Tucker (discussing role of nuclear power); Amarjit Singh, "The Future of Energy," *Leadership and Management Engineering* 9 (2009): 9–25; Kathleen Vaillancourt et al., "The Role of Nuclear Energy in Long-Term Climate Scenarios: An Analysis with the World-TIMES Model," *Energy Policy* 36 (2008): 2296–2307; Benjamin K. Sovacool, "Valu-

ing the Greenhouse Gas Emissions from Nuclear Power: A Critical Survey," *Energy Policy* 36 (2008): 2950–63 (study of total lifecycle emissions, not direct GHG emissions).

22. UNEP, see note 3, p. 111.

23. Mayors, see note 8, p. 9.

24. Ibid.

25. Ibid.

26. For a discussion of the topic, see Jerry Taylor, "An Economic Critique of Corn-Ethanol Subsidies," *Federal Reserve Bank of St. Louis, Regional Economic Development* 5(1) (2009): 78, http://www.cato.org/pubs/articles/jerrytaylor_aneconomiccritique-ofcornethanolsubsidies_2009.pdf.

27. Michael Faust, Sacramento Metro Chamber, Testimony before Sacramento Metropolitan Air Quality Management District regarding Wood Burning Rule 421 (Sept. 26, 2007), http://sacramentocacoc.weblinkconnect.com/cwt/external/wcpages/wcwebcontent/webcontentpage.aspx?contentid=1225.

28. "Port Activities and Wood Stoves Designate Tacoma as 'Non-Attainment' For Pollution," Tacoma Urbanist Blog, January 17, 2008, http://i.feedtacoma.com/Erik/port-activities-wood-stoves-designate/; Spokane County Air Pollution Control Authority, "DRAFT Technical Analysis Protocol for the Spokane PM10 Non-attainment Area PM10 Limited Maintenance Plan and Redesignation Request," http://www.spokanecleanair.org/documents/sip/Draft%20Spokane%20LMP%20TAP.pdf; Idaho Department of Environmental Quality, "Air Monitoring Overview: How DEQ Assesses Air Quality," http://www.deq.state.id.us/air/data_reports/monitoring/overview.cfm; Montana Department of Environmental Quality, "Citizens' Guide to Air Quality in Montana: Understanding Air Quality," http://www.deq.state.mt.us/AirMonitoring/citguide/understanding.asp.

29. Mayors, note 8, p. 9.

30. Ibid., p. 11.

31. See Timothy Searchinger et al., "Use of U.S. Croplands for Biofuels Increases Greenhouse Gases through Emissions from Land-Use Change," *Science* 319 (2008): 1240. We are aware of the controversy this paper sparked. See, e.g., pwintersatbio dotorg comment posting, "Biofuels and Climate Change," February 28, 2008, http://biofuelsandclimate.wordpress.com/2008/02/28/is-the-debate-on-land-use-over/#comments. The point is not whether Searchinger et al. are correct about the net impact but whether the green jobs literature acknowledges the active scientific controversy over these issues. It largely does not.

32. Conversion of habitat to cropland is generally deemed to be the most significant pressure on terrestrial species, habitat, and ecosystems. See Millennium Ecosystem Assessment, *Ecosystems and Human Well-Being* (Washington: Island Press, 2005), p. 67, http://www.millenniumassessment.org/documents/document.356.aspx.pdf; Indur M. Goklany, "Saving Habitat and Conserving Biodiversity on a Crowded Planet," *Bioscience* 48, 11 (1998): 13, 941; Likewise, diversions of freshwater for human uses are deemed to exert the greatest pressure on freshwater biodiversity. E.g., A. Brautigam, "The Freshwater Biodiversity Crisis," *World Conservation* 2 (1999): 4–5; IUCN, "Confirming the Global Extinction Crisis," press release, September 28, 2000, http://www.iucn.org/redlist/2000/news.html; see also MEA *Ecosystems*.

33. Searchinger et al., see note 31, p. 1,238 (carbon dioxide); G. Philip Robertson et al., "Sustainable Biofuels Redux," *Science* 322 (2008): 50 (nitrous oxide).

34. "Full of Sound and Fury," *The Economist*, July 14, 2007 (U.S. congressional debates over energy policy, ethanol, and other renewables, and taxation of oil compa-

nies); Paul B. Thompson, "The Agricultural Ethics of Biofuels: A First Look," *Journal of Agricultural and Environmental Ethics* (April 2008): 183–98.

35. UNEP, see note 3, p. 90.

36. Roger Bezdek, *Renewable Energy and Energy Efficiency: Economic Drivers for the 21st Century* (Boulder, CO: American Solar Energy Society, 2007), p. 29, http://www.misi-net.com/publications/ASES-EconomicDrivers07.pdf (noting that recycling is the second biggest "green job" in the United States).

37. UNEP, see note 3, p. 215 ("While recycling is of great value in terms of resource conservation, it can entail dirty, undesirable, and even dangerous and unhealthy work, and it is often poorly paid").

38. Ibid., p. 4.

39. Ibid., p. 219.

40. Ibid., p. 154.

41. CNW Marketing Research, Inc., "Dust to Dust: The Energy Cost of New Vehicles from Concept to Disposal," CNW Marketing Research Report, 2007, http://cnwmr.com/nss-folder/automotiveenergy/DUST%20PDF%20VERSION.pdf.

42. Bastian, see note 2, pp. 33–41.

43. See Mayors, note 8, p. 13.

44. Robert Pollin et al., "Green Recovery: A Program to Create Good Jobs and Start Building a Low Carbon Economy," Center for American Progress, Political Economy Research Institute, September 2008, p. 5.

45. UNEP, see note 3, p. 110.

46. "DOE Outlines HVAC Opportunities," *Air Conditioning, Heating and Refrigeration News*, April 13, 2009. The same issue notes that an HVAC contractor must be registered at www.recovery.gov to be eligible to participate in stimulus spending programs categorized as green.

47. UNEP, see note 3, p. 4.

48. Ibid.

49. Ibid., p. 28.

50. Ibid., p. 26.

51. Ibid., p. 101.

52. Jonathan H. Adler, "Rent Seeking behind the Green Curtain," *Regulation* 19 (1996): 26, (describing rent-seeking in 1990s ethanol programs); see also *U.S. Congress, Office of Technology Assessment, Innovation, and Commercialization of Emerging Technology,* OTA-BP-ITC-165 (Washington: U.S. Government Printing Office, September 1995), pp. 87–88 ("Regulations that are overly prescriptive can lock in existing technologies to the detriment of other technologies that might meet or exceed requirements").

53. Byron Swift, *Barriers to Environmental Technology and Use* (Washington: Environmental Law Institute, 1998), p. 6. For a general discussion, see Richard B. Stewart, "Environmental Regulation and International Competitiveness," *Yale Law Journal* 102 (1993): 2039.

54. UNEP, see note 3, p. 142.

55. Guy R. Newsham et al., "Do LEED-certified buildings save energy? Yes, but. . .," *Energy and Buildings*, 41 (2009): 897.

56. Ibid., p. 903.

57. Keynes did not actually say that. It is deduced from several points he made about the desirability of public projects to stimulate employment. See John Maynard Keynes, *The General Theory of Employment Interest and Money* (Classic House Books, 1935), pp. 129, 220. In a 1991 interview, Nobel laureate economist Milton Friedman called such hole-

digging harmful, because it produces no economic product. Interview, Milton Friedman, January 31, 1991, http://www.achievement.org/autodoc/printmember/fri0int-1.

58. Mayors, see note 8, p. 5.

59. UNEP, see note 3.

60. Roger H. Bezdek et al., "Environmental Protection, the Economy, and Jobs: National and Regional Analyses," *Journal of Environmental Management* 86 (2008): 66. Bezdek and his associates are primary authors of the ASES report.

61. Ibid., p. 76.

62. Mayors, see note 8, p. 5.

63. Ibid., p. 16.

64. The Pew Charitable Trusts, "The Clean Energy Economy," Pew Charitable Trusts Report, June 2009, p. 22, http://www.pewcenteronthestates.org/uploadedFiles/Clean_Economy_Report_Web.pdf.

65. Ibid.

66. UNEP, see note 3, pp. 136–37.

67. Pollin et al., see note 44, p. 16.

68. Ibid.

69. On the costs and benefits of alternative environmental policies, see Andrew P. Morriss and Roger E. Meiners, "Borders and the Environment," *Environmental Law* 39 (2009): 141.

70. UNEP, see note 3, p. 8.

71. As the title of this article indicates, the cost of having the government perform mundane tasks appears to be enormously expensive: Andrew Malcolm, "Obama's Federal Government Can Weatherize Your Home for Only $57,362 Each," *Los Angeles Times,* February 18, 2010, http://latimesblogs.latimes.com/washington/2010/02/obama-stimulus-weatherization.html.

Chapter 5

1. Daniel Stone, "What Green Jobs?" *Newsweek Web Exclusive*, July 28, 2009, http://www.newsweek.com/id/209073.

2. Phillip Bastian, "On the Grid: Careers in Energy," *Occupational Outlook Quarterly* (Washington: Government Printing Office, Fall 2008), p. 38.

3. United States Conference of Mayors, *U.S. Metro Economies: Current and Potential Green Jobs in the U.S. Economy* (Lexington, MA: Global Insight, 2008), pp. 6–7, http://www.usmayors.org/pressreleases/uploads/greenjobsreport.pdf.

4. Ibid., p. 7.

5. United Nations Environment Programme, *Green Jobs: Towards Decent Work in a Sustainable, Low-Carbon World* (Nairobi: U.N. Publishing Services Section, 2008), p. 6, http://www.unep.org/labour_environment/PDFs/Greenjobs/UNEP-Green-Jobs-Report.pdf.

6. U.S. Department of Energy, *20% Wind Energy by 2030: Increasing Wind Energy's Contribution to U.S. Electricity Supply* (Oak Ridge, TN: Department of Energy, 2008), p. 13, http://www.nrel.gov/docs/fy08osti/41869.pdf.

7. Roger Bezdek, *Renewable Energy and Energy Efficiency: Economic Drivers for the 21st Century* (Boulder, CO: American Solar Energy Society, 2007), p. 7, http://www.misi-net.com/publications/ASES-EconomicDrivers07.pdf.

8. Van Jones, *The Green-Collar Economy: How One Solution Can Fix our Two Biggest Problems* (New York: Harper Collins, 2008), p. 149.

9. Mayors, see note 3, pp. 6–7.

10. Ibid., p. 7.

11. EIA, "Renewable Energy 2007 Statistics." See Table 3 of this report for details of electricity generation from renewable sources.

12. Mayors, see note 3, p. 7.

13. Ibid., p. 8.

14. See Tom Wright, "India Windmill Empire Begins to Show Cracks," *Wall Street Journal*, April 18, 2008, http://online.wsj.com/article/SB120846287761023921.html; Michael Connellan, "Spinning to Destruction," *Guardian*, September 4, 2008, http://www.guardian.co.uk/technology/2008/sep/04/energy.engineering.

15. See Figure 1 in this chapter.

16. See the discussion in Chapter 3 about the technological problems with ethanol and for information about the size of the public subsidy.

17. Mayors, see note 3, p. 12.

18. American Wind Energy Association, "Wind Energy Grows by Record 8,300 MW in 2008," press release, January 27, 2009, http://www.awea.org/newsroom/releases/wind_energy_growth2008_27Jan09.html.

19. Vaclav Smil, *Energy at the Crossroads: Global Perspectives and Uncertainties* (Cambridge, MA: The MIT Press, 2003), p. 122.

20. Mayors, see note 3, p. 12.

21. Bezdek, see note 7; Roger Bezdek, *Green Collar Jobs in the U.S. and Colorado: Economic Drivers for the 21st Century* (Boulder, CO: American Solar Energy Society, 2009), pp. 7, 25. This report is an update to the ASES report used throughout this article, but the primary change is the section on Colorado; the November 2007 report cited routinely here had a similar section on Ohio, although Ohio was not worthy of mention in the title, unlike the Colorado version.

22. Mayors, see note 3, p. 12.

23. Bezdek, see note 7, p. 7.

24. Peter Fimrite, "Steps Taken toward Removing Klamath River Dams," *San Francisco Chronicle*, November 14, 2008, http://www.sfgate.com/cgi-bin/article.cgi?f=/c/a/2008/11/14/MNA21441S7.DTL. The plan to remove Klamath River dams includes a surcharge for customers of the electric utility, as it must find alternative electricity sources for the 70,000 customers the hydro sources serve. Solar and wind power would be considered. Hydro power sources are also being removed in Maine. See Colin Hickey, "Fort Halifax Dam Deal Rejected," *Kennebec (Maine) Journal*, June 29, 2007, http://kennebecjournal.mainetoday.com/news/local/4044480.html. There is no doubt dams have environmental consequences—as does the construction of any source of electricity.

25. Mayors, see note 3, p. 8.

26. Ibid., p. 12.

27. Ibid.

28. Ibid., p. 3.

29. "T. Boone Pickens Puts Texas Wind Farm Project on Hold," *Dallas Morning News*, November 12, 2008, http://www.dallasnews.com/sharedcontent/dws/bus/stories/111308dnbuspickens.ae1b50.html?npc.

30. UNEP, see note 5, p. 93.

31. See, e.g., Bernd Radowitz and Juan Montes, "Solar-Energy Loses Some Shine," *Wall Street Journal*, August 17, 2009, http://online.wsj.com/article/SB125047382306735797.html.

32. UNEP, see note 5, p. 93.

33. Ibid.

34. Ibid.

35. Ibid.

36. Ibid., p. 60.

37. Bezdek, see note 7, p. 36.

38. Robin Pagnamenta, "Scepticism Grows over the Viability of Green Projects," *Sunday Times (UK)*, January 29, 2009, http://business.timesonline.co.uk/tol/business/economics/wef/article5607996.ece.

39. UNEP, see note 5, p. 42.

40. Ibid., p. 37; the Mayors report sees a fourfold increase in the United States by 2018 and a tenfold increase by 2028; Mayors, see note 3, p. 12.

41. "Gigaton Throwdown" (2009), http://www.gigatonthrowdown.org/geothermal.php.

42. Robert Pollin et al., "Green Recovery: A Program to Create Good Jobs and Start Building a Low Carbon Economy," Center for American Progress, Political Economy Research Institute, September 2008, p. 6.

43. Adler, *Foul Winds*; Cape Wind, "America's First Wind Farm on Nantucket Sound," http://www.capewind.org/; Wendy Williams and Robert Whitcomb, *Cape Wind: Money, Celebrity, Class, Politics and the Battle for Our Energy Future on Nantucket Sound* (New York: Public Affairs, 2007).

44. http://www.doi.gov/news/doinews/Secretary-Salazar-Announces-Approval-of-Cape-Wind-Energy-Project-on-Outer-Continental-Shelf-off-Massachusetts.cfm. The Aquinnah tribe identified 14 legal concerns and may sue under federal laws, such as the National Historic Preservation Act. Beth Daley, "Aquinnah Tribe Says It Is Prepared to Sue If Cape Wind Is Approved," *Boston Globe*, Green Blog, April 26, 2010, http://www.boston.com/lifestyle/green/greenblog/2010/04/aquinnah_tribe_says_they_are_p.html.

45. Mayors, see note 3, p. 7.

46. U.S. Department of Energy, "North Dakota Wind Resource Map," http://www.windpoweringamerica.gov/maps_template.asp?stateab=nd.

47. Cristina L. Archer and Mark Z. Jacobson, "Supplying Baseload Power and Reducing Transmission Requirements by Interconnecting Wind Farms," *Journal of Applied Meteorology and Climatology* 46 (2007): 1701.

48. GE Wind Energy, LLC, "Advanced Wind Turbine Program Next Generation Turbine Development Project," National Renewable Energy Laboratory, Report No. NREL/SR-500-38752, 2006 (describing seven-year program to cut wind turbine-generated electricity costs to $0.025/kWh and inability to do so resorting to "high risk concepts" that were unmarketable).

49. Noelle Straub and Peter Behr, "Energy Regulatory Chief Says New Coal, Nuclear Plants May Be Unnecessary," *New York Times Greenwire*, April 22, 2009, http://www.nytimes.com/gwire/2009/04/22/22greenwire-no-need-to-build-new-us-coal-or-nuclear-plants-10630.html.

50. Ibid.

51. Mayors, see note 3, p. 7.

52. Ibid., pp. 7–8.

53. Ibid., p. 2

54. Ibid., p. 3.

55. Ibid., pp. 2–3 ("forecasting an average outflow of $240 billion per year, measured in 2006 dollars, to pay for imported oil through the year 2030 . . . acts very much as a tax . . . worse than a tax . . .").

56. Mark Gongloff, "Falling Gas Prices May Be Gone As a Stimulus," *Wall Street Journal,* February 12, 2009.

57. Samuel Sherraden, *Green Trade Balance* (2009), http://www.newamerica.net/publications/policy/green_trade_balance.

58. Ron Bailey, "How Green Is Your Crystal Ball?" *Reason Online,* August 4, 2009, http://www.reason.com/news/show/135213.html.

59. UNEP, see note 5, p. 149.

60. Ibid., p. 150.

61. Ibid., p. 236.

62. Roger H. Bezdek et al., "Environmental Protection, the Economy, and Jobs: National and Regional Analyses," *Journal of Environmental Management* 86 (2008): 69.

63. Pollin et al., see note 42, p. 11.

64. Ibid., p. 12.

65. Ibid., p. 11.

66. UNEP, see note 5, p. 186.

67. Hal R. Varian, "An iPod Has Global Value. Ask the (Many) Countries That Make It," *New York Times,* June 28, 2007, http://www.nytimes.com/2007/06/28/business/worldbusiness/28scene.html.

68. Market shares shift quickly; Chinese producers are expected to have a rapidly growing share of the market, but sales are likely to be domestic. Asari Efiong and Andrew Crispin, "Wind Turbine Manufacturers; Here Comes Pricing Power," Merrill Lynch Report, 2007, http://www.ohiowind.org/InsideOWWG/ActionTeams/.%5C.%5Cpdfs%5CMerrill%20Lynch%20Wind%20Power%20Report1.pdf. Merrill Lynch predicted little entry into the industry despite growth. Interestingly, GE's wind business was acquired from Enron in its bankruptcy: "G.E. to Buy Enron Wind-Turbine Assets," *New York Times,* April 12, 2002.

69. For a discussion of current wind market trends and events, see "The 'Who Is Who' of Wind Energy," http://www.windfair.net/.

70. In March 2010, Senators Schumer, Casey, Tester, and Brown requested that stimulus spending on wind energy be halted because 80 percent of the funding was going to foreign-owned companies. Brian Coppa, "Tensions Rise As Stimulus Funding Creates More Green Jobs Overseas," *Examiner.com,* March 25, 2010, http://www.examiner.com/x-8178-Phoenix-Green-Business-Examiner~y2010m3d25-Tensions-rise-as-stimulus-funding-creates-more-green-jobs-overseas

71. Matthew Dolan, "Gas Engines Get an Upgrade in Challenge to Hybrids," *Wall Street Journal,* January 14, 2009. However, U.S. demand for the Prius fell as retail gas prices declined dramatically in 2008. Kate Linebaugh, "Toyota Delays Mississippi Prius Factory amid Slump," *Wall Street Journal,* December 16, 2008; Peter Haldis, "GM Cuts Production, Toyota Cancels U.S. Prius Production," *World Refining and Fuels Today,* December 16, 2008.

72. "Auto Industry Plugs Electric-Car Subsidies," *Wall Street Journal,* April 15, 2010, http://online.wsj.com/article/SB10001424052702303348504575184261386174090.html.

73. Dolan, see note 71.

74. Ibid.

75. Bezdek, see note 7, p. 24. The study states that the calculation is by ASES and its consultant, Management Information Services, Inc.

76. Bastian, see note 2, p. 38.

77. UNEP, see note 5, p. 295.

78. Worldwatch Institute, "Worldwatch Mission Statement," http://www.world watch.org/node/24. Worldwatch was founded by Lester Brown, author of a number of alarmist books on population growth. See, e.g., Lester R. Brown, *Who Will Feed China? Wake-up Call for a Small Planet* (New York: WW Norton, 1995); Lester R. Brown, *Tough Choices: Facing the Challenge of Food Scarcity* (New York: WW Norton, 1998); Lester R. Brown et al., *Beyond Malthus: Nineteen Dimensions of the Population Challenge* (New York: WW Norton, 1999). In 1997, *The Economist* summarized Brown's record on population and food issues as follows:

> Lester Brown of the Worldwatch Institute began predicting in 1973 that population would soon outstrip food production, and he still does so every time there is a temporary increase in wheat prices. In 1994, after 21 years of being wrong, he said: "After 40 years of record food production gains, output per person has reversed with unanticipated abruptness." Two bumper harvests followed and the price of wheat fell to record lows. Yet Mr. Brown's pessimism remains as impregnable to facts as his views are popular with newspapers. The facts on world food production are truly startling for those who have heard only the doomsayers' views. Since 1961, the population of the world has almost doubled, but food production has more than doubled.

"Plenty of Gloom: Forecasters of Scarcity Are Not Only Invariably Wrong, They Think That Being Wrong Proves Them Right," *The Economist*, December 20, 1997.

79. The Pew Charitable Trusts, "The Clean Energy Economy," Pew Charitable Trusts Report, June 2009, p. 45, http://www.pewcenteronthestates.org/uploadedFiles/Clean_Economy_Report_Web.pdf.

80. Mayors, see note 3, p. 12.

81. Ibid., p. 15.

82. Ibid., p. 11.

83. John Ferak, "Ethanol Towns Also on Idle," *Omaha (NE) World-Herald*, January 30, 2009; Venita Jenkins, "Plans for Ethanol Plant Likely to Be Scrapped," *Fayetteville Observer*, January 31, 2009. But see Tom LoBianco and Edward Felker, "Ethanol Producers Aim to Lift Cap on 10% as Gas Additive," *Washington Times*, February 4, 2009, http://www.washingtontimes.com/news/2009/feb/04/ethanol-industry-wants-10-per-gallon-of-gas-limit-/.

84. UNEP, see note 5, pp. 94, 99; Ron Pernick and Joel Makower, *Harnessing San Francisco's Clean-Tech Future: A Progress Report*, Clean Edge, Inc. Report (2005).

85. Ibid., p. 99. The Renewable Energy Policy Project published several reports (available at http://www.repp.org/) that collectively found that "820,000 new good-paying manufacturing jobs could be created across the country." http://www.sierra club.org/energy/bluegreenjobs/.

86. UNEP, see note 5, p. 100; Brad Heavnor and Susannah Churchill, "Renewables Work: Job Growth from Renewable Energy Development in California," California Public Interest Research Group Charitable Trust, June 2002, p. 2.

87. UNEP, see note 5, p. 100; Peter Asmus, "Harvesting California's Renewable Energy Resources: A Green Jobs Business Plan," Center for Energy Efficiency and Renewable Technologies, 2008, p. 14.

88. UNEP, see note 5, p. 100; Solar Initiative of New York, "New York's Solar Roadmap: A Plan for Energy Reliability, Security, Environmental Responsibility and Economic Development in New York State," Solar Initiative of New York, 2007, p. 2, http://www.neny.org/download.cfm/NENY_Membership_Application.pdf?AssetID=225.

89. UNEP, see note 5, p. 100; Union of Concerned Scientists, "Cashing In on Clean Energy," Union of Concerned Scientists Fact Sheet, July 12, 2007 ("a 20% national renewable electricity standard would generate more than 185,000 renewable energy jobs nationally by 2020 in manufacturing, construction and other industries"). The UUC released an updated report in October 2007, assuming a 15% standard. Union of Concerned Scientists, "Cashing In on Clean Energy, October 2007 Update," Union of Concerned Scientists Fact Sheet, October 2007, http://www.ucsusa.org/assets/documents/clean_energy/cashing-in-national-15.pdf.

90. Apollo Alliance, "Our Mission," http://apolloalliance.org/about/mission/. Its funding appears to be mostly from left-wing foundations and labor organizations. See Apollo Alliance, "Funders," http://apolloalliance.org/about/funders/.

91. UNEP, see note 5, p. 99; Apollo Alliance, "New Energy for America: The Apollo Jobs Report: For Good Jobs and Energy Independence," Apollo Alliance, 2004, pp. 16–17, http://apolloalliance.org/downloads/resources_ApolloReport_022404_122748.pdf (investment in renewable energy markets and biofuels development yields expected to yield 419,042 jobs over 10 years); see also Jay Inslee, *Apollo's Fire: Igniting America's Clean-Energy Economy* (Washington: Island Press, 2008).

92. Pollin et al., see note 42, p. 10.

93. Ibid., p. 11. CAP's estimates are notable for its efforts to compare the impact of spending on green jobs to alternatives. More studies should attempt something similar. CAP also benchmarked its proposal against the February 2008 "stimulus" package, which simply gave consumers some additional cash. Economic Stimulus Act of 2008, Public Law 110-185, 122 Stat. 613. While we applaud the effort to benchmark, PERI's specific benchmark is deeply flawed.

94. Pew, see note 79, p. 18.

95. See discussion in Chapters 1 and 3.

96. Mayors, see note 3, p. 12.

97. Ibid., p. 13.

98. U.S. Energy Information Administration, *Annual Energy Review 2008* (Washington: Energy Information Administration, 2009), pp. 68–71, http://www.eia.doe.gov/aer/pdf/aer.pdf.

99. Ibid., p. 70.

100. "Consumption of nonmarketed solar, geothermal, and wind energy also increases dramatically in the projections; however, it continues to account for less than 1 percent of all delivered energy use in the residential and commercial sectors." Ibid., p. 58.

101. EIA projects that hydropower will decline from 7.1 percent of capacity in 2006 to 5.8 percent in 2030 because "environmental concerns and the scarcity of untapped large-scale sites limit its growth." Ibid., p. 71.

102. Mayors, see note 3, p. 16.

103. EIA, see note 98, p. 4.

104. Bezdek, see note 7, p. vii.

105. Ibid., p. 7.

106. Pollin et al., see note 42, p. 1.

107. Ibid., p. 27.

108. Mayors, see note 3, p. 5.

109. Ibid., p. 17.

110. Ibid., pp. 20–33.

111. See, e.g., Richard Florida, *The Rise of the Creative Class: And How It's Transforming Work, Leisure, Community and Everyday Life* (New York: Basic Books, 2002).

112. UNEP, see note 5, p. 17; similarly, "different approaches result in findings that cannot simply be aggregated or extrapolated," p. 36.

113. Ibid., p. 8.

114. Union of Concerned Scientists, "Renewing America's Economy: A 20 Percent National Renewable Electricity Standard Will Create Jobs and Save Consumers Money," Union of Concerned Scientists, 2004, http://www.ucsusa.org/assets/documents/clean_energy/ACFoDbPiL.pdf.

115. Ibid., p. 1.

116. Ibid., p. 2.

117. Ibid., pp. 1–2

118. Daniel M. Kammen, Kamal Kapadia, and Matthias Fripp, "Putting Renewables to Work: How Many Jobs Can the Clean Energy Industry Generate?" RAEL Report, University of California, Berkeley, 2006, p. 11, http://rael.berkeley.edu/old-site/renewables.jobs.2006.pdf.

119. Ibid., p. 15.

120. Bezdek et al., see note 62, p. 66.

121. DOE, see note 6, p. 205.

122. Ibid., p. 202.

123. See Cedric N. Hance, "Geothermal Industry Employment: Survey Results and Analysis," Geothermal Energy Association, Report for the Department of Energy, 2005, p. 7, http://www.geo-energy.org/publications/reports.asp.

124. Mayors, see note 3, p. 20.

125. Randall W. Eberts and Joe Allan Stone, *Wage and Employment Adjustment in Local Labor Markets* (Kalamazoo, MI: W.E. Upjohn Institute, 1992), Table 2.3.

Chapter 6

1. Chapter 6 incorporates, updates, and expands upon our earlier article: Roger Meiners et al., "Advocating Autarky: A Flaw in Green Jobs Policy Proposals as They Pertain to Renewable Energy," *Texas Journal of Oil, Gas, & Energy Law* 5 (2010): 155.

2. Emma Blake and A. Bernard Knapp, eds., *The Archaeology of Mediterranean Prehistory* (Oxford: Blackwell, 2005), p. 27 (discussing evidence of trade in Neolithic times) and p. 272 (discussing Eastern Mediterranean trade in the Bronze Age).

3. Apollo Alliance, "Make It in America: The Apollo Green Manufacturing Plan," Apollo Alliance, 2009, p. 6, http://apolloalliance.org/wp-content/uploads/2009/03/greenmap_proposal031109.pdf.

4. Robert Bradley and Richard Fulmer, *Energy: The Master Resource* (Dubuque, IA: Kendall/Hunt, 2004).

5. William T. Bogart, *The Economics of Cities and Suburbs* (New York: Prentice Hall, 1998) presents a textbook exposition of the Heckscher-Ohlin model and its application to trade among cities within the United States.

6. Installing backyard steel mills that weren't economically viable was part of China's policy in the Great Leap Forward of the late 1950s. David M. Bachman, *Bureaucracy, Economy, and Leadership in China* (Cambridge, UK: Cambridge University Press, 1991) refers to the Great Leap Forward as "one of the great disasters in the history of the People's Republic."

7. European Union GDP equaled $14.5 trillion in 2007, according to the International Monetary Fund, http://www.imf.org/external/pubs/ft/weo/2007/01/data/weorept.aspx?sy=2007&ey=2007&scsm=1&ssd=1&sort=country&ds=.&br=1&c=998&s=NGDP_RPCH%2CNGDPD%2CPPPWGT%2CPCPIPCH&grp=1&a=1&pr1.x=93&pr1.y=9. United States GDP was $14.1 trillion in 2007, according to the IMF, http://www.imf.org/external/pubs/ft/weo/2009/02/weodata/weorept.aspx?sy=2007&ey=2014&scsm=1&ssd=1&sort=country&ds=.&br=1&c=111&s=NGDPD&grp=0&a=&pr.x=69&pr.y=8. Intra-EU trade in 2006 was approximately 2.4 trillion euros, http://epp.eurostat.ec.europa.eu/cache/ITY_OFFPUB/KS-CV-07-001/EN/KS-CV-07-001-EN.PDF, Table 4A. Converting euros to dollars at the rate of 1.3197 dollars/euro, the spot rate on December 29, 2006, implies total trade of $1.8 trillion, or over 12 percent of GDP. Exchange rates can be found at http://www.federalreserve.gov/releases/h10/Hist/dat00_eu.txt.

8. Bogart, *Cities and Suburbs*, provides a textbook exposition of the trade among metropolitan areas in the United States.

9. See Gilles Duranton and Diego Puga, "Diversity and Specialization in Cities: Why, Where, and When Does It Matter?" *Urban Studies* 37 (2000): 553, for a general discussion of the theory behind urban specialization and citations to empirical evidence.

10. Edward Glaeser, "Reinventing Boston: 1640–2003," *Journal of Urban Geography* 5 (2005): 119. He has made a similar argument with respect to New York. Edward Glaeser, "The Reinventive City," *City Journal*, 2009, http://www.city-journal.org/2009/nytom_reinventive-city.html.

11. Gabriel Calzada, "Study of the Effects on Employment of Public Aid to Renewable Energy Sources," King Juan Carlos University, March 2009, http://www.juandemariana.org/pdf/090327-employment-public-aid-renewable.pdf. See Chapter 8 and related text for additional concerns raised by Calzada about the Spanish green jobs program.

12. Edward Glaeser and Matthew Kahn, "The Greenness of Cities: Carbon Dioxide Emissions and Urban Development," NBER Working Paper no. 14238, 2008.

13. Michael Szenberg et al., *Paul Samuelson: On Being An Economist* (New York: Jorge Pinto, 2005), p. 44.

14. A preference for retrofitting jobs that cannot be outsourced, food obtained from local, small, sustainable farms and videoconferencing instead of airline travel are a few examples of how green jobs proponents may not fully embrace the benefits of trade.

15. Robert Pollin et al., *Green Recovery: A Program to Create Good Jobs and Start Building a Low Carbon Economy*, Center for American Progress, Political Economy Research Institute, September 2008, p. 5.

16. United States Conference of Mayors, *U.S. Metro Economies: Current and Potential Green Jobs in the U.S. Economy* (Lexington, MA: Global Insight, 2008), pp. 18, 19–33, http://www.usmayors.org/pressreleases/uploads/greenjobsreport.pdf.

17. Ibid., p. 96.

18. Ibid., p. 98.

19. "Rest of The World Is Catching Up with U.S. Manufacturing Wages," *Manufacturing and Technology News,* January 4, 2006, p. 5, http://www.allbusiness.com/human-resources/compensation-salary/854351-1.html.

20. http://www.eia.doe.gov/cneaf/electricity/epm/tablees1b.html.

21. Anca D. Hansen and Lars H. Hansen, "Wind Turbine Concept Market Penetration over 10 Years (1995–2004)," *Wind Energy* 10 (2007): 89–90.

22. http://www.windfair.net/press/4193.html. India's Suzlon (#6 in the 2006 survey) is also mentioned as a major manufacturer in 2009.

23. http://www.windfair.net/press/4193.html. Total current Chinese turbine exports are zero.

24. http://www.associatedcontent.com/article/257473/new_york_steel_mill_undergoes_transformation_pg2.html?cat=8. This project apparently uses U.S.-made wind turbines, but at a cost of $4.5 million per turbine, the temptation to use turbines produced by an established foreign company is evident.

25. Large wind turbines are especially tempting for offshore wind projects, such as an attempt to put windmills in Lake Erie: http://blog.cleveland.com/business/2008/12/click_here_to_view_the.html. An analysis of the iPod illustrates how the country of assembly (China) captures only a fraction of the economic value compared to the country that controls the intellectual property (United States). See Greg Linden, Kenneth L. Kraemer, and Jason Dedrick, "Who Captures Value in A Global Innovation System? The Case of Apple's iPod," Personal Computing Industry Center Report, 2007, http://repositories.cdlib.org/pcic/403.

26. Pollin et al., see note 15, p. 11. No citation is provided for this incredibly precise measure of hugely complex portions of economic activity.

27. UNEP, *Green Jobs,* p. 136.

28. Ibid., p. 119.

29. Ibid., p. 4.

30. Ibid.

31. Michael I. Cragg and Matthew E. Kahn, "Carbon Geography: The Political Economy of Congressional Support for Legislation Intended to Mitigate Greenhouse Gas Production," NBER Working Paper no. 14963, 2009, p. 23.

32. See Andrew P. Morriss, "Litigating to Regulate: Massachusetts v. Environmental Protection Agency," *Cato Supreme Court Review* (2007): 211–12.

33. UNEP, *Green Jobs,* p. 162.

34. Ibid., p. 223.

35. Ibid.

36. Gregory Clark, *A Farewell to Alms: A Brief Economic History of the World* (Princeton, NJ: Princeton University Press, 2007).

37. Ibid., p. 3

38. E.g., Paul R. Ehrlich, *The Population Bomb* (New York: Ballantine Books, 1968); William Paddock, *Famine, 1975!: America's Decision: Who Will Survive?* (Boston: Little, Brown, 1967).

39. See Indur M. Goklany, *The Improving State of the World: Why We're Living Longer, Healthier, More Comfortable Lives on a Cleaner Planet* (Washington: Cato Institute, 2007).

40. Norman Borlaug, recipient of the Nobel Peace Prize in 1970 for his work on the "green revolution," summarized its history in a Nobel lecture in 2002, http://nobelprize.org/nobel_prizes/peace/articles/borlaug/borlaug-lecture.pdf.

41. UNEP, *Green Jobs,* p. 224.

42. Ibid.

43. See, e.g., Goklany, note 39, p. 109.

44. Adam Smith, *An Inquiry into the Nature and Causes of the Wealth of Nations*, vol. 2 (New York: Collier, 1902) p. 164.

45. Pierre Desrochers and Hiroko Shimizu, "Yes, We Have No Bananas: A Critique of the 'Food Miles' Perspective," Policy Primer no. 8, Mercatus Policy Series, Mercatus Center, George Mason University, 2008. Discussion of trade in medical services, p. 12.

46. "The Politics of Hunger: A Review," *Review of Austrian Economics* 3(1989): 253.

47. See, e.g., http://walmartwatch.com/ and http://wakeupwalmart.com/.

48. Jerry Hausman and Ephraim Leibtag, "CPI Bias from Supercenters: Does The BLS Know That Wal-Mart Exists?" NBER Working Paper no. 10712, 2004.

49. Emek Basker, "The Causes and Consequences of Wal-Mart's Growth," *Journal of Economic Perspectives* 21(3) (2007): 179.

50. The official website is http://www.cars.gov/.

51. Lucas W. Davis and Matthew E. Kahn, "International Trade in Used Vehicles: The Environmental Consequences of NAFTA," NBER Working Paper no. 14565, 2009.

52. Although it is enthusiastically practiced in North Korea under its Juche method of economic organization. See Juche Idea Study Group of England, http://www.korea-dpr.com/users/jisge/. (It compiles links to documents on the benefits of this method of anti-trade organization.)

53. Sean Higgins, "Buy American Policy Now Law as Critics Fear Global Reaction; Final Wording Spares EU, Japan, and Canada; Brazil Mulls WTO Case," *Investor's Business Daily*, February 18, 2009.

54. Martin Wolf, *Why Globalization Works* (New Haven, CT: Yale University Press, 2004), p. 188. He demolishes the link between trade and environmental problems on pp. 188–94.

55. Brian R. Copeland and M. Scott Taylor, "Trade, Growth, and the Environment," *Journal of Economic Literature* 42 (2004): 7.

56. Bryan Ward-Perkins, *The Fall of Rome and the End of Civilization* (Oxford: Oxford University Press, 2005), pp. 87–117.

57. http://devdata.worldbank.org/wdi2006/contents/Section6_1.htm.

Chapter 7

1. See, e.g., Michael Mandel, *Economics: The Basics* (New York: McGraw Hill, 2009), p. 398; Roger L. Miller and Roger E. Meiners, *Intermediate Microeconomics*, 3rd ed. (New York: McGraw Hill, 1986), pp. 581–82.

2. United Nations Environment Programme, *Green Jobs: Towards Decent Work in a Sustainable, Low-Carbon World* (Nairobi: U.N. Publishing Services Section, 2008), p. 225, http://www.unep.org/labour_environment/PDFs/Greenjobs/UNEP-Green-Jobs-Report.pdf.

3. Ibid., p. 233.

4. Ibid., p. 234.

5. Jack Neff, "What Wal-Mart Savings Claim Doesn't Tell You," *Advertising Age*, November 12, 2007, http://adage.com/article?article_id=121932. The "secret" is that one does not have to shop at Wal-Mart to gain the benefit.

6. Kent Garber, "The Growing Food Cost Crisis," *U.S. News and World Report*, March 17, 2008, http://www.usnews.com/articles/news/2008/03/07/the-growing-food-cost-crisis.html. See also Elisabeth Malkin, "Thousands in Mexico City Pro-

test Rising Food Prices," *New York Times,* February 1, 2007, http://www.nytimes.
com/2007/02/01/world/americas/01mexico.html?_r=1&scp=1&sq=Mexico+
tortilla+riots&st=nyt&oref=slogin; Opinion, "The Misguided Politics of Corn Ethanol," *International Herald Tribune,* September 19, 2007, http://www.iht.com/articles/
2007/09/19/news/edethanol.php.

7. UN Food and Agricultural Organization, "Bioenergy Policy, Markets and Trade
and Food Security," Technical Background Document from the Food and Agriculture
Organization of the United Nations Expert Consultation, Rome, February 2008, http://
www.fao.org/fileadmin/user_upload/foodclimate/HLCdocs/HLC08-bak-7-E.pdf;
Congressional Budget Office, *The Impact of Ethanol Use on Food Prices and Greenhouse-
Gas Emissions* (Washington: Congressional Budget Office, April 2009), http://www.
cbo.gov/doc.cfm?index=10057.

8. E.F. Schumacher, *Small Is Beautiful: A Study of Economics as if People Mattered*
(London: Blond and Briggs, 1973).

9. E.F. Schumacher, "Buddhist Economics," Smallisbeautiful.org, 1999, http://
www.smallisbeautiful.org/pdf/buddhist_economics/english.pdf.

10. Ibid.

11. UNEP, see note 2, p. 24.

12. See, e.g., Elizabeth Williamson and Paul Glader, "GE Pursues Pot of Government Stimulus Gold," *Wall Street Journal,* November 17, 2009, http://online.wsj.com/
article/SB125832961253649563.html.

13. See, e.g., Alan K. Ota, "Bioenergy Investors Flexing Political Clout," *CQ Today,*
November 16, 2007, http://public.cq.com/docs/cqt/news110-000002630067.html (describing ethanol industry's political connections).

14. See, e.g., Wendy Williams and Robert Whitcomb, *Cape Wind: Money, Celebrity,
Class, Politics and the Battle for Our Energy Future on Nantucket Sound* (New York: Public
Affairs, 2007).

15. See, e.g., Bruce Yandle, "Coase, Pigou, and Environmental Rights," in *Who
Owns the Environment?* eds. Peter Jensen Hill and Roger E. Meiners (Lanham, MD:
Rowman & Littlefield, 1998).

16. A classic episode in this regard is the Clean Air Act. See Bruce A. Ackerman and
William T. Hassler, *Clean Coal/Dirty Air: Or How the Clean Air Act Became a Multi-Billion
Dollar Bail-Out for High-Sulfur Coal Producers* (New Haven, CT: Yale University Press,
1981, 4th ed.).

17. Robert Pollin et al., "Green Recovery: A Program to Create Good Jobs and Start
Building a Low Carbon Economy," Center for American Progress, Political Economy
Research Institute, September 2008, p. 6–7.

18. Ibid., p. 16.

19. UNEP, see note 2, p. 131.

20. Ibid., p. 24.

21. Ibid., p. 139.

22. Ibid., p. 134.

23. Ibid., p. 159.

24. See, e.g., "Annual Hybrid Sales Drop for First Time," hybridCARS.com, http://
www.hybridcars.com/news/annual-hybrid-sales-drop-first-time-25388.html. ("The
best-selling hybrid, the Toyota Prius, posted 158,884 sales in 2008, a drop of 12.3 percent from 2007. In mid-year when gas prices spiked above $4 a gallon, customers joined
long waiting lists for the Prius. Those waiting lists, and general demand for hybrids,
evaporated as gas prices plunged, falling below $2 a gallon by the end of the year.")

25. Pollin et al., see note 17, pp. 6-7.

26. Ibid., see note 17, p. 9. CAP continues to report such benefits, in detail, from the 2009 stimulus plan. Will Straw, "The Nationwide Allocation of Recovery Funding: An Interactive Map on the Final House-Senate Compromise," Center for American Progress, http://www.americanprogress.org/issues/2009/02/compromise_map.html.

27. Ibid., p. 20.

28. Ibid., p. 21.

29. Ibid.

30. Ibid.

31. Ibid.

32. Ibid., p. 21, refers to Richard Hemming, Michael Kell, and Selma Mahfouz, "The Effectiveness of Fiscal Policy in Stimulating Economic Activity: A Review of the Literature," IMF Working Paper no. WP/02/208, 2002; Pollin et al., see note 62, p. 21.

33. Ibid.

34. Ibid., p. 22.

35. See, e.g., Michael J. Boskin, "An Alternative Stimulus Plan," *Wall Street Journal*, November 17, 2009, http://online.wsj.com/article/SB10001424052748704431804574541471162110460.html. Boskin notes that the $787 billion stimulus plan did not, as asserted, keep unemployment from rising above 8 percent. At the time Boskin wrote, it was 10.2 percent. See also Robert J. Barro and Charles J. Redlick, "Stimulus Spending Doesn't Work," *Wall Street Journal*, October 1, 2009, http://online.wsj.com/article/SB10001424052748704471504574440723298786310.html.

36. Pollin et al., see note 17, p. 8.

37. United States Conference of Mayors, *U.S. Metro Economies: Current and Potential Green Jobs in the U.S. Economy* (Lexington, MA: Global Insight, 2008), p. 11, http://www.usmayors.org/pressreleases/uploads/greenjobsreport.pdf.

38. UNEP, see note 2, p. 93.

39. Pollin et al., see note 17, p. 8.

40. Ibid.

41. UNEP, see note 2, p. 47.

42. Navigant Consulting, Inc., "Economic Impacts of the Tax Credit Expiration," report prepared for the American Wind Energy Association and the Solar Energy Research and Education Foundation, 2008, http://www.seia.org/galleries/pdf/Navigant_Tax_Credit_Impact.pdf.

43. Pollin et al., see note 17, p. 16.

44. Ibid.

45. Terry Macalister, "Blow to Brown as BP Scraps British Renewables Plan to Focus on US," *Guardian*, November 7, 2008, http://www.guardian.co.uk/business/2008/nov/07/bp-renewable-energy-oil-wind.

46. Danny Fortson, "Shell to Quit Wind Projects," *Sunday Times (UK)*, December 7, 2008, http://business.timesonline.co.uk/tol/business/industry_sectors/natural_resources/article5299195.ece.

47. UNEP, see note 2, p. 10.

48. Pollin et al., see note 17, p. 11.

49. Ibid., p. 9.

50. "$160,000 per Stimulus Job? White House Calls That 'Calculator Abuse,'" *ABC News*, October 31, 2009, http://blogs.abcnews.com/politicalpunch/2009/10/160000-per-stimulus-job-white-house-calls-that-calculator-abuse.html.

51. We are not arguing that a college education would necessarily be a better use of that much money (despite our self-interest in the growth of the higher-education industry), but the report gives no evidence that their prescription for the expenditure is better than the same amount spent on education or some other area of activity. Full tuition at York College of Pennsylvania in 2008–09 was $13,680. See http://ycp.edu/admissions/208.htm. Full tuition for an in-state student at Penn State in 2008–09 was $13,014 for a freshman or sophomore and $14,070 for a junior or senior. See http://tuition.psu.edu/Rates2008-09/UniversityPark.asp.

52. UNEP, see note 2, p. 170–71.

53. Ibid., p. 185.

54. Ibid., p. 3.

55. U.S. Department of Energy, *20% Wind Energy by 2030: Increasing Wind Energy's Contribution to U.S. Electricity Supply* (Oak Ridge, TN: Department of Energy, 2008), p. 203, http://www.nrel.gov/docs/fy08osti/41869.pdf.

56. The UNEP report occasionally considers job losses but generally finds them to be a positive effect. See, e.g., UNEP, see note 2, p. 150. ("In a sustainable economy, there will be fewer jobs in airplane manufacturing and air travel services than today. But from a macro-economic perspective, this is not necessarily a negative development. Many jobs in the aviation industry are effectively heavily subsidized, via exemptions from fuel duty, value added tax, and duty-free rules.")

57. Mayors, see note 37, p. 10.

58. Pollin et al., see note 17, p. 2.

59. Ibid., pp. 6–7.

60. UNEP, see note 2, p. 12.

61. Ibid., p. 138. The literature also notes that retrofitting would "stimulate jobs in the manufacturing of green building components and systems," p. 143.

62. Ibid., p. 140.

Chapter 8

1. Randy A. Becker and Ronald J. Shadbegian, "Environmental Products Manufacturing: A Look inside The Green Industry," *The B.E. Journal of Economic Analysis & Policy*, 9(1) (2009).

2. Robert Pollin et al., "Green Recovery: A Program to Create Good Jobs and Start Building a Low Carbon Economy," Center for American Progress, Political Economy Research Institute, September 2008, p. 2.

3. *Economic Report of the President (2010)*, p. 69. A critical view from outside the administration is found in John F. Cogan, John B. Taylor, and Volker Wieland, "The Stimulus Didn't Work," *Wall Street Journal*, September 17, 2009, http://online.wsj.com/article/SB10001424052970204731804574385233867030644.html.

4. Roger Bezdek, *Renewable Energy and Energy Efficiency: Economic Drivers for the 21st Century* (Boulder, CO: American Solar Energy Society, 2007), http://www.misi-net.com/publications/ASES-EconomicDrivers07.pdf.

5. United States Conference of Mayors, *U.S. Metro Economies: Current and Potential Green Jobs in the U.S. Economy* (Lexington, MA: Global Insight, 2008), p. 17, http://www.usmayors.org/pressreleases/uploads/greenjobsreport.pdf.

6. Douglas P. Woodward and Paulo Guimarães, "BMW in South Carolina: The Economic Impact of A Leading Sustainable Enterprise," Moore School of Business

Report, 2008, http://www.chattanoogachamber.com/PDF_Files/110308_BMWReport Sept2008.pdf.

7. A critical review of the literature along with case studies of specific cities is provided in Roger Noll and Andrew Zimbalist, eds., *Sports, Jobs, and Taxes: The Economic Impact of Sports Teams and Stadiums* (Washington: Brookings Institution Press, 1997).

8. John J. Siegfried et al., "The Economic Impact of Colleges and Universities," *Economics of Education Review* 26(2007): 546.

9. A relatively transparent example of the use of such a model (IMPLAN) in the context of green jobs is found in S. Tegen, M. Milligan, and M. Goldberg, "Economic Development Impacts of Wind Power: A Comparative Analysis of Impacts within the Western Governors' Association States," National Renewable Energy Laboratory Conference Paper no. NREL/CP-500-41808, 2007.

10. See Richard Hemming, Michael Kell, and Selma Mahfouz, "The Effectiveness of Fiscal Policy in Stimulating Economic Activity: A Review of the Literature," IMF Working Paper 02/208, 2002, p. 35.

11. Gabriel Calzada, "Study of the Effects on Employment of Public Aid to Renewable Energy Sources," King Juan Carlos University, March 2009, http://www.juandemariana.org/pdf/090327-employment-public-aid-renewable.pdf. A document leaked in May 2010 revealed that "even the socialist Spanish government now acknowledges the ruinous effects of green economic policy." Christopher Horner, "Leaked Doc Proves Spain's 'Green' Policies—the Basis for Obama's—an Economic Disaster," *Pajamas Media*, May 18, 2010, http://pajamasmedia.com/blog/spains-green-policies-an-economic-disaster/ (English translation, with link to the original Spanish document). Spain has been cited as a model for the type of green economy the United States should embrace.

12. Calzada, see note 11, p. 1.

13. Ibid., p. 32.

14. Robert J. Barro, *Macroeconomics: A Modern Approach* (Mason, OH: Thomson, 2008). He presents an argument against expectations of substantial impact from the stimulus in "Government Spending Is No Free Lunch," *Wall Street Journal*, January 22, 2009, http://online.wsj.com/article/SB123258618204604599.html.

15. Robert J. Barro and Charles J. Redlick, "Stimulus Spending Doesn't Work," *Wall Street Journal*, October 1, 2009, http://online.wsj.com/article/SB1000142405274870447 150457444072329878630.html. See also, Robert J. Barro and Charles J. Redlick, "Macroeconomic Effects from Government Purchases and Taxes," NBER Working Paper no. 15369, September 2009.

16. See, e.g., Wassily Leontief, *Input-Output Economics*, 2nd ed. (Oxford: Oxford University Press, 1986).

17. Ibid., p. 19.

18. Ibid.

19. Tegen, Milligan, and Goldberg, see note 9, pp. 9–10.

20. The ability to cost shift depends on relative elasticities of supply and demand. Harvey Rosen, *Public Finance*, 6th ed. (New York: McGraw Hill, 2002), p. 283.

21. Leontief, see note 16, p. 14.

22. See, e.g., United Nations Environment Programme, *Green Jobs: Towards Decent Work in a Sustainable, Low-Carbon World* (Nairobi: U.N. Publishing Services Section, 2008), p. 92, http://www.unep.org/labour_environment/PDFs/Greenjobs/UNEP-Green-Jobs-Report.pdf.

23. Linda Levine, "Job Loss and Infrastructure Job Creation Spending During the Recession," Congressional Research Service Report, October 2, 2009, p. 6, http://digitalcommons.ilr.cornell.edu/key_workplace/681/.

24. Ibid.

25. Ibid., p. 10.

26. Terry Buss, "The Case against Targeted Industry Strategies," *Economic Development Quartely* 13 (1999): 339.

27. Paul Courant, "How Would You Know a Good Economic Development Policy if You Tripped over One? Hint: Don't Just Count Jobs," *National Tax Journal* 47 (1994): 867.

28. Timothy J. Bartik, "Jobs, Productivity, and Local Economic Development," *National Tax Journal* 47 (1994): 852, 859.

29. This is the approach taken in three of the four studies that we most closely analyze and which estimate induced employment resulting from green jobs. See Pollin et al., note 2, pp. 24–26; Mayors, see note 5, pp. 12–17; and Bezdek, see note 4, pp. 30, 39, 46.

30. Pierre M. Picard, "Job Additionality and Deadweight Spending in Perfectly Competitive Industries: The Case of Optimal Employment Subsidies," *Journal of Public Finance* 79 (2001): 522.

31. Courant, see note 27, p. 872; Noll and Zimbalist, see note 7, pp. 61, 75. They go on to provide an example of incorrect analysis leading to vast overestimate of impact, pp. 497–498; see also William T. Bogart, *Don't Call It Sprawl: Metropolitan Structure in The Twenty-First Century* (Cambridge, UK: Cambridge University Press, 2006), p. 107 (on example of economic impact of new Cowboys stadium in Arlington not acknowledging spillovers from existing Cowboys stadium in Irving).

32. Noll and Zimbalist, see note 7, pp. 497–98; see also Bogart, see note 31.

33. A textbook exposition of deadweight loss can be found in Harvy Rosen and Ted Gayer, *Public Finance* (New York: McGraw Hill, 2008, 8th ed.). See also David Bradford, *Untangling the Income Tax* (Cambridge, MA: Harvard University Press, 1986), p. 135 (defining deadweight loss as "the effective waste of purchasing power owing to the distorting effects arising from the effort to avoid tax").

34. James C. Scott, *Seeing Like a State: How Certain Schemes to Improve the Human Condition Have Failed* (New Haven, CT: Yale University Press, 1999), pp. 47–48.

35. James Sallee, "The Incidence of Tax Incentives for Hybrid Vehicles," Harris School, University of Chicago, Working Paper no. 08.16, 2008.

36. Buss, see note 26, p. 347.

37. Picard, see note 30, p. 522, Table 1 (citing Foley).

38. EmployRES Project, "The Impact of Renewable Energy Policy on Economic Growth and Employment in the European Union," European Commission, DG Energy and Transport Report, 2006, p. 190, http://ec.europa.eu/energy/renewables/studies/doc/renewables/2009_employ_res_report.pdf.

39. Proponents of stadium projects tout increased employment from tourism, construction jobs, and increased localized spending. Richard W. Schwester, "An Examination of the Public Good Externalities of Professional Athletic Venues: Justifications for Public Financing?" *Public Budgeting and Finance* (September 2007): 90. ("A review of the literature shows that stadiums and arenas are insignificant in terms of creating employment. . . .")

40. Buss, see note 26, p. 347.

41. Bartik, see note 28, p. 856.

42. Woodward and Guimarães, see note 6, p. 9.

43. Dennis Coates and Brad Humphrey, "Professional Sports Facilities, Franchises and Urban Economic Development," *Public Finance and Management* 3 (2003): 335–57.

44. There are multiple analyses that discredit such studies. For example, Bruce Seaman's study of job claims in Atlanta found that the estimated average economic impact of several sports and cultural industries (commercial music, universities, professional sports) was $233 million in 1984, while the total personal income in the Atlanta metropolitan area was $32 billion. Bruce Seaman, "Arts Impact Studies: A Fashionable Excess," in *Economic Impact of the Arts: A Sourcebook,* eds. Anthony J. Radich and Sharon Schwoch (Washington: National Conference of State Legislatures, 1987). Thus, there could be at most 138 industries in the region before the entire income is accounted for.

45. See Jonathan H. Adler, "Clean Politics, Dirty Profits: Rent-Seeking behind the Green Curtain," in *Political Environmentalism: Going Behind the Green Curtain,* ed. Terry L. Anderson (Stanford: Hoover University Press, 2000).

46. That concept was first developed in Bruce Yandle, "Bootleggers and Baptists: The Education of a Regulatory Economist," *Regulation* (May–June 1983): 12.

47. See, e.g., Timothy Gardner, "150 Businesses Support Bill for U.S. Green Jobs," *Reuters,* August 5, 2009, http://www.reuters.com/article/internal_ReutersNews-Room_BehindTheScenes_MOLT/idUSTRE5746I820090805.

48. UNEP, see note 22, p. 4.

49. Ibid., p. 197.

50. Ibid., p. 228.

51. Ibid., p. 184.

52. Ibid., p. 92.

53. See Charles L. Schultze, *Other Times, Other Places: Macroeconomic Lessons from U.S. and European History* (Washington: Brookings Institution, 1986), pp. 27–33 (comparing U.S. and European labor productivity and economic policies).

54. Bezdek, see note 4, p. 14.

55. Ibid., p. iv.

56. Phillip Bastian, "On the Grid: Careers in Energy," *Occupational Outlook Quarterly* (Washington: Government Printing Office, Fall 2008), p. 38.

57. Indur M. Goklany, *The Improving State of the World: Why We're Living Longer, Healthier, More Comfortable Lives on a Cleaner Planet* (Washington: Cato Institute, 2007), pp. 44–48, 82–85.

58. UNEP, see note 22, p. 6.

59. Ibid., p. 9.

60. Ibid., p. 120.

61. Ibid., p. 102 (citing Kammen, Kapadia, and Fripp).

62. Ibid.

63. Ibid., p. 91. ("Extractive industries—the fossil fuel sector and other mining industries—do not employ many people.")

64. Ibid., p. 230. ("The trend towards consolidation and the growing market power of retailers that is occurring in the United States is also happening at the global level, and in some cases even more obviously so. Small 'greener' farmers are losing out to large capital-intensive producers and suppliers. This process has contributed to rural unemployment and accelerated urbanization.")

65. Ibid., p. 169. ("China's rail network grew by 24 percent in 1992–2002, but due to boosted labor productivity employment was cut almost in half . . . India's network grew only 1 percent, but due to radically different policies, employment stayed al-

most the same. . . . Increased labor productivity [in Africa] has led to reduced railway employment.")

66. Ibid., p. 166.

67. Kate Galbraith, "Europe's Way of Encouraging Solar Power Arrives in the U.S.," *New York Times*, March 12, 2009, http://www.nytimes.com/2009/03/13/business/energy-environment/13solar.html.

68. Manuel Frondel, Nolan Ritter, and Colin Vance, "Economic Impacts from the Promotion of Renewable Energies: The German Experience," Rhenisch-Westfälisches Institut für Wirtschaftsforschung, Final Report, 2009, http://www.instituteforenergyresearch.org/germany/Germany_Study_-_FINAL.pdf.

69. Ibid.

70. Goklany, see note 57, pp. 44–48, 82–85.

71. Bureau of the Census, U.S. Department of Commerce, *Statistical Abstract of the United States 2003* (Washington: Government Printing Office, 2003), Table HS-29, Employment Status of the Civilian Population: 1929 to 2002 (1929 figures); Bureau of the Census, U.S. Department of Commerce, *Statistical Abstract of the United States 2009* (Washington: Government Printing Office, 2003), Table 600, Employment by Industry 2000 to 2007 (2007 figures).

72. See, e.g., Bureau of the Census, U.S. Department of Commerce, *Statistical Abstract: Historical Statistics 2009* (Washington: Government Printing Office, 2009), Table HS-45 (comparing 1900 production in corn (2,662 mil. bu. vs. 9,008 mil. bu.), wheat (599 mil. bu. vs. 1,616 mil. bu.), and cotton (10,124 thousand bales vs. 17,100 thousand bales).

73. J. Paul Leigh et al., "Costs of Occupational Injuries in Agriculture," *Public Health Report* 116 (2001): 236.

74. Martin Wolf, *Why Globalization Works* (New Haven, CT: Yale University Press, 2004), p. 196.

75. W.G. Hettinga et al., "Understanding the Reductions in US Corn Ethanol Production Costs: An Experience Curve Approach," *Energy Policy* 27 (2008): 201.

76. UNEP, see note 22, p. 4 ("good jobs which offer adequate wages"); p. 22 (praising green certification programs for leading to "increased wages"); p. 65 (green jobs need to be "decent with regard to wages").

77. H.J. Habakkuk, *American and British Technology in the Nineteenth Century: The Search for Labour-Saving Inventions* (Cambridge, UK: Cambridge University Press, 1967), p. 101. (quoting *Parliamentary Papers* 51 (1854)); George Rogers Taylor, *The Transportation Revolution, 1815–1860* (Armonk, NY: ME Sharp, 1977), p. 224. ("Americans excelled especially in inventions increasing the speed of machine operation and making processes so automatic that they required less and less attention from the operatives.")

78. Douglass C. North, *The Economic Growth of the United States, 1790–1860* (Englewood Cliffs, NJ: Prentice Hall, 1966), p. 173.

79. Habakkuk, see note 77, p. 13; Paul Wallace Gates, *The Farmer's Age: Agriculture, 1815–1860* (Armonk, NY: ME Sharp, 1968), p. 271. ("In the early decades of the nineteenth century, the greatest difference between farming in the Old World and farming in the New was that in American agriculture labor was scarce and its cost relatively high."; in 1840 the Massachusetts Commissioner of Agricultural Survey noted that "the price of labor is enormous.")

80. Habakkuk, note 77, p. 47.

81. Ibid., p. 51.

82. See, e.g., E.F. Schumacher, *Small Is Beautiful: A Study of Economics as if People Mattered* (London: Blond and Briggs, 1973), (the best-seller of its day).,

83. See Schultze, note 53.

84. David S.J. Jones and Peter R. Pujadó, eds., *Handbook of Petroleum Processing* (New York: Springer, 2006), p. 1; U.S. Government Accountability Office, *Motor Fuels: Understanding the Factors That Influence the Retail Price of Gasoline* (Washington: Government Accountability Office, 2005), p. 1.

85. See, e.g., SenterNovem, *The Dutch Waste Profile 1990–2005* (Waste Management Authority, 2006), p. 7, www.senternovem.nl. ("The environmental regulations lead to increased capital intensity, increase in scale of the installations and economy of scale.")

86. Kirkpatrick Sale, "Avowedly Low-Tech: America's New Luddites," *Le Monde Diplomatique*, February 1997, http://mondediplo.com/1997/02/20luddites (describing efforts to create a coalition including environmentalists "to establish the legitimacy of resisting technological change").

Chapter 9

1. Portions of this chapter draw heavily on Andrew P. Morriss, "The Next Generation of Mobile Source Regulation," *New York University Environmental Law Journal* 17 (2008): 325.

2. United States Senate, Committee on Environment and Public Works, *Legislative History of The Clean Air Amendments of 1970, Volume 2* (Washington: Government Printing Office, 1974), p. 835.

3. J. Robert Mondt, *Cleaner Cars: The History and Technology of Emission Control Since the 1960s* (Warrendale, PA: SAE International, 2000), p. 57.

4. For an exposition on this point, see Indur Goklany, *Clearing the Air* (Washington: Cato Institute, 1999).

5. Steven F. Hayward, *Index of Leading Environmental Indicators,* 14th ed. (San Francisco: Pacific Research Institute, 2009), p. 22.

6. Iain Carson and Vijay Vaitheeswaran, *ZOOM: The Global Race to Fuel the Car of the Future* (New York: Twelve, 2007), p. 38.

7. W. Stanley Jevons, *The Coal Question,* 3rd ed. (London: Macmillan, 1906), p. 140. ("It is wholly a confusion of ideas to suppose that the economical use of fuel is equivalent to a diminished consumption. The very contrary is the truth.") There is empirical support for the Jevons Paradox with respect to automobile mileage. See Kenneth A. Small and Kurt Van Dender, "The Effect of Improved Fuel Economy on Vehicle Miles Traveled: Estimating The Rebound Effect Using U.S. State Data, 1966–2001," University of California Energy Institute, Working Paper no. EPE-014, 2005. See also John Polimeni et al., *The Jevons Paradox and the Myth of Resource Efficiency Improvements* (London: Earthscan, 2008).

8. Kenneth Small and Kurt Van Dender, "Fuel Efficiency and Motor Vehicle Travel: The Declining Rebound Effect," *Energy Journal* 28 (2007): 25 (estimating that—with variables at 1997–2001 levels—the rebound effect is somewhere between 2.2 percent and 10.7 percent).

9. On indoor air pollution, see Majid Ezzati and Daniel M. Kammen, "Evaluating the Health Benefits of Transitions in Household Energy Technologies in Kenya," *Energy Policy* 30 (2001): 815 (summarizing studies showing indoor air pollution's role in disease burden for developing countries); World Health Organization, *Fuel for Life: Household Energy and Health* (Geneva: WHO Press, 2006).

10. U.S. Department of Transportation, Federal Highway Administration, *Freight Facts and Figures 2006* (Washington: Department of Transportation, 2006),

Table 5-7, http://ops.fhwa.dot.gov/freight/freight_analysis/nat_freight_stats/docs/06factsfigures/table5_7.htm. "VMT" is vehicle miles traveled and is the standard unit of measure of trucking volume.

11. Patricia Jiayi Ho, "China Auto Sales Soar," *Wall Street Journal,* June 10, 2009, http://online.wsj.com/article/SB124454555379697583.html.

12. Stacy C. Davis, Susan W. Diegel, and Robert G. Boundy, *Transportation Energy Data Book,* 26th ed. (Oak Ridge, TN: Oak Ridge National Laboratory, 2007).

13. Andrew Peaple, "Car Makers Are Facing a Traffic Jam in China," *Wall Street Journal,* April 22, 2010.

14. Carson and Vaitheeswaran, see note 6, p. 202.

15. Japan International Transport Institute (JITI), "The Impact of Motorization in Fast-Growing Developing Nations Such as China and India," Institute of Economic Research Report, Kyoto University, 2005, pp. 5, 18, http://www.jitidc.com/conferences/2005/11/seminar_report.pdf.

16. Ibid., p. 20.

17. "China's '09 Auto Sales Forecast to Hit 12.6M," *China Daily,* September 25, 2009, http://www.chinadaily.com.cn/china/2009-09/25/content_8737881.htm.

18. JITI, "Impact of Motorization," p. 25.

19. See, e.g., "Rs 1 Lakh Car a Threat to Environment: Pachauri," *The Economic Times (India),* December 15, 2007, http://economictimes.indiatimes.com/Rs_1_lakh_car_a_threat_to_nature_Pachauri/articleshow/2624634.cms.

20. Carson and Vaitheeswaran, see note 6, p. 233.

21. Emissions standards for a gasoline and diesel 2005 car are:

	Gasoline	Diesel
Total HC	1.25 g/mi.	0.58 g/mi.
Exhaust CO	12.57 g/mi.	1.57 g/mi.
Exhaust NO_X	0.92 g/mi.	1.32 g/mi.

SOURCE: U.S. Department of Transportation, Federal Highway Administration, *Freight Facts and Figures 2006* (Washington: Department of Transportation, 2006), Table 5-11, http://ops.fhwa.dot.gov/freight/freight_analysis/nat_freight_stats/docs/06factsfigures/table5_11.htm.

22. See Mondt, note 3, p. 28 ("Compared to spark-ignition (Otto-cycle) engines, Diesel-cycle engines produce larger quantities of particulates because the fuel charge is injected into a combustion space that is essentially filled with air. At the end of the combustion event, the flame front is cooled before all the fuel is oxidized, and the unburned carbon in the fuel is oxidized by surrounding air, producing particules or particulates.")

23. For a sympathetic account of the ZEV program in California, see Union of Concerned Scientists, "California's Zero Emission Vehicle Program," http://www.ucsusa.org/clean_vehicles/solutions/advanced_vehicles_and_fuels/californias-zero-emission-1.html. For more skeptical analyses, see H. Gruenspecht, "Zero Emission Vehicles: A Dirty Little Secret," *Resources* 142 (2001): 7–10; L. Dixon et al., *Driving Emissions to Zero: Are The Benefits of California's Zero Emission Vehicle Program Worth The Cost?* (Santa Monica, CA: RAND, 2002). The official description is available at California Air Resources Board, Zero Emission Vehicle (ZEV) Program (2009), http://www.arb.ca.gov/msprog/zevprog/zevprog.htm.

24. On the life cycle trade-offs between a Prius and a Hummer, see CNW Marketing Research, "Dust to Dust" (a controversial report contending that the net environmental impact of a Toyota Prius was greater than of a Hummer H1). For a summary of the critiques of the study, see Bengt Halvorson, "Prius Versus Hummer: Exploding the Myth," *The Car Connection*, April 16, 2007, http://www.thecarconnection.com/tips-article/1010861_prius-versus-hummer-exploding-the-myth.

25. United Nations Environment Programme, *Green Jobs: Towards Decent Work in a Sustainable, Low-Carbon World* (Nairobi: U.N. Publishing Services Section, 2008), p. 14, http://www.unep.org/labour_environment/PDFs/Greenjobs/UNEP-Green-Jobs-Report.pdf.

26. Ibid., pp. 14, 152, 167.

27. Ibid., p. 162.

28. Ibid., p. 149.

29. Ibid., pp. 13, 166. For example, the UNEP criticized China for making its rail network more efficient: "China's rail network grew by 24 percent in 1992–2002, but due to boosted labor productivity employment was cut almost in half . . . India's network grew only 1 percent, but due to radically different policies, employment stayed almost the same. . . . Increased labor productivity [in Africa] has led to reduced railway employment," p. 169.

30. United States Conference of Mayors, *U.S. Metro Economies: Current and Potential Green Jobs in the U.S. Economy* (Lexington, MA: Global Insight, 2008), p. 16, http://www.usmayors.org/pressreleases/uploads/greenjobsreport.pdf; U.S. Energy Information Administration, *Annual Energy Review 2008* (Washington: Energy Information Administration, 2009), p. 4, http://www.eia.doe.gov/aer/pdf/aer.pdf.

31. Executive Office of the President, Council of Economic Advisors (CEA), *Economic Analysis of The Car Allowance Rebate System* (Washington: Council of Economic Advisors, September 10, 2009), http://www.whitehouse.gov/assets/documents/CEA_Cash_for_Clunkers_Report_FINAL.pdf.

32. Bracken Hendricks and Benjamin Goldstein, "Retiring Old Cars, Creating New Jobs," Center for American Progress, March 23, 2009, http://www.americanprogress.org/issues/2009/03/cash_for_clunkers.html.

33. Joe Romm, "Cash for Clunkers Is a Double Economic Stimulus That Pays for Itself in Oil Savings So CO_2 Savings Are Free," *Climate Progress*, August 27, 2009, http://climateprogress.org/2009/08/27/cash-for-clunkers-double-economic-stimulus-oil-savings-co2-greenhouse-gas/. CAP heavily promoted the idea while it was being considered in Congress as well.

34. CEA, see note 31, p. 4.

35. EIA forecasts a $2.94/gallon price in 2010, for example. See Energy Information Administration, "Short Term Energy Outlook," November 10, 2009, http://www.eia.doe.gov/emeu/steo/pub/contents.html.

36. See also Burton Abrams and George Parsons, "Is Cars a Clunker?" *The Economists' Voice* 6.8 (2009) (using a conventional cost/benefit analysis and finding that the total enviro benefits of each car taken off the road works out to $596 per vehicle compared to a cost of $2,600 to retire that vehicle); Chistopher Knittel, "The Implied Cost of Carbon Dioxide Under the Cash for Clunkers Program," CSEM Working Paper no. 189, Center for the Study of Energy Markets, University of California Energy Institute, August 2009 (concluding that the implied cost of carbon dioxide emissions in this program range from $237 per ton to $365 per ton); Lee Schipper et al., "When It Comes to Being Green, Cash for Clunkers Is a Lemon," *Washington Post*, August 9, 2009.

37. "Cash for Clunkers Results Finally In: Taxpayers Paid $24,000 per Vehicle Sold," Edmunds.com, October 28, 2009, http://www.edmunds.com/help/about/press/159446/article.html.

38. Atif Miar and Amin Sufi, "The Effects of Fiscal Stimulus: Evidence from the 2009 'Cash for Clunkers' Program," NBER Working Paper No. 16351 (Sept. 2010); http://papers.nber.org/papers/w16351.

39. Macon Phillips, "Busy Covering Car Sales on Mars, Edmunds.com Gets It Wrong (Again) on Cash for Clunkers," The White House Blog, October 29, 2009, http://www.whitehouse.gov/blog/2009/10/29/busy-covering-car-sales-mars-edmundscom-gets-it-wrong-again-cash-clunkers; Joseph Plocek, "Analysis: US Q3 GDP Revised Lower, to 2.8%; Final Sales +1.9%; Q4 Weaker?" *iMarketNews.com*, November 24, 2009, http://imarketnews.com/node/5117.

40. Peter Tertzakian, *A Thousand Barrels A Second* (New York: McGraw Hill, 2007), p. 208.

41. Carson and Vaitheeswaran, see note 6, p. 3.

42. Robert Zubrin, *Energy Victory: Winning the War on Terror by Breaking Free of Oil* (Amherst, NY: Prometheus Books, 2007), p. 63.

43. Ibid.

44. Devlin Barrett, "Sen. Clinton Pitches Ethanol Energy Plan," *San Francisco Chronicle*, May 23, 2006, http://www.sfgate.com/cgi-bin/article/article?f=/n/a/2006/05/23/politics/p085135D20.DTL.

45. D.V. Spitzley et al., "Automotive Life Cycle Economics and Replacement Intervals," Report no. CSS04-01, Center for Sustainable Systems, University of Michigan, January 7, 2004, http://css.snre.umich.edu/css_doc/CSS04-01.pdf.

46. Davis, Diegel, and Boundy, see note 12.

47. Andrew P. Morriss, Bruce Yandle, and Andrew Dorchak, *Regulation by Litigation* (New Haven, CT: Yale University Press, 2009), pp. 74–75.

48. Zubrin, see note 42, p. 23.

49. See, e.g., Sharon Terlap, "Electric Cars Face a Battery of Hurdles," *Detroit News*, February 19, 2008, http://www.detnews.com/apps/pbcs.dll/article?AID=/20080219/AUTO01/802190349/1148/rss25 (describing technological challenges).

50. Vehicles that burn fossil fuels cause air pollution in three ways. First, and most obviously, the consumption of fuel results in emissions of byproducts of the consumption and of partially consumed fuel. Second, vehicles can emit pollutants through leaks in the fuel storage and consumption systems within the vehicle (e.g., evaporation from fuel tanks). Third, fueling vehicles can cause pollution through contact between the fuel and the atmosphere during fueling (e.g., evaporation from gasoline pumps during fueling). Cars and trucks today emit much less from each of these sources than they did in the past. There is no low hanging fruit to pick in any of these instances.

51. Carson and Vaitheeswaran, see note 6, p. 264.

52. Ibid.

53. Bernard Challen and Rodica Baranescu, eds., *Diesel Engine Reference Book,* 2nd ed. (Woburn, MA: Butterworth Heinemann, 1999), p. 93. See also Hajime Fujimoto et al., "New Concept on Lower Exhaust Emission of Diesel Engine" in *Diesel Engine Combustion and Emissions from Fuel to Exhaust Aftertreatment* (Warrendale, PA: Society of Automotive Engineers, 1995), p. 65.

54. *Diesel Engine Reference Book*, p. 93. See also Kathleen M. Nauss, "Critical Issues in Assessing the Carcinogenicity of Diesel Exhaust: A Synthesis of Current Knowl-

edge," in *Diesel Exhaust: A Critical Analysis of Emissions, Exposure, and Health Effects* (Boston, MA: Health Effects Institute, 1995), p. 24. ("One of the problems with controlling diesel emissions is the tradeoff between emissions of particulate matter and emissions of oxides of nitrogen.")

55. EPA, Memorandum of Law of the United States of America in Support of Motion to Enter Consent Decree and Response to Public Comments, *United States of America v. Caterpillar, Inc.*, Civil Action no. 1:98CV02544, April 30, 1999, p. 13.

56. Mondt, see note 3, p. 22.

57. Motor Vehicle Nitrogen Oxides Standard Committee, Assembly of Engineering, National Research Council, NO_x *Emission Controls for Heavy-Duty Vehicles: Toward Meeting a 1986 Standard* (Washington: National Academy Press, 1981), p. 23.

58. See Linsey C. Marr and Robert A. Harley, "Spectral Analysis of Weekday-Weekend Differences in Ambient Ozone, Nitrogen Oxide, and Non-Methane Hydrocarbon Time Series in California," *Atmospheric Environment* 36 (2002): 2334; N.A. Kelly and R.F. Gunst, "Response of Ozone to Changes in Hydrocarbon and Nitrogen Oxide Concentrations in Outdoor Smog Chambers Filled with Los Angeles Air," *Atmospheric Engineering* 24a (1990): 2991.

59. D.J. Peterson and Sergej Mahnovski, *New Forces at Work in Refining: Industry Views of Critical Business and Operations Trends* (Santa Monica, CA: RAND, 2003), p. 21 (quoting a "technology and services executive").

60. The arguments in this section are developed in greater detail in Andrew P. Morriss and Nathaniel Stewart, "Market Fragmenting Regulation: Why Gasoline Costs So Much (and Why It's Going to Cost Even More," *Brooklyn Law Review* 72 (2007): 939.

61. Paul H. Giddens, *Standard Oil Company (Indiana): Oil Pioneer of The Middle West* (New York: Appleton-Century-Crofts, 1976), pp. 287–92.

62. *Federal Register* 37 (February 23, 1972): 3882. The final rule was issued in January 1973. *Federal Register* 38 (January 10, 1973): 1254. Although the lead additive makers challenged EPA's actions, the en banc D.C. Circuit upheld the rule. Ethyl Corp. v. EPA, 541 F.2d 1 (D.C. Cir. en banc), cert. den., 426 U.S. 941 (1976).

63. See Thomas O. McGarity, "MTBE: A Precautionary Tale," *Harvard Enviromental Law Review* 28 (2004): 294. (When Congress set automotive emissions standards with the Clean Air Act Amendments of 1970, it "assumed that the automobile manufacturing industry would meet those standards by installing catalytic converters in the exhaust stream.")

64. The authority was phrased broadly, however, allowing EPA to control the use of additives on environmental grounds generally. See 42 U.S.C. 7574(c)(1)(A) (2000).

65. In 1971, the newly formed EPA announced consideration of restrictions on lead as an additive, *Federal Register* 32 (1971): 1486. In 1972, the agency proposed regulations, *Federal Register* 37 (1972): 11786, and in 1973, EPA exercised its Clean Air Act § 211(c)(1)(A) authority to require a series of lead additive reductions beginning January 1, 1975, to a final level of no more than 0.5 grams per gallon by January 1979, *Federal Register* 38 (1973): 33,734. Refiners challenged EPA's actions and lost, Amoco Oil Co. v. EPA, 501 F.2d 722 (D.C. Cir. 1974), although the challenge resulted in a less restrictive phase-out schedule. Robert L. Bradley Jr., *Oil, Gas, and Government: The U.S. Experience, Volume 2* (Lanham, MD: Rowman and Littlefield, 1996), pp. 1252–1253.

66. Morriss and Stewart, see note 60, pp. 1023–1024 (summarizing small refiner biases in lead phase-out). For a thorough public choice analysis of the history of petroleum regulation, see Bradley, note 65.

67. *Federal Register* 38 (1973): 33,734, 33,740.

68. Clean Air Act Amendments of 1977, Public Law no. 95-95, sec. 223, 91 Stat. 685, 764 codified at 42 U.S.C. 7545(g).

69. Thomas O. McGarity, "Radical Technology Forcing in Environmental Regulation," *Loyola of Los Angeles Law Review* 27 (1994): 950.

70. See Adler, *Clean Fuels, Dirty Air.* The interaction of the environmental regulation with 1970s economic regulation of energy prices also caused problems for refiners. The price controls did not allow refiners to fully pass through to consumers the additional costs of producing unleaded gasoline; as a result, "most oil companies chose to go slow in expanding their unleaded gasoline capacity." Richard B. Mancke, *Performance of the Federal Energy Office* (Washington: American Enterprise Institute, 1975), p. 35. This then produced periodic shortages of unleaded gasoline in the 1970s. These shortages prompted EPA to slow down the lead phase-out. McGarity, *Radical Technology Forcing,* p. 949.

71. William L. Leffler, *Petroleum Refining in Nontechnical Language* (Tulsa: PenWell, 2000), p. 141.

72. Ibid.

73. Ibid.

74. McGarity, see note 63, p. 296. See also Arthur M. Reitze Jr., "The Regulation of Fuels and Fuel Additives under Section 211 of the Clean Air Act," *Tulsa Law Journal* 29 (1994): 506–07.

75. McGarity, see note 74, p. 296.

76. Ibid. MMT, approved after EPA testing, is legal, if not widely used, in all states except California and Nevada, as of April 2010. Cy Ryan, "Battle over Gasoline Additive Sparks Debate." *Las Vegas Sun,* April 27, 2010, http://www.lasvegassun.com/news/2010/apr/27/battle-over-gasoline-additive-sparks-debate/.

77. 42 U.S.C. 7545(m), 7512a(b)(3).

78. McGarity, see note 63, p. 306.

79. Ibid., p. 309. See also Reitze, note 74, pp. 526–28 (describing interest group maneuvering over oxygenates).

80. Reitze, see note 74, p. 528 (noting that rule-making ultimately had "a tilt away from a fuel neutral approach to one that carved a place for ethanol").

81. National Academy of Sciences, *Ozone-Forming Potential of Reformulated Gasoline* (Washington: National Academy Press, 1999), p. 108. One problem was that the EPA allowed vehicles to be certified with lower volatility gasoline than was used in practice, leading to higher emissions than anticipated. See Reitze, *Fuels,* pp. 515–16.

82. Reitze, see note 74, p. 516 (describing efforts of Northeast States for Coordinated Air Use Management, an eight-state coalition, and a subgroup of the coalition to impose volatility requirements in 1989). Before the 1990 Amendments, California refiners led a push toward "cleaner" fuels out of concern that the state not mandate a mixture of 85 percent methanol and 15 percent gasoline and ultimately introduced a wide range of fuels built around the addition of MTBE. McGarity, see note 74, pp. 305–06.

83. NAS, see note 81, p. 109.

84. Ibid. The 1990 amendments allowed the EPA to impose a baseline set of requirements for gasoline, including mandating reformulated gasoline (RFG) to help meet federal standards for ground level ozone. The 1990 amendments specified a wide range of characteristics of "base" gasoline, 42 U.S.C. 7581(4). The first set of RFG requirements were applied in 1995, with a second, tighter phase following in 2000.

The EPA initially required the RFG formulations in nine metropolitan areas, although others were added later. 42 U.S.C. 7545.

85. U.S. Environmental Protection Agency, Office of Compliance, *Profile of The Petroleum Refining Industry* (Washington: Environmental Protection Agency, 1995), p. 91. Most commonly, the additional steps were additional catalytic cracking and alkylation of the gasoline. Because n-butane also raises the average octane, however, a substitute was needed to maintain the blend's octane level. Needless to say, refineries also found themselves with seasonal surpluses of n-butane. James H. Gary and Glenn E. Handwerk, *Petroleum Refining: Technology and Economics,* 4th ed. (New York: Marcel Dekker, 2001), pp. 8–9.

86. EPA, *Petroleum Refining Industry,* p. 91. In particular, blending of lower volatility compounds into the gasoline increased.

87. Ibid.

88. J.G. Calvert et al., "Achieving Acceptable Air Quality: Some Reflections on Controlling Vehicle Emissions," *Science* 261 (1993): 42 (reducing sulfur content both lowers sulfur oxide emissions and makes catalytic reduction of HCs, CO, and NO_x more efficient).

89. Reitze, see note 74, pp. 507–12. 40 C.F.R. §80.195 et seq. contain the gasoline sulfur requirements.

90. D.R. Blackmore, "Gasoline And Related Fuels," in *Modern Petroleum Technology, Volume 2,* ed. Alan G. Lucas (Hoboken, NJ: Wiley, 2002), p. 248 (describing model).

91. Ibid.

92. NAS, see note 81, pp. 126–27. The problem was ultimately solved by the EPA's "in situ' sample audits, which led most refiners blending at refinery.

93. See Environmental Protection Agency, "Reformulated Gasoline," http://www .epa.gov/otaq/rfg/faq.htm (discussing SIP revisions for state-mandated gasoline formulations).

94. U.S. Senate, Committee on Government Affairs, Majority Staff of the Permanent Subcommittee on Investigations, *Gas Prices: How Are They Really Set?* 2002, p. 94.

95. See, e.g., Hawaii Rev. Stat. 486J-10 (requiring 10 percent ethanol content for all unleaded gasoline sold after April 2, 2006).

96. See Jennifer Brown et al., "Reformulating Competition? Gasoline Content Regulation and Wholesale Gasoline Prices," CUDARE Working Papers no. 1010, 2006.

97. U.S. Federal Trade Commission, *Gasoline Price Changes: The Dynamic of Supply, Demand, And Competition* (Washington: Federal Trade Commission, 2005), pp. 88–89.

98. Brown et. al., see note 96, pp. 4–5. An EPA analysis found that boutique requirements are not a factor in increasing gasoline prices, claiming that the refining and distribution network is "able to provide adequate quantities of boutique fuels, as long as there are no disruptions in the supply chain." See H. Josef Herbert, "Gas Blends Don't Raise Prices," *Associated Press,* June 23, 2006, quoting the EPA report. As this quote suggests, the agency focused on the wrong question. It is precisely when there are disruptions in the supply chain that a broad, deep market makes a difference. The agency concluded that "[t]he timing of price changes . . . suggests that they may bear some relationship to the introduction of Phases I (1992) and II (1996) of the stringent and specialized CARB requirements for gasoline sold in California" (p. 90). While the FTC study found evidence of a boutique fuel price effect in California, it did not in the Gulf Coast, where the agency concluded that the larger amount of refinery capacity in the Gulf Coast region and greater interconnection

of that region with other areas reduced the impact of disruptions at any particular facility (p. 94). The FTC found similar results in the East Coast, Rocky Mountain, and Midwestern states.

99. P. Ellis Jones, "Introduction," see note 90, pp. xv, xxiii.

100. See A. Ogden-Swift, "Control and Optimization," see note 90, p. 181. ("Refinery planning and scheduling, optimization, process control and monitoring are essential to achieving [maximum profits]. Typically savings from improvements in these areas exceed $20 million per year for a world-scale refinery by choosing the best feedstocks, the best way to operate the refinery, effective control at the best point, and efficient detection and management of abnormalities.")

101. See Jones, "Introduction," see note 90, p. xxi. ("The development of products that meet the required quality standards has not generally been unduly difficult; where problems have arisen they have frequently arisen from the need to 'trade off' one characteristic against another.")

102. Britt A. Holmen and Debbie A. Niemeier, "Characterizing The Effects of Driver Variability on Real-World Vehicle Emissions," *Transportation Research*, D 3 (1998): 127.

103. See Craig N. Oren, "Getting Commuters Out of Their Cars: What Went Wrong?" *Stanford Environmental Law Journal* 17 (1998): 141 (describing failure of 1990 Act measures).

104. Todd A. Stewart, "E-Check: A Dirty Word in Ohio's Clean Air Debate," *Capital University Law Review* 29 (2001): 285–96.

105. Urea $((NH_2)_2CO)$ is the primary "reducing agent" injected into exhaust streams in selective catalytic reduction systems to reduce nitrogen oxide emissions. For a description, see Tom Gelinas, "Diesel Engine Technology: Emissions Control—2010," *GreenDieselTechnology.com*, January 1, 2009, http://www.greendieseltechnology.com/content/diesel-engine-technology-emissions-control-%E2%80%93-2010. On Mercedes' use of urea, see Derrick Y. Noh, "EPA to Set Urea Guidelines by October," Autobloggreen, August 29, 2009, http://green.autoblog.com/2006/08/29/epa-to-set-urea-guidelines-by-october/; Tim Moran, "Urea Must Flow or New Diesels Won't Go," *Automotive News*, October 20, 2008, http://www.autonews.com/article/20081020/ANA03/810200294/1186; Sam Abuelsamid, "Mercedes' New BlueTEC Diesels Will Not Start If Urea Runs Out," Autobloggreen, October 20, 2008, http://green.autoblog.com/2008/10/20/mercedes-new-bluetec-diesels-will-not-start-if-urea-runs-out/. The Mercedes system allows 20 restarts after the tank is "critically low."

106. Charles Sterling Pope, *Standard Oil Company (New Jersey) in World War II* (New York: Standard Oil Company, 1952), p. 30. (Hundred octane aviation fuel allowed British fighters to outmaneuver German planes during Battle of Britain.) See also Tim Palucka, "The Wizard of Octane," *Invention and Technology*, Winter 2005, http://www.americanheritage.com/articles/magazine/it/2005/3/2005_3_36.shtml; Richard Overy, *Why the Allies Won* (New York: W.W. Norton, 1997), p. 234. ("Hundred octane fuels produced much better performance than the 87 octane fuel used by the Luftwaffe. It allowed aircraft longer range, greater maneuverability, and those surges of power that gave Spitfires the edge over the Messerschmitt-109 in 1940.") It also aided tank warfare, leading Stalin to offer a toast at a birthday party for Churchill during the Tehran conference in 1943, "This is a war of engines and octanes. I drink to the American auto industry and the American oil industry" (p. 234).

107. Louis C. Hunter, "Industry in the Twentieth Century," in *The Growth of the American Economy*, ed. Harold F. Williamson, 2nd ed. (New York: Prentice Hall, 1951), pp. 699, 712–13.

108. Richard H.K. Vietor, *Energy Policy in America since 1945: A Study of Business-Government Relations, Volume 2* (Cambridge, UK: Cambridge University Press, 1984), p. 28.

109. Pope, see note 106, p. 10.

110. Hunter, see note 107, p. 713.

111. U.S. Department of Commerce, Office of Domestic Commerce, "United States Petroleum Refining: War and Postwar," Industrial Series no. 73, Department of Commerce, 1947, p. 9.

112. Pope, see note 106, p. 21.

113. Ibid., pp. 21–23.

114. Ibid., p. 25.

115. Ibid., pp. 21–23; H.C. Miller and G.B. Shea, "Gains in Oil and Gas Production Refining and Utilization Technology," Technical Paper no. 3, National Resources Planning Board, 1941, p. 30.

116. Pope, see note 106, p. 37.

117. Miller and Shea, see note 115, p. 36.

118. Shell Oil Company, *Shell, Soldier and Civilian* (New York: Shell Oil Company, 1945), p. 5.

119. Energy Information Agency, "U.S. Refinery Production of Finished Gasoline," http://tonto.eia.doe.gov/dnav/pet/hist/mgfrpus2a.htm (all figures except 1900); Affordability of Cleaner Fuels (2000), p. C-1 (1900 figures).

120. National Petroleum Council, *Impact of New Technology on the U.S. Petroleum Industry 1946–1965* (Washington: National Petroleum Council, 1967), p. 293.

121. Ibid., p. 256.

122. Ibid.

Chapter 10

1. The map showing the proposed corridors can be found at http://www.fra.dot.gov/us/content/203.

2. Average mpg is for U.S. passenger cars in 2006, found at http://www.bts.gov/publications/national_transportation_statistics/html/table_04_23.html.

3. There were 2.59 people per household in 2000 according to the Census, found at http://quickfacts.census.gov/qfd/states/00000.html.

4. Ian Parry, Margaret Walls, and Winston Harrington, "Automobile Externalities and Policies" *Journal of Economic Literature* 45 (2007), p. 373, Table 2.

5. This is estimated by reviewing available fares on Orbitz.com. In order to get a low fare, the flight was investigated as a round-trip departing on a Thursday and returning on a Sunday at least one month in advance.

6. The passenger-mile estimate is from http://www.earthlab.com/carbon-calculator.html.

7. The official Ohio Hub website is http://www2.dot.state.oh.us/ohiorail/Ohio%20Hub/Website/ordc/index.html. The plan reports an auto travel time of a little less than four hours, consistent with the estimates used in our earlier discussion.

8. Ibid., Executive Summary, p. 5.

9. Amtrak provides a calculator to assist passengers in purchasing carbon offsets at http://www.carbonfund.org/site/pages/land/amtrak.

10. Edward Glaeser looked at a hypothetical Houston-Dallas high-speed rail route in some detail at Edward Glaeser, "Running The Numbers on High-Speed Trains," *New York Times* Economix Blog, http://economix.blogs.nytimes.com/2009/08/04/running-

the-numbers-on-high-speed-trains/; Edward Glaeser, "How Big Are the Environmental Benefits of High-Speed Rail?" *New York Times* Economix Blog, http://economix.blogs .nytimes.com/2009/08/12/how-big-are-the-environmental-benefits-of-high-speed-rail/.

11. Bent Flyvbjerg, Mette Skamris Holm, and Søren Buhl, "How (In)accurate Are Demand Forecasts in Public Works Projects?" *Journal of the American Planning Association* 71 (2005): 131–46, present general results regarding the systematic overestimation of ridership in transit projects; Donald Pickrell, "A Desire Named Streetcar—Fantasy and Fact in Rail Transit Planning," *Journal of the American Planning Association* 58 (1992): 158–76, had found a similar result studying projects from the 1970s and 1980s.

12. Ohio Hub Plan, Executive Summary, p. 8.

13. Fares and schedule information can be found at Greyhound's website, http:// www.greyhound.com/home/.

14. The estimate is from CarbonFund, at http://www.carbonfund.org/site/pages/ carbon_calculators/category/Assumptions/.

15. Andrea Sachs, "Back on the Bus," *Washington Post*, August 30, 2009, http://www .washingtonpost.com/wp-dyn/content/article/2009/08/27/AR2009082703374 .html?referrer=emailarticle.

16. Edward Glaeser, see note 9. He estimated CO_2 emissions of 157 pounds per passenger in a car (at an average of 1.6 passengers per car), 134 pounds per passenger in an airplane, and 32 pounds per passenger in trains. He did not review buses.

17. Ohio Development Rail Commission, http://www.dot.state.oh.us/Divisions/ Rail/Programs/passenger/3CisME/Pages/default.aspx.

18. David Levinson, "Some Thoughts on High-Speed Rail—Part 7: Summary and Conclusions," The Transportationist Blog, April 28, 2010, http://blog.lib.umn.edu/ levin031/transportationist/.

19. For a book-length treatment of modern metropolitan structure, see William T. Bogart, *Don't Call It Sprawl: Metropolitan Structure in The Twenty-First Century* (Cambridge, UK: Cambridge University Press, 2006).

20. Paul Bairoch, *Cities And Economic Development: From the Dawn of History to the Present* (Chicago: University of Chicago Press, 1988), p. 280, on origins of mass transit.

21. Kenneth Jackson, *Crabgrass Frontier: The Suburbanization of the United States* (New York: Oxford University Press, 1985), provides evidence of the decentralization of metropolitan areas beginning in the middle 1800s as mass transit is introduced.

22. Bogart, see note 17, p. 41. Cleveland's Regional Transit Authority posts signs reminding riders that the average paid fare covers about 20 percent of the cost of the trip. Sales tax revenue and government subsidies and grants are the other primary sources of revenue, with passenger fares accounting for 20–25 percent of revenue. *Budget Challenges,* available at http://www.riderta.com/budgetchallenges/.

23. Sam Staley and Adrian Moore, *Mobility First: A New Vision for Transportation in a Globally Competitive Twenty-First Century* (Landham, MD: Rowman and Littlefield, 2009), p. 46.

24. John Meyer, John Kain, and Martin Wohl, *The Urban Transportation Problem* (Cambridge, MA: Harvard University Press, 1965).

25. Robert Pollin, James Heintz, and Heidi Garrett-Peltier, "The Economic Benefits of Investing in Clean Energy: How The Economic Stimulus Program and New Legislation Can Boost U.S. Economic Growth and Employment," Political Economy Research Institute (PERI), University of Massachusetts, Amherst, June 18, 2009, http:// www.peri.umass.edu/economic_benefits/.

26. Arthur C. Nelson, "Toward a New Metropolis: The Opportunity to Rebuild America," Brookings Institution Metropolitan Policy Program, Discussion Paper, December 2004.

27. Randall Bartlett, "Testing the 'Popsicle Test': Realities of Retail Shopping in New 'Traditional Neighborhood Developments,'" *Urban Studies* 40 (2003): 1471–85.

28. Marlon Boarnet and Saksith Chalermpong, "New Highways, House Prices, and Urban Development: A Case Study of Toll Roads in Orange County, CA," *Housing Policy Debate* 12 (2001): 575–605.

29. Gilles Duranton and Matthew Turner, "The Fundamental Law of Road Congestion: Evidence from US Cities," NBER Working Paper no. 15376, 2009.

30. Robert Pollin et al., "Green Recovery: A Program to Create Good Jobs and Start Building a Low Carbon Economy," Center for American Progress, Political Economy Research Institute, September 2008, pp. 7–8.

31. Ibid., p. 8.

32. Ibid., p. 7.

33. United Nations Environment Programme, *Green Jobs: Towards Decent Work in a Sustainable, Low-Carbon World* (Nairobi: U.N. Publishing Services Section, 2008), p. 13, http://www.unep.org/labour_environment/PDFs/Greenjobs/UNEP-Green-Jobs-Report.pdf.

34. Ibid.

35. Ibid., p. 164.

36. Randal O'Toole, "Does Rail Transit Save Energy or Reduce Greenhouse Gas Emissions?" Cato Institute Policy Analysis no. 615, April 14, 2008, pp. 14–15.

37. Ibid., p. 15.

38. Ibid.

39. Ibid.

40. Ibid.

41. Ibid.

42. Ibid., p. 16.

43. Ibid.

44. U.S. Department of Transportation, Bureau of Transportation Statistics, "National Transportation Statistics 2008," 2008, Tables 1-37 and 3-30b, http://www.bts.gov/publications/national_transportation_statistics/pdf/entire.pdf.

45. Bob Johnson, "For Road Crews, Stimulus Promises More Opportunity," *Washington Post*, February 15, 2009, http://www.washingtonpost.com/wp-dyn/content/article/2009/02/15/AR2009021500551.html?hpid=sec-business.

46. U.S. Department of Transportation, see note 42, Tables 1-37 and 3-30b.

47. Clifford Winston and Vikram Maheshri, "On the Social Desirability of Urban Rail Transit Systems," *Journal of Urban Economics* 62 (2007): 362–83; O'Toole, p. 34.

48. Winston and Maheshri, see note 47, p. 362.

49. Sam Bass Warner, *Streetcar Suburbs: The Process of Growth in Boston, 1870–1900* (Cambridge, MA: Harvard University Press, 1962), provides an example of development of specialized neighborhoods in Boston along streetcar routes. Jackson, *Crabgrass Frontier,* provides evidence of this pattern in multiple U.S. cities.

50. See Flyvbjerg et al., note 10, and Pickrell, note 10.

51. Winston and Maheshri, see note 47, p. 379.

52. BART ridership from http://www.bart.gov/news/articles/2009/news20091029.aspx, regular Bay Bridge use from http://www.kcra.com/traffic/21495070/detail.html.

53. Winston and Maheshri, see note 47, p. 381.

54. Robert Wassmer, "Causes of Urban Sprawl in the United States: Auto Reliance as Compared to Natural Evolution, Flight from Blight, and Local Revenue Reliance," *Journal of Policy Analysis and Management* 27 (2008): 536.

55. These calculations and much of the discussion are based on Gilbert Metcalf, "Tax Policies for Low Carbon Technologies," *National Tax Journal* 62 (2009): 519–33. The geothermal and wind comparison is from Table 3 on p. 526. The car comparison is from Table 2 on p. 525.

Chapter 11

1. James Parks, "AFL-CIO Announces Center for Green Jobs," AFL-CIO NOW Blog, February 5, 2009, http://blog.aflcio.org/2009/02/05/afl-cio-announces-center-for-green-jobs/.

2. On the Issues, "John McCain on Environment," http://www.ontheissues.org/domestic/John_McCain_Environment.htm.

3. United States Department of Labor, "US Department of Labor Announces Nearly $55 Million in Green Jobs Training Grants through Recovery Act," Press Release, November 18, 2009, http://www.dol.gov/opa/media/press/eta/eta20091439.htm.

4. U.S. Senator Bernie Sanders, "Green Jobs for Vermont," Press Release, November 18, 2009, http://sanders.senate.gov/newsroom/news/?id=8c468876-07dd-4b59-b8d7-9207d5039577.

5. Ann O'Dea, "GE's Jeff Immalt on Green Jobs," Business and Leadership, February 2, 2009, http://www.businessandleadership.com/news/article/17121/ges-jeff-immelt-on-green-jobs.

6. Kate Galbraith, "Pickens Drops Plans for Largest Wind Farm," *New York Times,* July 7, 2009, http://greeninc.blogs.nytimes.com/2009/07/07/pickens-drops-plan-for-largest-wind-farm/?apage=3.

7. As early as 1995, Cato had declared ADM the largest recipient of corporate welfare in the United States. James Bovard, "Archers Daniel Midland: A Case Study in Corporate Welfare," Cato Policy Analysis No. 241, September 26, 1995, http://www.cato.org/pubs/pas/pa-241.html. In 1997, Cato scholar Doug Bandow again flagged ADM's addiction to subsidies. Doug Bandow, "Ethanol Keeps ADM Drunk on Tax Dollars," *Investor's Business Daily*, October 2, 1997. More recently, left groups have joined in condemning ADM's subsidies. See Sasha Lilley, "Green Fuel's Dirty Secret," CorpWatch, June 1, 2006, http://www.corpwatch.org/article.php?id=13646.

8. Elizabeth Williamson and Paul Glader, "General Electric Pursues Pot of Government Stimulus Gold," *Wall Street Journal*, November 17, 2009, http://online.wsj.com/article/SB125832961253649563.html.

9. See, e.g., Philip Mattera, "High Road or Low Road? Job Quality in the New Green Economy," Good Jobs First, February 2009, http://www.goodjobsfirst.org/pdf/gjfgreenjobsrpt.pdf (calling for restrictions to favor unions).

10. See, e.g., Jay Yarrow, "Unions Block Non-Union Solar Projects," *The Business Insider,* June 19, 2009, http://www.businessinsider.com/in-california-solar-projects-go-union-or-else-2009-6 (describing how unions file ESA objections to nonunion projects).

11. We do not want to be accused of being the pot calling the kettle black, as we are all in higher education, an industry notorious for lobbying for higher revenues regardless of net benefits to society from the revenues. So the named parties are no different than other actors in our political economy.

12. The website of almost every member of Congress reports the details of money flowing to constituents in the state or district. One senator's bridge to nowhere is another senator's project of critical importance.

13. See, e.g., Amy Lorentzen, "White House Hopefuls Love Iowa Ethanol," *USA Today*, August 30, 2007, http://www.usatoday.com/news/politics/election2008/2007-08-30-ethanol-candidates_N.htm. ("Don't expect to hear much talk about farming from the presidential candidates who regularly tour Iowa, one of the nation's premier agriculture states. Instead, prepare for three words: I love ethanol."); "The Caucuses: Ethanol Politics," Iowa Public TV, January 3, 2008, http://www.iptv.org/iowajournal/story.cfm/143. (Collecting pro-ethanol quotes by candidates and noting, "In truth it may not be the make or break issue that many campaigns think it is, but few of the candidates have dared to spurn the state's leading distillate."); Robert Bryce, "The Iowa Imperative," *The Energy Tribune*, November 6, 2007, http://www.energytribune.com/articles.cfm?aid=404&idli=3. ("When looking for a root cause of the ongoing ethanol scam, look no further than Iowa. Indeed, the dearth of rationality in America's choice of motor fuels can be blamed on a single fact: the Iowa Caucus is the first presidential primary."); Robert W. Hahn, "Ethanol: Law, Economics, and Politics," Reg-Markets Center Working Paper no. 08-02, 2008.

14. Bruce Yandle, "Bootleggers and Baptists: The Education of a Regulatory Economist," *Regulation* (May–June 1983): 12. See also Bruce Yandle, "Bootleggers and Baptists in Retrospect," *Regulation* 22(3) (1999): 5–7.

15. Francesco Guerrera, "GE Doubles 'Green' Sales in Two Years," *Financial Times*, May 23, 2007, http://www.ft.com/cms/s/0/1f6db26a-0951-11dc-a349-000b5df10621,dwp_uuid=e8477cc4-c820-11db-b0dc-000b5df10621.html?nclick_check=1.

16. "GE's Green Business Rakes In $17B for 2008—a 21 Percent Jump in Revenue," Greenbiz.com, May 27, 2009, http://www.greenbiz.com/news/2009/05/27/ges-green-business-rakes-17b-2008-21-percent-jump-revenue. This does not mean that all the sales were from pork projects, nor does it mean that the quality of goods and services provided is not fine; the issue is how much business revenue comes from political sources that would not otherwise exist.

17. "Energy Tech Sales Help Siemens Beat Profit Estimates," *Environmental Leader*, April 30, 2009, http://www.environmentalleader.com/2009/04/30/energy-tech-sales-help-siemens-beat-profit-estimates/.

18. See Terry L. Anderson and Donald R. Leal, *Enviro-Capitalists: Doing Good While Doing Well* (Lanham, MD: Rowman and Littlefield, 1997).

19. Robert L. Bradley, "Enron v. Exxon Mobil: Polar Approaches to Energy and Public Policy," MasterResource.org, June 15, 2009, http://www.masterresource.org/2009/06/enron-vs-exxon-mobil-houston-chronicle-op-ed/. The details of how Enron used its wind operations to be a "qualifying facility" and so reap benefits under federal energy law is described in Bethany McLean and Peter Elkind, *The Smartest Guys in the Room* (New York: Protfolio, 2003), pp. 166–67, and Kurt Eichenwald, *Conspiracy of Fools* (New York: Broadway, 2005), pp.142–44. Bradley plans to describe the issues in detail in *Enron and Ken Lay: An American Tragedy* (M & M Scriveners Press, forthcoming, 2011).

20. Charles Forelle, "French Firm Cashes In under U.N. Warming Program," *Wall Street Journal*, July 23, 2008 http://online.wsj.com/article/SB121677247656875573.html?mod=googlenews_wsj.

21. Bjorn Lomborg, "The Climate Industrial Complex," *Wall Street Journal*, May 22, 2009, http://online.wsj.com/article/SB124286145192740987.html. Germany's energy

companies have used renewables to trade their CO_2 emission permits to plants elsewhere, prompting a *Der Spiegel* analysis to conclude that "The climate hasn't in fact profited from these developments. As astonishing as it may sound, the new wind turbines and solar cells haven't prohibited the emission of even a single gram of CO_2." Anselm Waldermann, "Wind Turbines in Europe Do Nothing for Emissions-Reduction Goals," *Der Spiegel Online International*, February 10, 2009, http://www.spiegel.de/international/business/0,1518,606763,00.html.

22. Stephen Power, "Debate Arises on 3 Wheeler," *Wall Street Journal*, September 14, 2009, http://online.wsj.com/article/SB125288146359206959.html.

23. Ibid.

24. "Congress OKs Bill Making 3-Wheelers Eligible for Funds," *Automotive News*, October 16, 2009, http://www.autonews.com/apps/pbcs.dll/article?AID=/20091016/ANA02/910169976/1186; Edward Niedermeyer, "It's Official: Three-Wheelers Are Cars Too. For Subsidy Purposes," The Truth About Cars, October 19, 2009, http://www.thetruthaboutcars.com/its-official-three-wheelers-are-cars-too-for-subsidy-purposes/.

25. See, among others, the website of Citizens Against Government Waste (www.cagw.org) for a laundry list of specific pork projects.

26. See Edward Kleinbard, "The Congress within The Congress: How Tax Expenditures Distort our Budget and our Political Processes," *Ohio Northern Law Review* 36 (2010) (discussing tax disbursements to the energy sector and finding them to be larger than direct fiscal outlays).

27. Alexis Madrigal, "Bailout Bill Is Rife with Tasty Green Pork," *Wired*, October 8, 2008, http://www.wired.com/wiredscience/2008/10/bailout-bill-ri/.

28. Siobhan Hughes, "First Ever Smart Grid Tax Breaks Hitch Ride on Bailout Bill," *Dow Jones Newswires*, October 9, 2008, http://www.drsgcoalition.org/news/media/2008-10-09.pdf.

29. H.R. 1424, sec. 504 (110th Congress). The primary beneficiary of the tax break is Rose City Archery of Myrtle Point, Oregon. Both senators from Oregon denied having anything to do with it. See Matthew Daly, *Associated Press*, "What's This about 'Wooden Arrows' in the Bailout Bill?" *KATU.com*, October 3, 2008, http://www.katu.com/news/30342874.html.

30. H.R. 1424, sec. 205.

31. The $5,000 incremental credit divided by the 12 kWh of capacity in the Volt over the 4 kWh base.

32. "The Energy Tax Credits in the Bailout Bill, Part 1: Solar Power and Plug In Hybrids Win Big," *Climate Progress*, October 5, 2008, http://climateprogress.org/2008/10/05/the-bailout-bills-part-1-solar-power-and-plug-in-hybrids-win-big/. As a comment to one online report noted, "Sneaky these Senators – putting the minimum battery size just above that of the new Prius. . . . It really is a give away to the Volt." Comment, "Senate Version of Bailout Bill Has PHEV Credits," *Green Car Congress*, October 2, 2008, http://www.greencarcongress.com/2008/10/senate-version.html. Not all analysts caught the GM bias. The dean of Duke's School of the Environment missed it in his "scorecard" of the bill, giving the plug-in hybrid provision a "green rating" despite its pork attributes and exclusion of hybrid technology pioneer Toyota. See Bill Chameides, "The $700 Billion Bailout Bill Goes Green?" *The Green Grok*, October 7, 2008, http://nicholas.duke.edu/thegreengrok/the-700-billion-bailout-bill-goes-green-not-quite.

33. See David Mayhew, *Congress: The Electoral Connection*, 2nd ed. (New Haven, CT: Yale University Press, 2004).

34. Data from Opensecrets.org, the Center for Responsive Politics' website, listing campaign contributions, available at http://www.opensecrets.org/orgs/summary. php?id=D000000125&cycle=2010 as of November 30, 2009. The methodology is described at http://www.opensecrets.org/industries/methodology.php.

35. "Enron Slipping off the Top 100 Campaign Contributors of All Time," Bloggingstocks.com, January 21, 2009, http://www.bloggingstocks.com/2009/01/21/enron-slipping-off-the-top-100-campaign-contributors-of-all-time/. Enron's investment did not appear to pay off at the end of the company's existence. See John Samples, "Three Myths about Enron and Campaign Finance," Cato.org, February 1, 2002, http://www. cato.org/pub_display.php?pub_id=3384 (describing inability of company to get help from recipients). However, it does appear to have paid off earlier, when the company was lobbying for green pork.

36. League of Conservation Voters National Environmental Scorecard, http:// www.lcv.org/scorecard/. There are issues concerning whether the LCV Scorecard is accurate. See, e.g., National Center for Policy Analysis, "League of Conservation Voters Makes Traditional Misleading Attack on Republicans, Promotes Democratic Party Candidates," October 30, 2002, http://www.nationalcenter.org/TSR103002.html.

37. See James T. Hamilton, "Taxes, Torts, and the Toxics Release Inventory: Congressional Voting on Instruments to Control Pollution," *Economic Inquiry* 35(4) (1997): 754 (exploring differences in votes on technical amendments and on final passage for a bill).

38. See, e.g., Defenders of Wildlife Action Fund, *Endorsements* [for 2008], http:// defendersactionfund.org/political_campaigns/endorsements.html. Environmental organizations produce audiences for members of Congress as well as favorable publicity. Visit the website of an organization such as the Sierra Club (www.sierraclub .org) and type "Senator" in the search box. It will provide more than 1,000 links to Sierra Club activities involving speeches and political action by the organization with members of the U.S. Senate.

39. See Robert Duffy, *The Green Agenda in American Politics: New Strategies for The Twenty-First Century* (Lawrence, KS: University Press of Kansas, 2003); U.S. Senate, Environment and Public Works Committee, Majority Staff, "Political Activity of Environmental Groups and Their Supporting Foundations," September 2004, http://epw .senate.gov/repwhitepapers/Political.pdf.

40. See John Cadigan, "Interest Groups and Get Out the Vote Drives," *Topics in Economic Analysis & Policy*, 4 (2004): 1333.

41. Fred McChesney, *Money for Nothing: Politicians, Rent Extraction, and Political Extortion* (Cambridge, MA: Harvard University Press, 1997).

42. Quoted in Daniel A. Farber, "Environmental Protection as a Learning Experience," *Loyola of Los Angeles Law Review* 27 (1994): 793; see also Willett Kempton et al., *Environmental Values in American Culture* (Cambridge, MA: The MIT Press, 1995), p. 5. ("The majority of Americans now" consider themselves "environmentalists."); Mark Dowie, *Losing Ground: American Environmentalism at the Close of the Twentieth Century* (Cambridge, MA: The MIT Press, 1995), pp. 3–4. ("A Gallup poll in 1970 showed that 53 percent of Americans viewed 'reduction of air and water pollution' as a national priority, up from 17 percent in 1965. By the 1990s well over 80 percent of Americans, according to recent polls, were comfortable calling themselves environmentalists.").

43. James Q. Wilson, "Why They Don't Campaign about the Environment," *Slate*, October 27, 2000, http://www.slate.com/id/92005/.

44. Hal K. Rothman, *Saving The Planet: The American Response to the Environment in the Twentieth Century* (Chicago: Ivan R. Dee, 2000), p. 110. Rothman distinguishes

the two approaches as follows: "While conservation had focused on society, on the greatest good for the greatest number in the long run, environmentalism often had ambiguous social connotations. It reflected the growing obsession with individualism that had come to dominate American society, but it also embraced a contradictory sense of community effort in support of collective goals," (p. 111). Rothman's language illustrates our point despite his evident confusion between the Declaration of Independence's "pursuit of happiness" language and the Constitution's text.

45. Ibid., p. 3 (internal citations omitted).

46. Robert H. Nelson, "How Much Is God Worth? The Problems—Economic and Theological—of Existence Value," Competitive Enterprise Institute, May 1996, p. 25, http://cei.org/pdf/1456.pdf.

47. Philip Shabecoff, *Earth Rising: American Environmentalism in The 21st Century* (Washington: Island Press, 2000), p. 6. Similarly, Kempton et al., p. 9, cite a variety of analysts who make the case that modern environmentalism represents something new.

48. Dowie, see note 42, p. 226.

49. Al Gore, *Earth in the Balance: Ecology and the Human Spirit* (New York: Penguin, 2006), p. 231.

50. Bill Devall and George Sessions, *Deep Ecology: Living as if Nature Mattered* (Layton, UT: Gibbs Smith, 1985), p. 48.

51. Rothman, see note 44, p. 134–35.

52. Linda H. Graber, *Wilderness as Sacred Space* (Washington: Association of American Geographers, 1976), p. 50.

53. See Kempton et al., note 42, p. 42.

54. Rachel Carson, *Silent Spring* (New York: Houghton Mifflin, 1962).

55. John Bellamy Foster, *The Vulnerable Planet: A Short Economic History of The Environment* (New York: Cornerstone Books, 1994), pp. 11–12.

56. Devall and Sessions, see note 50, p. 74.

57. Shabecoff, see note 47 p. 177.

58. John McPhee, *Encounters with The Archdruid* (New York: Farrar, Straus and Giroux, 1971), pp. 79, 83.

59. Former Vice President Al Gore, Policy Address at New York University School of Law on Solving the Climate Crisis, September 18, 2006, http://www.nyu.edu/community/gore.html.

60. Thomas R. Dunlap, *Faith in Nature: Environmentalism as Religious Quest* (Seattle: University of Washington Press, 2004), p. 35.

61. Nelson, see note 46, p. 9.

62. Robert H. Nelson, *Economic vs. Environmental Religion: The New Holy Wars* (University Park, PA: Penn State Press, 2010), pp. 66–67. See also Robert H. Nelson, "Dick Cheney Was Right: The Energy Debate Is about Virtue," *Weekly Standard,* June 11, 2001, pp. 18–20 (elaborating on theme of sacrifice in ANWR).

63. Scott Slovic, "Epistemology and Politics in American Nature Writing: Embedded Rhetoric and Discrete Rhetoric," in *Green Culture: Environmental Rhetoric in Contemporary America,* eds. Carl. G. Herndl and Stuart C. Brown (Madison, WI: University of Wisconsin Press, 1996), p. 86.

64. Samuel P. Hays, *A History of Environmental Politics since 1945* (Pittsburg: University of Pittsburg Press, 2000), p. 108.

65. Shabecoff, see note 47, p. 127.

66. Arne Naess, "Identification as a Source of Deep Ecological Attitudes," in *Deep Ecology*, 2d ed., ed. Michael Tobias (San Francisco: Pfeiffer, 1988), p. 25.

67. Ken Ward, "Liberal Democrats Desert Climate in Droves: Understanding Polling in Terms of Core vs. General Public," Grist, February 23, 2009, http://www.grist.org/article/Liberal-democrats-desert-climate-in-droves.

68. Quoted in Helen M. Ingram et al., "Interest Groups and Environmental Policy," in *Environmental Politics and Policy: Theories and Evidence*, 2nd ed., ed. James P. Lester (Durham, NC: Duke University Press, 1995), p. 120.

69. Quoting Michael Frome in Tom Knudson, "Fat of the Land Movement's Prosperity Comes at a High Price," *Sacramento Bee*, April 22, 2001, http://enviro-lies.org/sacbee_01-04-22.htm.

70. Ibid.

71. Chris Goodall, *How to Live a Low Carbon Life* (London: Earthscan, 2007), p. 63. ("[I]ncreasing numbers of people do make the effort to segregate their recyclable wastes and do so out of a sense of moral duty.").

72. Frederick Buell, *From Apocalypse to Way of Life: Environmental Crisis in the American Century* (New York: Routledge, 2003).

Chapter 12

1. World Health Organization, "Indoor Air Pollution and Health," Fact Sheet no. 292, June 2005, http://www.who.int/mediacentre/factsheets/fs292/en/index.html.

2. Indur M. Goklany, *The Improving State of the World: Why We're Living Longer, Healthier, More Comfortable Lives on a Cleaner Planet* (Washington: Cato Institute, 2007), p. 140. Between 1940 and 1970, four of the five major indoor air pollutants dropped by more than 80 percent; the fifth, nitrous oxide, took longer to decline, dropping by 60 percent by 2000.

3. Envirofit—Making the World Fit for Humanity, www.envirofit.org.

4. Ibid.

5. David G. Victor, "Climate Accession Deals: New Strategies for Taming Growth of Greenhouse Gases in Developing Countries," Discussion Paper no. 08-18, Harvard Project on International Climate Agreements, 2008, p. 20, http://irps.ucsd.edu/dgvictor/publications/Victor_Chapter_2009_Climate%20Acession%20Deals.pdf.

6. Ibid.

7. Envirofit notes that it has also developed a direct-injection retrofit for dirty two-stroke engines. That is one more potential improvement to deal with one more environmental problem.

8. This is a very rough calculation, but it is clear the potential emission reduction is huge. Department of Energy, "Carbon Dioxide Emissions from the Generation of Electric Power in the United States," Department of Energy, July 2000, http://www.eia.doe.gov/cneaf/electricity/page/co2_report/co2report.html.

9. "We're all Democrats now," says the CEO of GE, who is a registered Republican. Elizabeth Williamson and Paul Glader, "GE Pursues Pot of Government Stimulus Gold," *Wall Street Journal*, November 17, 2009, http://online.wsj.com/article/SB125832961253649563.html.

10. See Kate Sheppard, "A Green Tinged Stimulus Bill," *Grist*, February 12, 2009, http://gristmill.grist.org/story/2009/2/12/83439/6486. The numbers are a bit slippery; when checked in May 2010, the White House blog asserted that $80 billion for

green jobs projects is included in the stimulus bill. See http://www.whitehouse.gov/issues/energy-and-environment.

11. United Nations Environment Programme, *Green Jobs: Towards Decent Work in a Sustainable, Low-Carbon World* (Nairobi: U.N. Publishing Services Section, 2008), p. 306, http://www.unep.org/labour_environment/PDFs/Greenjobs/UNEP-Green-Jobs-Report.pdf.

12. U.S. Geological Survey, "Cement Statistics," in *Historical Statistics for Mineral and Material Commodities in the United States*, comps. T.D. Kelly and G.R. Matos (Washington: U.S. Geological Survey Data Series no. 140, 2008), http://minerals.usgs.gov/ds/2005/140/cement.pdf.

13. UNEP, see note 11, p. 203.

14. Vice President Biden asserted that green jobs "pay 10 to 20 percent more than other jobs." Joseph R. Biden, "The Case for Green Jobs," White House Blog, February 27, 2009, http://www.whitehouse.gov/blog/09/02/27/The-case-for-green-jobs/.

15. Manuel Frondel, Nolan Ritter, and Colin Vance, "Economic Impacts from the Promotion of Renewable Energies: The German Experience," Rhenisch-Westfälisches Institut für Wirtschaftsforschung, Final Report, 2009, p. 5, http://www.institutefor energyresearch.org/germany/Germany_Study_-_FINAL.pdf.

16. Ibid.

17. Ibid.

18. Ibid., p. 6.

19. Ibid., p. 7.

20. Ibid., p. 6.

21. Pete Harrison, "Once-Hidden EU Report Reveals Damage from Biodiesel," *Reuters*, April 21, 2010, http://www.alertnet.org/thenews/newsdesk/LDE63J1FP.htm.

22. Clean Energy Jobs and American Power Act, May 27, 2010, http://kerry.senate.gov/cleanenergyjobsandamericanpower/intro.cfm. This website links to several documents, including the full text of Senate Bill 1733, endorsed by a coalition of "business, political, and religious leaders."

23. Spending on green jobs is consistently called an investment. See, e.g., speech by Vice President Biden, "The Case for Green Jobs," White House Blog, February 27, 2009, http://www.whitehouse.gov/blog/09/02/27/The-case-for-green-jobs/.

Index

About the Authors

Andrew P. Morriss is the D. Paul Jones Jr. and Charlene Jones Chairholder in Law and professor of business at the University of Alabama. He received an A.B. from Princeton, a J.D. from the University of Texas at Austin, and a Ph.D. in economics from MIT. He is the author of many articles and the editor of numerous books, including *Global Labor and Employment Law for the Practicing Lawyer* (Kluwer 2010) and *Regulatory Competition and Offshore Financial Centers* (AEI Press 2010). He is a senior fellow at the Property and Environment Research Center in Bozeman, Montana, and a reporter for the American Law Institute's Restatement of Employment Law project.

William T. (Tom) Bogart became president of Maryville College in 2010. He previously served as dean of academic affairs at York College of Pennsylvania and as a member of the economics faculty in the Weatherhead School of Management at Case Western Reserve University. Dr. Bogart earned a B.A. in economics and mathematical sciences from Rice University and a Ph.D. in economics from Princeton University. He is the author of two previous books, *Don't Call It Sprawl: Metropolitan Structure in the Twenty-first Century* (Cambridge University Press 2006) and *The Economics of Cities and Suburbs* (Prentice Hall 1997), and his work has been published in scholarly journals such as the *Review of Economics and Statistics, National Tax Journal, Urban Studies, Environmental Management*, and the *Journal of Urban Economics*.

Andrew Dorchak has served as head of reference and foreign/international law specialist since 2000 at the Case Western Reserve University School of Law's Judge Ben C. Green Law Library. He provides research instruction and assistance for law students, with a focus on international law topics and legal memoranda for various international war crimes tribunals. He is co-author of *Regulation by Litigation* (Yale University Press 2008).

Roger Meiners is Goolsby Distinguished Professor of Economics and Law at the University of Texas at Arlington. He was previously a member of the faculty at Clemson University, Emory University, the University of Miami, and Texas A&M University. His articles have appeared in *Environmental Law,* the *Journal of Law and Economics, Administrative Law Review,* and other journals. He is also a senior fellow at the Property and Environment Research Center, Bozeman, Montana.

Cato Institute

Founded in 1977, the Cato Institute is a public policy research foundation dedicated to broadening the parameters of policy debate to allow consideration of more options that are consistent with the traditional American principles of limited government, individual liberty, and peace. To that end, the Institute strives to achieve greater involvement of the intelligent, concerned lay public in questions of policy and the proper role of government.

The Institute is named for *Cato's Letters*, libertarian pamphlets that were widely read in the American Colonies in the early 18th century and played a major role in laying the philosophical foundation for the American Revolution.

Despite the achievement of the nation's Founders, today virtually no aspect of life is free from government encroachment. A pervasive intolerance for individual rights is shown by government's arbitrary intrusions into private economic transactions and its disregard for civil liberties.

To counter that trend, the Cato Institute undertakes an extensive publications program that addresses the complete spectrum of policy issues. Books, monographs, and shorter studies are commissioned to examine the federal budget, Social Security, regulation, military spending, international trade, and myriad other issues. Major policy conferences are held throughout the year, from which papers are published thrice yearly in the *Cato Journal*. The Institute also publishes the quarterly magazine *Regulation*.

In order to maintain its independence, the Cato Institute accepts no government funding. Contributions are received from foundations, corporations, and individuals, and other revenue is generated from the sale of publications. The Institute is a nonprofit, tax-exempt, educational foundation under Section 501(c)3 of the Internal Revenue Code.

CATO INSTITUTE
1000 Massachusetts Ave., N.W.
Washington, D.C. 20001
www.cato.org